Gayatri Chakravorty Spivak is University Professor at Columbia University. She has written a few books, received a few prizes, and include a few honorary degrees. For many years, she has been grappling with finishing a book on W. E. B. Du Bois and writing an afterword to the first English translations of Antonio Gramsci's conversation with Julia and Tatiana Schucht while imprisoned. Humanities for social justice is her obsession. Translation is the medium of this work.

Aron Aji is Director of MFA in Literary Translation at the University of Iowa. A native of Turkey, he has translated works by Turkish writers, including Karasu's *The Garden of Departed Cats*, and *A Long Day's Evening*. Aji was president of the American Literary Translators Association between 2016 and 2019. He leads the Translation Workshop, and teaches courses on retranslation, poetry and translation, theory, and contemporary Turkish literature.

Emily Apter is Silver Professor of French and Comparative Literature at New York University. Her books include *Unexceptional Politics: On Obstruction, Impasse and the Impolitic* (2018); *Against World Literature: On the Politics of Untranslatability* (2013); *Dictionary of Untranslatables: A Philosophical Lexicon* (co-edited with Barbara Cassin, Jacques Lezra, and Michael Wood) (2014); and *The Translation Zone: A New Comparative Literature* (2006). In 2017–18 she served as president of the American Comparative Literature Association. In fall 2014 she was a Humanities Council Fellow at Princeton and in 2003–04 she was a Guggenheim Fellowship recipient.

Avishek Ganguly is Associate Professor in the Department of Literary Arts and Studies at the Rhode Island School of Design in Providence, Rhode Island. He has a co-edited volume (with Kélina Gotman), *Translation and Performance in a Global Age*, forthcoming from Cambridge University Press. He is currently working on a monograph on "Global Englishes," another co-edited volume tentatively titled "Decolonizing the Imagination," and a new research project at the intersection of humanities and design.

Mauro Pala is Professor of Comparative Literature at the University of Cagliari (Italy), where he coordinates the PhD program in Philological and Literary, Historical and Cultural Studies. He has been a Fulbright Lecturer at the University of Notre Dame, Visiting Professor at the Universities of Aarhus,

Limoges, UAM (Mexico City), Guest Professor at the University of Malta, and has published extensively on critical theory, cultural studies and postcolonial literature. He is currently working with Prof. Roberto Dainotto (Duke University) on a monograph about literature and subalternity.

Surya Parekh is Assistant Professor in the Department of English at Binghamton University. His monograph *Black Enlightenment* (under contract to Duke University Press) investigates the necessity of the Black subject to the Enlightenment. He has published in *19th Century Literature* and *Postcolonial Directions in Education*. He is also a co-editor of the volume *Spivak Moving* (forthcoming from Seagull Books).

Maureen Robertson is Director Emerita of the MFA in Literary Translation at the University of Iowa, and Professor Emerita of Comparative Literature and Asian Languages. She received her PhD in Chinese Literature from the University of Washington in 1970. Dr. Robertson's work focuses on materials by educated women of the governing class in seventeenth–nineteenth-century dynastic China, identifying, contextualizing, and translating poetry by pseudonymous or anonymous authors who remain unincorporated into the canonical understanding of Chinese literature. She has held research appointments at the National Diet Library in Tokyo, Meiji University, Harvard University, and Fudan University.

Gayatri Chakravorty Spivak

Living Translation

Edited by

EMILY APTER, AVISHEK GANGULY, MAURO PALA, and SURYA PAREKH

With a Foreword by EMILY APTER

A Preface by ARON AJI and MAUREEN ROBERTSON

An Afterword by AVISHEK GANGULY

and an Essay by MAURO PALA

Seagull
BOOKS

LONDON NEW YORK CALCUTTA

Seagull Books, 2022

Essays © Gayatri Chakravorty Spivak

All essays first published in other volumes and journals have been reproduced in this volume with the kind permission of the author.

Foreword © Emily Apter, 2022

Preface © Aron Aji and Maureen Robertson, 2022

Afterword © Avishek Ganguly, 2022

"Gramsci and Spivak" © Mauro Pala, 2022

This compilation © Seagull Books, 2022

ISBN 978 1 8030 9 113 6

British Library Cataloguing-in-Publication Data
A catalogue record for this book is available from the British Library

Typeset by Seagull Books, Calcutta, India

Contents

Foreword

EMILY APTER

Gayatri Chakravorty Spivak, one of the most moving thinkers of the twentieth and twenty-first centuries, has contributed uniquely to comparative literature, global feminism, subaltern studies, postcolonial theory, electoral education, and the ethics of planetarity. In this volume, which performs the invaluable service of gathering for the first time her wide-ranging writings on translation, we can see in sharp relief the extent to which, throughout her long career, she has made translation a central concern of the comparative humanities. Starting with her landmark "Translator's Preface" to Jacques Derrida's *De la grammatologie* (*Of Grammatology*) in 1976, and continuing with her "Translator's Foreword" to Mahasveta Devi's "Draupadi" (and Afterword to Devi's *Chotti Munda and His Arrow*) Spivak tackled translatability as such from the ground up and at the political limit; at border checkpoints, at sites of colonial pedagogy, in acts of resistance to monolingual regimes of national language, at the borders of minor literature and schizo-analysis, in the deficits of cultural debt and linguistic expropriation, and, more generally, at theory's edge, which is to say, where practical criticism yields to theorizing in Untranslatables.[1] (This volume also provides

---

1 Drawing on it as the engine of her monumental *Dictionary of Untranslatables: A Philosophical Lexicon* (2004), Barbara Cassin used the notion of the "Untranslatable" (*l'intraduisible*) to designate how a term or syntactic structure springs to life, becomes, as it were, fully activated, only when the reader or speaker encounters its resistance to translation, its recesses of opacity and obstinate meaning. For

information about how her institution-building as director of Comparative Literature at the university of Iowa—and in her subsequent places of employment—began at the same time.) From this perspective, Spivak takes her place within a distinguished line-up of translator-theorists that includes Walter Benjamin, George Steiner, Jacques Derrida, Binoy Majumdar, François Cheng, Louis-Jean Calvet, Samuel Weber, Susan Bassnett, Abdelfattah Kilito, Barbara Cassin, Abdessalam Benabdelali, Jean-Jacques Lecercle, François Jullien, Lydia Liu, and Lydia Davis, all of them particularly attuned to the processes of cognizing in languages, all of them alive to the co-productivity of thinking, translating, writing.

Cassin, the Untranslatable is not an exceptional category reserved for select keywords; it applies quite even-handedly to any term or concept in the throes of mistranslation, non-translation, or interminable retranslation.

Very early on, in her preface to *Of Grammatology,* Spivak picked up on the potential of the Untranslatable as a point of departure for theoretical work:

> It is customary at this point to say a few words about the problem of translation. Derrida's text certainly offers its share of "untranslatable" words. I have had my battles with "exergue" and "proper." My special worry is "entamer." As we have seen, it is an important word in Derrida's vocabulary. It means both to break into and to begin. I have made do with "broach" or "breach" with the somewhat fanciful confidence that the shadow-word "breach" or "broach" will declare itself through it [. . .].
> (p. 32 in this volume, henceforth cited in this essay with page numbers in parentheses)

In "Translating into English" (2005), the Untranslatable reemerges as a productive site, this time in relation to the problem of the Marxist value-form:

> When Marx wrote about the commensurability of all things, that it was "contentless and simple" (*inhaltslos und einfach*) he was speaking as a materialist speaks of form. Not as *form*, but as a thing without content. Generations of empiricist English translators have missed the point, not resonating with Marx's philosophical presuppositions, translated *inhaltslos* as "slight in content," and thus made nonsense out of the entire discussion of value. Marx's insight could have taken on board today's transformation of all things into data—telecommunication rendering information indistinguishable from capital. (pp. 90–91)

Like many in this company, but in ways unparalleled, Spivak developed a singular focus on the *politics of translation*. A watershed essay of 1992 on "The Politics of Translation" kicks off with the avowal that "The idea for this title comes from the British sociologist Michele Barrett's feeling that the politics of translation takes on a massive life of its own if you see language as the processes of meaning-construction." Spivak would lend heft to translation politics' "massive life of its own," starting with this essay, in which she situates language within an ensemble of "gestures, pauses [. . .] chance, [and] subindividual force-fields of being which click into place in different situations [and] swerve from the straight or true line of language-in-thought" (p. 36). Taking recourse to translation as conceived in this expanded field, Spivak will underscore the importance of *gendered agency* as a mode of resisting "capitalist multiculturalism's invitation to self-identity." "The task of the feminist translator," she writes, "is to consider language as a clue to the workings of gendered agency."[2] When Walter Benjamin coined the expression "task of the translator" (*die Aufgabe des Übersetzers*) in the foundational essay of 1923, gender and agency were predictably absent as conceptual levers of meaning-construction, subject formation and *Überleben* (*sur-vie,* afterlife, survival, living on, or as Sam Weber renders

---

2 Spivak here anticipates Judith Butler's relatively recent focus on gender and translation: "I now believe that gender is a problem of translation, and we probably shouldn't be thinking about gender outside of the context of translation," (Butler, "The CounterText Interview," *CounterText* 3[2] [2017]: 127). In another piece, Butler attacks the issue of "gender" (in English) as a so-called "foreign" term, capable, on the one hand, of arousing exorbitant fear and censorship or, on the other, of functioning as some kind of universal cipher in feminist and LGBTQ theory ("a generalizable concept no matter the language into which it enters"). Butler makes the forceful case that "there is no 'gender theory' without a problem of translation," and that "the fear of 'gender' as a destructive cultural imposition from English (or from the Anglophone world) manifests a resistance to translation that deserves critical attention." See Judith Butler, "Gender in Translation: Beyond Monolingualism," in Jude Browne (ed.) *Why Gender?* (Cambridge: Cambridge University Press, 2021), pp. 15–37.

it, "living away"). Spivak's insistence on placing them at the heart of the translator's task is no small move. It opens the way to a translation practice that is decidedly unsafe in the way intimate reading—which demands surrender to regions outside the self's comfort zone—de-secures foundational knowledge and identitarian footholds. In the name of an untameable literarity and in response to the summons to unpack the Foucauldian doublet of *puissance/connaissance*, Spivak writes evocatively of the frayed "selveges" of the language-fabric. Its raggedy threads, when pulled apart, weave the kind of uncanny relation to alterity that enables prompts Melanie Klein to look "at the violent translation that constitutes the subject in responsibility" (pp. 71–72) and enables Derrida to insist that speaking in a language not his own (English) "will be more just." Derrida's phrase inspires Spivak to claim the right "to the same dignified complaint for a woman's text in Arabic or Vietnamese" (p. 40), a claim echoed later on in her call for an eco-political planetary justice.[3]

Spivak's translational model of "planetarity" overrides difference-shattering globalisms (translatese) and taps into the spirit-orientation

---

3 In Lee Cataldi and Peggy Rockman Napaljarri's chapter "On Transcoding," in the context of a discussion of the philosopheme "lost our language" used by the Australian Aboriginals of the East Kimberly region, Spivak reads an account of how the ecopolitics of translation proceeds under conditions of settler-colonialism. Shifting to the Walpiri people of Central North Australia, Spivak observes:

> Cataldi and Napaljarri, our translators, inhabit an *aporia*, a catch. Some of their material 'is derived from land-claim documents,' already a site of transcoding a mnemonic geography into the semiosis of land as property. [. . .] What is the relationship between standardized environmentalism, on the one hand, and traditional knowledge systems on the other? Mnemonic geography and satellite positioning technology? This is also a transcoding question. Just as we cannot content ourselves with collecting examples of diasporic hybridity, so also can we not just read books translating "other cultures." (pp. 77–78)

Spivak's intuition that the trajectory of translation is from the performative to performance is useful here (*A Critique of Postcolonial Reason: Toward the History of the Vanishing Present* [Cambridge, MA: Harvard University Press, 1999], pp. 18, 404).

of animism, native cosmos and a "native space" of the third world translator who self-others by no longer remaining oblivious to class privilege or susceptible to the majority-pleasing dictates of the translation market. This alterity, associated by Spivak with seeing oneself as a "planetary accident" rather than as a "global agent" or entity, might be seen as a version of the untranslatable inasmuch as it is underivable ("alterity remains underived from us, it is not our dialectical negation, it contains us as much as it flings us away").[4] Like an etymology without a radical, or a metaphysics without first philosophy, or a civilizational history without "step-wise connections" between "sowing cereals in our primeval past and waiting in line at the Department of Motor Vehicles," alterity is non-derivating,[5] inhabiting a space-time of indeterminacy between the human and the natural (Spivak's condition of the Aboriginal), and between discrete languages.[6] In its cosmic dissemination, alterity models a kind of antiphilology.

The impress of antiphilology can be discerned in an approach to intellectual history and literary genealogy that bypasses influence paradigms in favor of novel conjunctures: Immanuel Kant, Friedrich Schiller, Karl Marx, Antonio Gramsci, Melanie Klein, Emanuel Levinas, and Jacques Derrida appear alongside Binoy Majumdar, Rabindranath Tagore, James Joyce, J. M. Coetzee, Mahasweta Devi, Assia Djebar,

---

4 Gayatri Chakravorty Spivak, "Imperative to Re-imagine the Planet," in *An Aesthetic Education in the Era of Globalization* (Cambridge, MA: Harvard University Press), p. 339.

5 Kwame Anthony Appiah uses the phrase "step-wise connection" in his review of *The Dawn of Everything: A New History of Humanity*, a book co-authored by David Graeber and David Wengrow that challenges the "cereals to-states arrow of history" and the presumption that "a mode of production comes "with a predetermined politics" ("Digging for Utopia," *New York Review of Books* 68[20] [December 2021]: 80.

6 In its anti-foundationalism, this antiphilology, which pushes against inheritance models of philological genesis and transmission, bears pronounced affinities with antiphilosophy, associated in the western tradition with the work of Kierkegaard, Nietzsche, Wittgenstein, Derrida, Lacan, and Laruelle among others.

Oe Kenzaburo, Wilson Harris, Maryse Condé, Farhad Mazhar, Toni Morrison, and numerous Bengali poets, lately Sankha Ghosh. This is not just an eclectic array; these figures engage in agonistic dialogue, producing *a dialectics of cultural translation* that allows conflict, irresolution and interpretive difficulty to have standing. "Cultural translation" in Spivak's ascription is no mere blandishment for differences adjudicated according to standardized measures of moral equivalence or specious criteria of same. To translate in the Spivakian mode is to ensure that the translator has effaced her "voice," always insufficiently, to be haunted, perhaps, by an "original":

> Knowledge depends on cooking the soul with slow learning, not a one size-fits all toolkit. You cannot produce a toolkit for a "moral metric," or if you do you will be disappointed.
>
> What is it, then, to translate? Deep language learning of the original, straining to be haunted by it as it can be learned before reason. Effacing oneself, being as little as possible so the text speaks. Never to translate from an imperial language translation, never. (p. 182)

The commitment to counter epistemicide by translating away from imperial languages prompts a profound rethinking of what translation *is* and *does* and *for whom it serves*.[7] The imperative "Never to translate from an imperial language" points to a postcolonial politics of translating that often relies on strategic uses of marked failure or withholding. We see this at work in Spivak's discussion of dilemmas faced when translating Mahasweta Devi's *Chotti Munda ebong tar tir* (1980). Expressing dissatisfaction with her rendering of the phrase *hoker kotha bollo na Chotti* as "Didn't Chotti speak of 'rights'?" she notes:

---

7 In the chapter "Necessary, Yet Impossible," Spivak writes: "In our time, in postcolonial countries, decolonizing the mind in translation practices has mostly not yet been activated or achieved. We tend to translate from translations into imperial languages." (p. 159)

Hok, in Bengali, a *totshomo* or identical loan word from the Arabic *al haq,* is not rights alone but a peculiar mix of rights and responsibilities that goes beyond the individual. Anyone who has read the opening of Mahasweta's novel knows that the text carries this presupposition. *I have failed in this detail. Translation is as much a problem as a solution.* I hope the book will be taught by someone who has enough sense of the language *to mark this kind of unavoidable failure, and that the rare reader will be led to the Bengali.* (p. 94, emphasis added)

The political tasking of translation in a Spivakian mold—with critical pedagogy urgently foregrounded—is fully in play and on display, soldered to expressions of hope and love:

I myself prepare my translations in the distant and unlikely hope that my texts will fall into the hands of a teacher who knows Bengali well enough to love it, so that the students will know that the best way to read this text is to push through to the original. Of course, not everyone will learn the language, but one might, or two! And the problem will be felt. (p. 94)

And the problem will be felt. This little phrase packs a great political punch. For it outlines the dimensions of a larger project for translation studies today—how to effectively translate into and from little-taught languages, often of "the Global South"—while addressing, indeed repairing, those weaknesses in contemporary liberal education that hail from North America, specifically curricula that promote packaged sound-bites, standardized deliverables, frictionless learning processes based on supposedly value-neutral data and monocultural accessibility at the expense of plurilingual difficulty.[8] (Spivak's initiation of a Bengali

---

8 The theme of repair features strongly in "Living Translation." Drawing on the work of Melanie Klein (much as Eve Kosofsky Sedgwick does for her concept of "reparative reading"), Spivak observes: "This originary *Schuldigsein*—being indebted in the Kleinian sense—the guilt in seeing that one can treat one's mother

bilingual series with Columbia University Press, with glossary and critical introduction is proof of another kind of institution-building.)

When we read the essays assembled in *Living Translation* from beginning to end (and even out of the chronological order in which they were written), what emerges is a picture of translation theory as a critical praxis traversing the history of colonialism and its aftermath, and transforming a range of postwar isms and movements: poststructuralism, deconstruction, global feminism, subaltern studies, anthropocentric humanism, ecocriticism. Throughout, there is an attentiveness to translation as pedagogy—in some ways the only pedagogy—capable of challenging monolingual protocols in the Euro-American academy. In Spivak's public call for a curriculum in which all students would already know or study a non-European language, what is at stake is not just a way of working in world literatures that acknowledges the risks of translation-as-violation or cultural appropriationism, but a politics of pedagogy that fastens on the singularities and withholdings of each and every idiom.

Translation withheld, marked as failed, and *not*-translated qualify as hallmarks of Spivakian untranslatability even if untranslatability is not a term Spivak herself would necessarily subscribe to—her practice as teacher and translator roundly affirms translatability as a precondition of transnational literacy.[9] If I make the case here for a Spivakian

---

tongue as one language among many—gives rise to a certain obligation for reparation" (p. 72). In *Ambiguities of Witnessing: Law and Literature in the Time of a Truth Commission* (Stanford, CA: Stanford University Press, 2007), Mark Sanders builds on Spivak's Kleinian model of reparative translation in a discussion of the role of languages in testimonies given to the South African Truth and Reconciliation Commission. On this topic, see also Emily Apter, "Afterword: Towards a Theory of Reparative Translation," in Francesco Giusti and Benjamin Lewis Robinson (eds), *The Work of World Literature* (Berlin: ICI Berlin Press, 2020), pp. 209–28.

9 In referring to Spivakian untranslatability, let me affirm the obvious: there are many untranslatabilities in her own work, and in my own as well, even if I have at times implicitly restricted the term's usage by applying it to fugitive dimensions of untranslatability, it is in the interest of marking something very particular to her way of working *as a translator*, something we might think of as a *self-resistance* (or autoimmunity?) that maps onto and derives vibrancy from that which is resistant in language itself.

This double helix of self-resistance/language resistance is on display in Spivak's preface to her translation from Bengali into English of Mahasweta Devi's story collection *Breast Stories*. In the story "Drapaudi" Spivak confronts the caste term for "untouchables," always problematic in Indian languages (and giving rise to Mahatma Gandhi's assimilation of untouchables to tribals through the name Harijan, "God's people," a mistranslation insofar as tribals should not be confused with untouchables) (p. 130). Spivak notes Devi's decision to follow "the Bengali practice of calling each so-called untouchable caste by the name of its menial and unclean task within the rigid structural functionalism of institutionalized Hinduism" (p. 130). And yet she chooses to go with the phrase: "The untouchables don't get water," admitting bluntly "I have been unable to reproduce this in my translation" (p. 130). The defeated translator finds strength in the caste term's resistance to translation because it sets the stage for a pedagogical scene, one that demonstrates, first, how translating prevents autochthonous meaning from shining through, and second, how the withholding of content can be strategically deployed to disrobe the posture of all-knowingness and entitled access directed by western Anglophone readers towards texts in Indian languages. "I have been unable to reproduce this in translation" is a gesture that points to reserves of untranslatability that lie in the deep

---

style and form, theopolitical interdictions, ethnonationalist ontology as it takes root in linguistic nativism, and language passporting at the checkpoint. The diversity of approaches to the untranslatable is fully on display in Cassin's *Dictionary of Untranslatables*, a work that I helped edit and translate into English. Each entry, one could say, represents one of many ways of looking at the blackbird of the untranslatable.

structure of discursive hierarchies, themselves imbricated in a specific politics of history.

Spivak channels undercurrents of resistance within language as such by tapping into the untranslatability effects produced by colonial language policy, racial injustice, caste discrimination, religious wars, ethnic cleansing, apartheid, ecocide, cultural globalization, and ethno-nationalism. Consider, by way of example, her analysis of Farhad Mazhar's *Ashomyer Noteboi* (1994). In response to Mazhar's lines:

> Untimely notebook, I'm giving a fatwa,
>> you're murtad
> I'll dorra you a hundred and one times
>> you're shameless (p. 97)

Spivak avows:

> I am unable to access *murtad* and *dorra* because they are *tatshomo* words from Arabic. [. . .] *Tat* in these two words signifies "that" or "it," and refers to Sanskrit, one of the classical languages of India, claimed by the Hindu majority. They are descriptive of two different kinds of words. *Tadbhabo* means "born of it." *Tatshomo* means "just like it." I am using these two words by shifting the shifter *tat*—that or it—to refer to Arabic as an important loan-source. (p. 98)

Spivak expatiates often on Bengali-Arabic shared etymologies, often obscured by politicized philology. Her attention to loanwords, as in Tamara Chin's recent work on Silk Road loanwords in antiquity, brings together pre and postcolonial approaches to the politics of historical semantics.[10] Spivak's semantics bears little in common with that of the positivist nineteenth-century philologists who tracked a meaning to its mythic origin or *Ursprung* with the aim of shoring up linguistic

---

10 Tamara Chin, "The Afro-Asian Silk Road: Chinese Experiments in Postcolonial Premodernity," *PMLA* 136(1) (January 2021): 17–38.

genetics and the "genius" of a people. As I have already suggested, Spivak practices instead a kind of antiphilology that dredges up histories of linguistic conquest and erasure primarily for the sake of translational justice. To this end, she will call out "the fashioners of the new Bengali prose [who] purged the language of the Arabic-Persian content" by Sanskritizing Bengali (p. 99). With its Arabic and Persian components reduced to little more than local color within the refined contemporary Bengali that Spivak was taught in school, terms such as *murtad* and *dorra* are rendered opaque, effectively untranslatable.

The story does not end here however. *Murtad* and *dorra* lead Spivak to subtle insights into how partition operates in language politics. In abstract terms it refers to a partitive, parthenogenetic process in language, like a splitting of the word's atomic particles which, once combusted, shower the world with potentially toxic elements. As a historically grounded particular, it canonizes the event of Partition, applicable on the subcontinent to the division of West and East Bengal in 1947 and the secession of East Pakistan as the People's Republic of Bangladesh in 1971. Spivak's gloss on partition dissects how untranslatability—in this case the suppression of Arabic and Persian roots— becomes a visible symptom of the violent and bloody history of ethnic cleansing:

> If the establishment of a place named Bangladesh in a certain sense endorses the Partition of 1947, the language policy of the state, strangely enough, honors that other partition—the gradual banishment of the Arabic and Persian elements of the language that took place in the previous century—and thus paradoxically undoes the difference from West Bengal. The official language of the state of Bangladesh, over 90 percent Muslim, is as ferociously Sanskritized as anything to be found in Indian Bengali.
>
> It is over against and all entwined in this tangle that the movement to restore the Arabic and Persian element of Bengali, away from its century-old ethnic cleansing, does its work. And

it is because I grew up inside the tangle that, in spite of my love of Bengali, I could not translate *murtad* and *dorra*—though I could crack *ashomoyer* with Nietzsche. (p. 101)

Not-translating *murtad* and *dorra*, grappling with resistant translation in contexts of political violence and ethnic cleansing, is a *worrying task*, with "worry" understood as symptom of anxiety tracing all the way back to Spivak's preface to *Of Grammatology*, possibly her earliest reflection on the auto-inflicted afflictions of the translator:

Derrida's text certainly offers its share of "untranslatable" words. I have had my battles with "exergue" and "proper." My special worry is "entamer." As we have seen, it is an important word in Derrida's vocabulary. It means both to break into and to begin. I have made do with "broach" or "breach" with the somewhat fanciful confidence that the shadow-word "breach" or "broach" will declare itself through it. (p. 32)

When Spivak mentions "my special worry," we could take it in an anodyne way to mean problem-solving, or thinking within the constraints of language. But we could equally well pick up on its more aggressive significations; worrying in the sense of twisting, pulling, biting or cutting away at the verbal thing to arrive at the *right target, le mot juste*. In this case, that which is cut out—the alternative word choice—haunts the translation like a phantom limb. Spivakian "worrying" in this scenario, enters the world of Derridian hauntology.

Living in the cuts where meanings fork and self-divide, living in the break of translation (which implies *living on* its worry-spots, its flesh-wounds), entails experiences of pain and suffering that must be fully tasted because they put us in touch with traumatic hauntings. But these same breaks afford breakthroughs in thinking. This is what happens with the untranslatable loanword *haq*, which Spivak knows is particularly conducive to lucky finds. Taking off on Patrick Wolfe's surmise that it may have a connection to the English word "hock" (connoting extortion, ransom or bounty), with a history in the violent

Crusades narrative of hostage-taking and age-old conflicts between Christians and Saracens, Spivak embarks on a path leading from "hock" to *al-Haq*, the Arabic expression for truth (in the sense of genuine, real, right or righteously) that sometimes stands in for the name of Allah in the Qur'an (p. 94n9). She then takes a leap, translating haq into a notion of "para-individual structural responsibility" into which we are born— that is, our true being, with the proviso that "responsibility" be taken as an approximative translation for a "structural positioning" associated with birth-right.[11] It is this approximate space, this "not quite English sense of my haq" that hatches the invention of a new theoreme of global criticality—planetarity, a term predicated on "a precapitalist feeling of responsibility for the planet" that eludes "a rationally justifiable teleology." "You will indulge me, [writes Spivak] if I say that the 'planet' is, here, as perhaps always, a catachresis for inscribing collective responsibility as right."[12] This catachresis—a rhetorical figure signaling mistranslation (as when one uses mitigate for militate)—seeds an outline for a planetary bill of rights that "speaks" in a language—pre-capitalist and para-individual—that the translator must train herself to hear and to transcribe.

There are many untranslatabilities operative in Spivak's writings on translation, but they arguably converge in a model of concept-labor— Spivak's signature task as a translator—that translates towards alterity; towards episteme-logics that do not yet exist.

New York University
January 2022

---

11 Spivak, "Imperative to Re-imagine the Planet," p. 341.
12 Spivak, "Imperative to Re-imagine the Planet," p. 341.

Preface

Earliest Engagements with Translation: Institution-Building

ARON AJI and MAUREEN ROBERTSON

I engaged with translation from my earliest encounter with English, which was of course the imperial language, but not the language spoken at home. I did not go to a convent school in Calcutta, and had no native English-speaking teachers until the few months of postgraduate instruction in 1960. In 1959, preparing hard for my BA in English Honors, I translated Book I of Edmund Spenser's *The Faerie Queene* into Bengali to keep myself working all night, night after night in that mosquito-ridden heat. The next big undertaking was, as this essay written by Aron Aji and Maureen Robertson testifies, institution-building at the University of Iowa, even as I had taken up the practice of translation by way of Jacques Derrida's *De la grammatologie* as permission to write the Introduction! Aji and Robertson beautifully describe the transition from a spectacular academic tourist facility into a much more nose-to-the-ground unit of intellectual labor. (This is not to undermine the International Writing Program; I met Okot p'Bitek, Ngũgĩ wa Thiong'o, and Sankha Ghosh through it.) I should mention here the work with Steven Ungar and Rudi Kuenzli during those early years to enrich the work of the program. The authors of this essay have no reason to know that I had also succeeded, partly through ignorance of institutional racism, in having Sheldon Pollock, the eminent Sanskritist who is now my colleague at Columbia, hired through the Classics Department rather than Southern Asia Studies!—**GCS**

In the mid 1970s, while continuing to work on her translation of Derrida's *Of Grammatology* at the University of Iowa, Gayatri Chakravorty Spivak founded the MFA in Translation (1974) in collaboration with Daniel Weissbort, director of the Iowa Translation Workshop. Soon, Spivak would also become the director of Iowa's Comparative Literature Program, and make several faculty hires that decidedly counteracted the traditional Eurocentric/Orientalist scope of comparative literature. Reflecting, however briefly, on these early actions by Spivak in Iowa seems fitting on the occasion of this collection of her writings on translation.

A decade earlier, the University had introduced the first translation workshop ever offered at a US university, spurred by Paul and Hualing Nieh Engle's ambitious project to establish an international residency program—now the world-renowned International Writing Program. The Iowa Translation Workshop, as it was quickly christened, enlisted the students in the Writers' Workshop to collaboratively translate works by the international writers in residence. While capitalizing on this creative energy, Spivak's new MFA in Translation had greater ambitions. Introduced inside the Comparative Literature Program, the new MFA approached translation as a field of both practice and discipline, balancing the workshops in the writerly art of translation with coursework in translation theory and history, comparative literature, and literary studies in the source languages. This curricular emphasis on the source languages and cultures is especially noteworthy. Whereas earlier translation practice generally prioritized fluency and readability in English, a domesticating approach, the new MFA program treated translation as a complex bi-directional operation between the source and target languages and cultures, one that engaged, critically and creatively, the essential foreignness of the original, to resist subordinating it all too quickly to the linguistic and literary norms of English. For Spivak and Weissbort, translation was itself a generative act that resulted in a new literary form. What a previous generation would have regarded as fatal inaccuracy, the new generation celebrated: translation's necessary but impossible attempt at faithfulness creates a new object which could not exist without the translator.[1] In this critical shift, it is hard to miss the intellectual fingerprints of the future author of "Can the Subaltern Speak?" and "The Politics of Translation."

The translation degree, an MFA no less, also served as a catalyst in the transformation of comparative literature at Iowa. At the time, the program was housed in the English department; Spivak's three faculty hires in 1976 underscored, on the one hand, the intersection of scholarship and translation, and introduced, on the other, areas of expertise that were conspicuously different from the Anglo- and Eurocentric make-up of the faculty: Vladimir Padunov, a Russian cinema and narrative theory scholar; Maureen Robertson, a classical Chinese literature scholar; and Steve Ungar, a French cinema and Barthes scholar. All of these scholars challenged the received purpose and intent of the discipline of Comparative Literature, which for a century had recapitulated the colonialist epistemology of Europe, encountering and rendering legible the world against European referents and forms. For all of them, comparative literature shed its anxiety of regulating the relationship between European literature and its others—the work of disarming potentially counterhegemonic forms by addressing them through mere "comparison." Instead, these scholars embraced the impossibility of clean passages and unproblematic referents. This was comparative literature's excitement and urgency, not its downfall.

Indeed, translation and comparison are both intimately concerned with the anxiety over the disappearance of the original and the impossibility of its full reproduction or comparison. Ungar and Padunov, as film scholars, worked to expand the conception of what counted as

---

1 Daniel and I had a running discussion here, my own feelings leaning much more toward a necessary but impossible "faithfulness," with which Maureen was sympathetic, so I mark the moment.—GCS

"literary" in the same way that Spivak's approach to translation did, and not without the same kind of opposition from established scholars. Robertson's focus on medieval women poets in China was exemplary of Spivak's direct challenge to the conventions of both translation and Comparative Literature. Robertson focused on the Ming and early Qing dynasties, during which women were forbidden to publish or to be literate; she found and translated a wealth of women's literature published in secret, under pseudonyms, or by relatives. This project of identifying and translating legally voiceless women, in a context with no relevant European referent, so far in the past, is so ridden with aporetic moments that the technical question of accuracy in comparison and translation is necessarily subordinated to the literary act of passage in representing these women's voices in the present day.

But here as elsewhere, gender relations had shaped the landscape of possibility. Spivak's mentorship of Robertson specifically created the space for her to move from her earlier work on well-known male poets to the work of finding the voice and identity in women writers. Both Spivak and Robertson came up in academic settings without women, in which a young woman scholar could not accept the help of a senior male scholar without the risk of becoming a protégé. Indeed, accepting help from male colleagues was perilous. Robertson focused her own mentorship at Iowa on expanding the spaces Spivak had established for women to advance in scholarship, banishing the leers and condescension of the greying Orientalists and Jesuit sinologists who had haunted her graduate years.

Spivak wrote that Comparative Literature, once shed of its urge to regulate legibility against a European criterion, is itself a "translation before translation": "Comparative Literature imagines that each language may be activated in this special way and makes an effort to produce a simulacrum through the reflexivity of language as habit. Here we translate not the content but the very moves of languaging. We can provisionally call this peculiar form of translation before translation, the 'comparison' in comparative literature."[2] Spivak's vision has retained its currency at Iowa, long after she left, by the people she had originally hired to shape and define the two disciplines. Despite the unfortunate elimination of Iowa's comparative literature degree programs (sad casualties of the winds of efficiency and reorganization sweeping the US academy), the discipline still represents a large intellectual community across the humanities at Iowa, with faculty members in cinematic arts, English, area studies, religious studies, world languages, literatures and cultures, and of course, translation. Iowa's MFA in literary translation, in particular, is where Spivak's articulation of comparative literature continues to thrive, as we train US and international students in the creative art and critical, reflective practice of literary translation.

I never was given so strong an opportunity to build institutionally at Texas–Austin, or, indeed, Emory—my places of employment after Iowa. I could, therefore, say that my constructive institutional work began with translation. In my sustained work with comparative literature, however, I have insisted that the act of translation should be a practice rather than a convenience. I was interested to see that Wyatt Mason, as, in his review of Lydia Davis's *Essays Two*, he quotes a powerful passage by Javier Marías, and manages to miss the reference to teaching translation, as well as to the deep double bind in teaching, reflected in the phrase "God forbid", involved in the teaching of something as critically intimate as translation, as he goes on to identify the writing of novels and essays on translation, eliminating the reference to practice with the position expressed by Marías in this passage: "Were he ever to have a creative-writing school—*God forbid*, he said—he would accept only students who knew at least one language besides their own. 'And the only thing I would make them do,' he explained, 'is to translate and to translate and to translate. Because I think that's the best possible school for

---

2 See "What Is It, Then, to Translate?" in this volume, pp. 162–82.

someone who wants to become a writer."[3] My first instinct in the mid 70s, when I became director of the Comparative Literature Program at Iowa, was to believe that this practice was also part of the best possible training for someone who wanted to become a serious comparativist. By the time I came to Pittsburgh, where once again I had the permission to intervene institutionally, I established a Cultural Studies Program—times had changed, but language and translation remained crucial. They were of course part of the initial principles upon which Andreas Huyssen and I, later aided by Rosalind Morris, founded the Institute for Comparative Literature and Society at Columbia in 1998.—**GCS**

---

3 Wyatt Mason, Review of *Essays Two* by Lydia Davis, *New York Times*, December 3, 2021. Available at: https://nyti.ms/3tcephS (last accessed on January 11, 2022).

POLITICS OF TRANSLATION

Translator's Preface to *Of Grammatology* by Jacques Derrida

(1976)*

If you have been reading Derrida, you will know that a plausible gesture would be to begin with a consideration of "the question of the preface." But I write in the hope that for at least some of the readers of this volume Derrida is new; and therefore take it for granted that, for the moment, an introduction can be made.

Jacques Derrida is maitre-assistant in philosophy at the Ecole Normale Supérieure in Paris. He was born forty-five years ago of Sephardic Jewish parents in Algiers.[1] At nineteen, he came to France as a student. He was at Harvard on a scholarship in 1956–57. In the sixties he was among the young intellectuals writing for the avant-garde journal *Tel Quel*.[2] He is now associated with GREPH (Groupe de Recherche

---

* Selection from Translator's Preface to Jacques Derrida, *Of Grammatology* (Gayatri Chakravorty Spivak trans.) (Baltimore, MD: Johns Hopkins University Press, 2016[1976]), pp. xxvii–cxii.

1 For Derrida's interest in his own Jewish tradition, see "Edmond Jabès et la question du livre," and "Ellipse," both in *L'écriture et la différence* (hereafter cited in the text as ED) (Paris: Seuil, 1967), pp. 99–116, 429–36, and, of course, *Glas*. At the end of "Ellipse" he signs as he quotes Jabès—"Reb Dérissa." The few provocative remarks in response to Gérard Kaleka's questions after Derrida's paper "La question du style" (*Nietzsche aujourd'hui*? VOL. 1 [Paris: UGE, 1973], p. 289; hereafter cited as QS) can provide ideas for the development of an entire thematics of the Jew.

2 For an account of the *Tel Quel* group, see Mary Caws, "*Tel Quel*: Text and Revolution," *Diacritics* 3(1) (Spring 1973): 2–8.

de l'Enseignement Philosophique)—a student movement that engages itself with the problems of the institutional teaching of philosophy. He was for a time a visiting professor on a regular basis at the Johns Hopkins University, and now occupies a similar position at Yale. He has an affection for some of the intellectual centers of the Eastern seaboard—Cambridge, New York, Baltimore—in his vocabulary, "America." And it seems that at first these places and now more and more of the intellectual centers all over the United States are returning his affection.

Derrida's first book was a translation of Edmund Husserl's *Origin of Geometry*, with a long critical introduction. This was followed by *La voix et le phénomène*, a critique of Husserl's theory of meaning. In-between appeared a collection of essays entitled *L'écriture et la différence*. *De la grammatologie* came next, followed by two more collections—*La dissémination* and *Marges de la philosophie*. There was a little-noticed introduction to the *Essai sur l'origine des connaissances humaines* by Condillac, entitled "L'archéologie du frivole," and *Positions*, a collection of interviews. This year his monumental *Glas* has appeared.[3]

---

3 Edmund Husserl, *L'origine de la géométrie* (Jacques Derrida trans.) (Paris: Presses universitaires de France, 1962).

Jacques Derrida, *La Voix et le phénomène: introduction au problème du signe dans la phénoménologie de Husserl* (Paris; Presses universitaires de France, 1967), hereafter cited in the text as VP; translated as *Speech and Phenomena and Other Essays on Husserl's Theory of Signs* by David B. Allison (Evanston, IL: Northwestern University Press, 1973), hereafter cited in the text as SP. *L'écriture et la différence* (Paris: Seuil, 1967). *De la grammatologie* (Paris: Minuit, 1967), hereafter cited simply by page numbers in the text, page references to the French followed by references to the present edition in bold-face type. *La dissémination* (Paris: Seuil, 1972), hereafter cited as Dis. *Marges de la philosophie* (Paris: Minuit, 1972), hereafter cited as MP. *Positions* (Paris: Minuit, 1972), hereafter cited as Pos F; parts of this book have been translated in *Diacritics* 2(4) (Winter 1972): 6–14 (hereafter cited in the text as Pos E I) and *Diacritics* 3(1) (Spring 1973) : 33–46 (hereafter cited in the text as Pos E II). "L'archéologie du frivole," in Condillac, *Essai sur l'origine des connaissances humaines* (Paris: Galilée, 1973). Finally, *Glas* (Paris: Galilée, 1974).

Four important essays that are as yet uncollected are "Le parergon," *Digraphe* 2 (1974): 21–57; "La question du style," "Le facteur de la vérité," *Poétique* 21 (1975):

Jacques Derrida is also this collection of texts.

In an essay on the Preface to Hegel's *Phenomenology of the Mind*, Jean Hyppolite writes:

> When Hegel had finished the *Phenomenology* [. . .] he reflected retrospectively on his philosophic enterprise and wrote the "Preface." [. . .] It is a strange demonstration, for he says above all, "Don't take me seriously in a preface. The real philosophical work is what I have just written, the *Phenomenology of the Mind*. And if I speak to you outside of what I have written, these marginal comments cannot have the value of the work itself. [. . .] Don't take a preface seriously. The preface announces a project and a project is nothing until it is realized."[4]

It is clear that, as it is commonly understood, the preface harbors a lie. "Prae-fatio" is "a saying before-hand" (*Oxford English Dictionary*; OED). Yet it is accepted as natural by Hyppolite, as indeed by all of us, that "Hegel reflected *retrospectively* on his philosophic enterprise and wrote his 'Preface.'" We may see this as no more than the tacit acceptance of a fiction. We think of the Preface, however, not as a literary, but as an expository exercise. It "involves a norm of truth," although it might well be the insertion of an obvious fiction into an ostensibly "true" discourse. (Of course, when the preface is being written by someone other than the author, the situation is yet further complicated. A pretense at writing *before* a text that one must have read *before* the preface can be

---

96–147 (soon to appear in translation in Yale French Studies), and "Le sens de la coupure pure (Le parergon II)," *Digraphe* 3 (1975): 5–31.

4 Jean Hyppolite, "Structure du langage philosophique d'après la 'Préface' de la 'Phénoménologie de l'esprit' de Hegel," available in English translation as: "The Structure of Philosophic Language According to the 'Preface' to Hegel's *Phenomenology of the Mind*," in Richard Macksey and Eugenio Donato (eds), *The Languages of Criticism and the Sciences of Man: The Structuralist Controversy* (Baltimore, MD: Johns Hopkins University Press, 1970), pp. 157–68, hereafter cited in the text as SC. The passage cited is on p. 159.

written. Writing a postface would not really be different—but that argument can only be grasped at the end of this preface.)

Hegel's own objection to the Preface seems grave. The contrast between abstract generality and the self-moving *activity* of cognition appears to be structured like the contrast between preface and text. The method of philosophy is the structure of knowing, an activity of consciousness that moves of itself; this activity, the method of philosophical discourse, structures the philosophical text. The reader of the philosophical text will recognize this self-movement in his consciousness as he surrenders himself to and masters the text. Any prefatory gesture, abstracting so-called themes, robs philosophy of its self-moving structure. "In modern times," Hegel writes, "an individual finds the abstract form ready made."[5] Further,

> let [modern man] read reviews of philosophical works, and even go to the length of reading the prefaces and first paragraphs of the works themselves; for the latter give the general principles on which everything turns, while the reviews along with the historical notice provide over and above the critical judgment and appreciation, which, being a judgment passed on the work, goes farther than the work that is judged. This common way a man can take in his dressing-gown. But spiritual elation in the eternal, the sacred, the infinite, moves along the high way of truth in the robes of the high priest.[6]

---

5 Georg Wilhelm Friedrich Hegel, *Phänomenologie des Geistes* (Frankfurt am Main: Suhrkamp, 1970), p. 37; *The Phenomenology of the Mind* (J. B. Baillie trans.) (New York: Harper Torchbooks, 1967), p. 94. My general policy in quoting from English translations has been to modify the English when it seems less than faithful to the original. I have included references to both the original and the English, and generally included the original passage in the text when I have modified the translation.

6 Hegel, *Phänomenologie*, p. 65; Baillie, pp. 127–28.

Yet, as Hyppolite points out, Hegel damns the preface in general even as he writes his own "Preface." And Derrida suggests that a very significant part of Hegel's work was but a play of prefaces (Dis 15f). Whereas Hegel's impatience with prefaces is based on philosophical grounds, his excuse for continuing to write them seems commonsensical:

> Having in mind that the general idea of what is to be done, if it precedes the attempt to carry it out, facilitates the comprehension of this process, it is worth while to indicate here some rough idea of it, with the intention of eliminating at the same time certain forms whose habitual presence is a hindrance to philosophical knowledge [*in der Absicht zugleich, bei dieser Gelegenheit einige Formen zu entfernen, deren Gewohnheit ein Hindernis fur das philosophische Erkennen ist*].[7]

Hegel's objection to prefaces reflects the following structure: preface/text = abstract generality/self-moving activity. His acceptance of prefaces reflects another structure: preface/text = signifier/signified. And the name of the "=" in this formula is the Hegelian *Aufhebung*.

Aufhebung is a relationship between two terms where the second at once annuls the first and lifts it up into a higher sphere of existence; it is a hierarchial concept generally translated "sublation" and now sometimes translated "sublimation." A successful preface is *aufgehoben* into the text it precedes, just as a word is *aufgehoben* into its meaning. It is as if, to use one of Derrida's structural metaphors, the son or seed (preface or word), caused or engendered by the father (text or meaning) is recovered by the father and thus justified.

But, within this structural metaphor, Derrida's cry is "dissemination," the seed that neither inseminates nor is recovered by the father, but is scattered abroad.[8] And he makes room for the prefatory gesture in quite another way:

---

7 Hegel, *Phänomenologie*, p. 22; Baillie, p. 79.
8 See "La dissémination," Dis, II.x. "Les greffes, retour au surjet," pp. 395–98, and pp. lxv–lxvi of the full Preface, from which this is an extract.

The preface is a necessary gesture of homage and parricide, for the book (the father) makes a claim of authority or origin which is both true and false. (As regards parricide, I speak theoretically. The preface need make no overt claim—as this one does not—of destroying its pre-text. As a preface, it is already surrendered to that gesture . . .) Human-kind's common desire is for a stable center, and for the assurance of mastery—through knowing or possessing. And a book, with its pon-derable shape and its beginning, middle, and end, stands to satisfy that desire. But what sovereign subject is the origin of the book? "I was not one man only," says Proust's narrator,

> but the steady advance hour after hour of an army in close for-mation, in which there appeared, according to the moment, impassioned men, indifferent men, jealous men. [. . .] In a com-posite mass, these elements may, one by one, *without our noticing it*, be replaced by others, which others again eliminate or reinforce, until in the end a change has been brought about which it would be impossible to conceive if we were a single person.[9]

What, then, is the book's identity? Ferdinand de Saussure had remarked that the "same" phoneme pronounced twice or by two differ-ent people is not identical with itself. Its only identity is in its difference from all other phonemes (77–78, **52–54**). So do the two readings of the "same" book show an identity that can only be defined as a difference. The book is not repeatable in its "identity": each reading of the book produces a simulacrum of an "original" that is itself the mark of the shifting and unstable subject that Proust describes, using and being used by a language that is also shifting and unstable. Any preface com-memorates that difference in identity by inserting itself between two

---

9 Marcel Proust, "La fugitive," in *A la recherche du temps perdu* (Paris: Pléiade edition, 1954), VOL. 3, p. 489; "The Sweet Cheat Gone" (C. K. Scott Moncrieff trans.) (New York: Vintage, 1970), p. 54, emphasis added.

readings-in our case, my reading (given of course that my language and I are shifting and unstable), my rereading, my rearranging of the text—and your reading. As Hegel (and other defenders of the authority of the text) wrote preface on preface to match re-editions and revised versions, they unwittingly became a party to this identity in difference:

> From the moment that the circle turns, that the book is wound back upon itself, that the book repeats itself, its self-identity receives an imperceptible difference which allows us to step effectively, rigorously, and thus discreetly, out of the closure. Redoubling the closure, one splits it. Then one escapes it furtively, between two passages through the same book, through the same line, following the same bend. [. . .] This departure outside of the identical within the same remains very slight, it weighs nothing, it thinks and weighs the book *as such*. The return to the book is also the abandoning of the book. (ED 430)

The preface, by daring to repeat the book and reconstitute it in another register, merely enacts what is already the case: the book's repetitions are always other than the book. There is, in fact, no "book" other than these ever-different repetitions: the "book" in other words, is always already a "text," constituted by the play of identity and difference. A written preface provisionally localizes the place where, between reading and reading, book and book, the inter-inscribing of "reader(s)," "writer(s)," and language is forever at work. Hegel had closed the circle between father and son, text and preface. He had in fact suggested, as Derrida makes clear, that the fulfilled concept—the end of the self-acting method of the philosophical text—was the pre-dicate—pre-saying—preface, to the preface. In Derrida's reworking, the structure preface-text becomes open at both ends. The text has no stable identity, no stable origin, no stable end. Each act of reading the "text" is a preface to the next. The reading of a self-professed preface is no exception to this rule.

It is inaccurate yet necessary to say that something called *De la grammatologie* is (was) the provisional origin of my preface. And, even as I write, I project the moment, when you, reading, will find in my preface the provisional origin of your reading of *Of Grammatology*. There can be an indefinite number of variations on that theme.

Why must we worry over so simple a thing as preface-making? There is, of course, no real answer to questions of this sort. The most that can be said, and Derrida has reminded us to say it anew, is that a certain view of the world, of consciousness, and of language has been accepted as the correct one, and, if the minute particulars of that view are examined, a rather different picture (that is also a no-picture, as we shall see) emerges. That examination involves an enquiry into the "operation" of our most familiar gestures. To quote Hegel again:

> What is "familiarly known" is not properly known, just for the reason that it is "familiar. "When engaged in the process of knowing, it is the commonest form of self-deception, and a deception of other people as well, to assume something to be familiar, and to let it pass [*gefallen zu lassen*] on that very account. Knowledge of that sort, with all its talking around it [*Hin- und Herreden*] never gets from the spot, but has no idea that this is the case. [. . .] To display [*auseinanderlegen*] an idea in its original [*ursprünglich*] elements means returning upon its moments, [. . .][10]

When Derrida writes that since Kant, philosophy has become aware of taking the responsibility for its discourse, it is this reexamination of the familiar that he is hinting at. And this is one of the reasons why he is so drawn to Mallarmé, "that exemplary post," who invested every gesture of reading and writing—even the slitting of an uncut double page with a knife—with textual import.[11]

---

10 Hegel, *Phänomenologie*, p. 35; Baillie, p. 92.
11 Stéphane Mallarmé, "Le Livre, instrument spirituel," in *Quant au Livre, Oeuvres complètes* (Paris: Pléiade edition, 1945), p. 381; *Mallarmé* (Anthony Hartley ed. and trans.) (Harmondsworth: Penguin, 1965), p. 194.

And if the assumption of responsibility for one's discourse leads to the conclusion that all conclusions are genuinely provisional and therefore inconclusive, that all origins are similarly unoriginal, that responsibility itself must cohabit with frivolity, this need not be cause for gloom. Derrida contrasts Rousseau's melancholy with Nietzsche's affirmative joy precisely from this angle:

> Turned toward the presence, lost or impossible, of the absent origin, the structuralist thematic of broken immediateness is thus the sad, *negative*, nostalgic, guilty, Rousseauist aspect of the thought of play of which the Nietzschean *affirmation*—the joyous affirmation of the play of the world and of the innocence of becoming, the affirmation of a world of signs without fault, without truth, without origin, offered to an active interpretation—would be the other side. (ED 427, SC 264)

There is, then, always already a preface between two hands holding open a book. And the "prefacer," of the same or another proper name as the "author," need not apologize for "repeating" the text.

I

"It is inaccurate yet necessary to say," I have written above, "that something called *De la grammatologie* is (was) the provisional origin of my preface." Inaccurate yet necessary. My predicament is an analogue for a certain philosophical exigency that drives Derrida to writing "sous rature," which I translate as "under erasure." This is to write a word, cross it out, and then print both word and deletion. (Since the word is inaccurate, it is crossed out. Since it is necessary, it remains legible.) To take an example from Derrida that I shall cite again: "[. . .] the sign is[x] that ill-named thing[x] [. . .] which escapes the instituting question of philosophy [. . .] " (31, **19**).

In examining familiar things we come to such unfamiliar conclusions that our very language is twisted and bent even as it guides us. Writing "under erasure" is the mark of this contortion.

Derrida directs us to Martin Heidegger's *Zur Seinsfrage* as the "authority" for this strategically important practice,[12] which we cannot understand without a look at Heidegger's formulation of it.

Zur Seinsfrage is ostensibly a letter to Ernst Junger which seeks to establish a speculative definition of nihilism. Just as Hegel, writing a preface, philosophically confronted the problem of prefaces, so Heidegger, establishing a definition, philosophically confronts the problem of definitions: in order for the nature of anything in particular to be defined as an entity, the question of Being is general must always already be broached and answered in the affirmative. That something *is*, presupposes that *anything* can be.

What is this question of Being that is necessarily precomprehended in order that thinking itself occur? Since it is always anterior to thinking, it can never be formulated as an answer to the question "what is [. . .]:." "The 'goodness' of the rightfully demanded 'good definition' finds its confirmation in our giving up the wish to define in so far as this must be established on assertions in which thinking dies out. [. . .] No information can be given about nothingness and Being and nihilism, about their essence and about the (verbal) essence [it *is*] of the (nominal) essence [it is] which can be presented tangibly in the form of assertions [it is . . .]." (QB 80–81) This possibility of Being must be granted (or rather is already of itself granted) for the human being to say "I am," not to mention "you are," "she is." Even such negative concepts as "nothingness" or "nihilism" are held within this precomprehended question of Being which is asked and answered nonverbally, nonnominally, and without agency. This question, therefore, cannot be constructed to match an assertive answer. And the human being is the place or zone where this particular problem has its play; not the human being as an

---

12 Martin Heidegger, *The Question of Being* (William Kluback and Jean T. Wilde trans), bilingual edition (New York: New College and University Press, 1958), hereafter cited in the text as QB.

individual, but the human being as *Dasein*—simply being-there—as the principle that asks and posits: "Man does not only stand *in* the critical zone. [. . .] He himself, but not he for himself and particularly not through himself alone, *is* this zone [. . .]" (QB 82–83). But, Heidegger cautions us, this is not mysticism. It is the baffling result of an examination of the obvious, the lifting of the most natural forgetfulness.

"What if even the [propositional] language of metaphysics and meta-physics itself, whether it be that of the living or of the dead God, *as* metaphysics, formed that barrier which forbids a crossing over (*Übergehen*) the line [from the assertion, to the question, of Being]?" (Elsewhere Heidegger suggests, as does, of course, Nietzsche before him, that the propositional language of the sciences is just as forgetful of the question of Being.) "If that were the case, would not then the crossing [out] [diagonally—*Überqueren*] of the line necessarily become a transformation of language and demand a transformed relationship to the essence of language?" (QB 70–71)

As a move toward this transformation, Heidegger crosses out the word "Being," and lets both deletion and word stand. It is inaccurate to use the word "Being" here, for the differentiation of a "concept" of Being has already slipped away from that precomprehended question of Being. Yet it is necessary to use the word, since language cannot do more:

A thoughtful glance ahead into this realm of "Being" can only write it as Being[x]. The drawing of these crossed lines at first only wards off (*abwehrt*), especially the habit of conceiving "Being" as something standing by itself. [. . .] The sign of crossing through [*Zeichen der Durchkreuzung*] can, to be sure, [. . .] not be a merely negative sign of crossing out [*Zeichen der Durchstreichung*. . . .] Man in his essence is the memory [or "memorial," *Gedächtnis*] of Being, but of Being[x] This means that the essence of man is a part of that which in the crossed intersected lines of Being[x] puts thinking under the claim of a more originary command [*anfänglichere Geheiss*]. (QB 80–81, 82–83)

Language is indeed straining here. The sentence "Man in his essence is the memory (memorial) of Being" avoids ascribing an agent to the unaskable question of Being. Heidegger is working with the resources of the old language, the language we already possess, and which possesses us. To make a new word is to run the risk of forgetting the problem or believing it solved: "That the transformation of the language which contemplates the essence of Being is subject to other demands than the exchanging of an old terminology for a new one, seems to be clear." This transformation should rather involve "crossing out" the relevant old terms and thus liberating them, exposing "the presumptuous demand that [thinking] know the solution of the riddles and bring salvation" (QB 72–73).

Now there is a certain difference between what Heidegger puts under erasure and what Derrida does. "Being" is the master-word that Heidegger crosses out. Derrida does not reject this. But his word is "trace" (the French word carries strong implications of track, footprint, imprint), a word that cannot be a master-word, that presents itself as the mark of an anterior presence, origin, master. For "trace" one can substitute "arche-writing" ("archi-écriture"), or "differance," or in fact quite a few other words that Derrida uses in the same way. But I shall begin with "trace/track," for it is a simple word; and there also seems, I must admit, something ritually satisfying about beginning with the "trace."

To be sure, when Heidegger sets Being before all concepts, he is attempting to free language from the fallacy of a fixed origin, which is also a fixed end. But, *in a certain way*, he also sets up Being as what Derrida calls the "transcendental signified." For whatever a concept might "mean," anything that is conceived of in its being-present must lead us to the already-answered question of Being. In that sense, the sense of the final reference, Being is indeed the final signified to which all signifiers refer. But Heidegger makes it clear that Being cannot be contained by, is always prior to, indeed transcends, signification. It is therefore a situation where the signified commands, and is yet free of, all signifiers—a recognizably theological situation. The end of philosophy, according to Heidegger, is to restore the memory of that free and commanding signified, to discover *Urwörter* (originary words) in the languages of the world by learning to waylay the limiting logic of signification, a project that Derrida describes as "the other side of nostalgia, which I will call Heideggerian *hope* [. . .] I [. . .] shall relate it to what seems to me to be retained of metaphysics in [Heidegger's] 'Spruch des Anaximander,' namely, the quest for the proper word and the unique name" (MP 29, SP 159–60).

Derrida seems to show no nostalgia for a lost presence. He sees in the traditional concept of the sign a hetereogeneity—"the other of the signified is never contemporary, is at best a subtly discrepant inverse or parallel—discrepant by the time of a breath—of the order of the signifier" (31, **18**). It is indeed an ineluctable nostalgia for presence that makes of this heterogeneity a unity by declaring that a sign brings forth the presence of the signified. Otherwise it would seem clear that the sign is the place where "the completely other is announced as such— without any simplicity, any identity, any resemblance or continuity— in that which is not it" (69, **47**). Word and thing or thought never in fact become one. We are reminded of, referred to, what the convention of words sets up as thing or thought, by a particular arrangement of words. The structure of reference works and can go on working not because of the identity between these two so-called component parts of the sign, but because of their relationship of difference. The sign marks a place of difference.

One way of satisfying the rage for unity is to say that, within the phonic sign (speech rather than writing) there is no structure of difference; and that this nondifference is felt as self-presence in the silent and solitary thought of the self. This is so familiar an argument that we would accept it readily if we did not stop to think about it. But if we did, we would notice that there is no necessary reason why a particular sound should be identical with a "thought or thing"; and that the argument applies even when one "speaks" silently to oneself. Saussure was accordingly obliged to point out that the phonic signifier is as conventional as the graphic (74, **51**).

Armed with this simple yet powerful insight—powerful enough to "deconstruct the transcendental signified"—that the sign, phonic as well as graphic, is a structure of difference, Derrida suggests that what opens the possibility of thought is not merely the question of being, but also the never-annulled difference from "the completely other." Such is the strange "being" of the sign: half of it always "not there" and the other half always "not that." The structure of the sign is determined by the trace or track of that other which is forever absent. This other is of course never to be found in its full being. As even such empirical events as answering a child's question or consulting the dictionary proclaim, one sign leads to another and so on indefinitely. Derrida quotes Lambert and Peirce: "'[philosophy should] reduce the *theory of things* to the *theory of signs*.' [. . .] 'The idea of *manifestation* is the idea of a sign'" (72, **49**), and contrasts them to Husserl and Heidegger. On the way to the trace/track, the word "sign" has to be put under erasure: "the sign is[x] that ill-named thing[x]; the only one, that escapes the instituting question of philosophy: 'What is . . . ?'"

Derrida, then, gives the name "trace" to the part played by the radically other within the structure of difference that is the sign. (I stick to "trace" in my translation, because it "looks the same" as Derrida's word; the reader must remind himself of at least the track, even the spoor, contained within the French word.) In spite of itself, Saussurean linguistics recognizes the structure of the sign to be a trace-structure. And Freud's psychoanalysis, to some extent in spite of itself, recognizes the structure of experience itself to be a trace-, not a presence-structure. Following an argument analogical to the argument on the sign, Derrida puts the word "experience" under erasure:

As for the concept of experience, it is most unwieldy here. Like all the notions I am using, it belongs to the history of metaphysics and we can only use it under erasure. "Experience" has always designate the relationship with a presence, whether that relationship had the form of consciousness or not. Yet we must, by means of the sort of contortion and contention that discourse is obliged to undergo, exhaust the resources of the concept of experience before attaining and in order to attain, by deconstruction, its ultimate foundation. It is the only way to escape "empiricism" and the "naive" critiques of experience at the same time. (89, **60**)

Now we begin to see how Derrida's notion of "sous rature" differs from that of Heidegger's. Heidegger's Being[x] might point at an inarticulable presence. Derrida's trace[x] is the mark of the absence of a presence, an always already absent present, of the lack at the origin that is the condition of thought and experience. For somewhat different yet similar contingencies, both Heidegger and Derrida teach us to use language in terms of a trace-structure, effacing it even as it presents its legibility. We must remember this when we wish to attack Derrida or, for that matter, Heidegger, on certain sorts of straightforward logical grounds; for, one can always forget the invisible erasure, "act as though this makes no difference" (MP 3, SP 131).[13]

Derrida writes thus on the strategy of philosophizing about the trace:

The value of the transcendental arche [origin] must make its necessity felt before letting itself be erased. The concept of the

---

13 Because it overlooks the invisible erasure, the usual superficial criticism of Derrida goes as follows: he says he is questioning the value of "truth" and "logic," yet he uses logic to demonstrate the truth of his own arguments! (A characteristic example would be Lionel Abel, "Jacques Derrida: His 'Difference' with Metaphysics," *Salmagundi* 25 [Winter 1974]: 3–21.) The point is, of course, that the predicament of having to use resources of the heritage that one questions is the overt concern of Derrida's work, and as such is prepared for, as I shall show, by the fundamental questionings of Nietzsche, Freud, and Heidegger.

arche-trace must comply with both that necessity and that era-sure. It is in fact contradictory and not acceptable within the logic of identity. The trace is not only the disappearance of origin, [. . .] it means that the origin did not even disappear, that it was never constituted except reciprocally by a non-origin, the trace, which thus becomes the origin of the origin. From then on, to wrench the concept of the trace from the classical scheme which would derive it from a presence or from an originary non-trace and which would make of it an empirical mark, one must indeed speak of an originary trace or arche-trace. (90, **61**)

At once inside and outside a certain Hegelian and Heideggerian tradition, Derrida, then, is asking us to change certain habits of mind: the authority of the text is provisional, the origin is a trace; contradicting logic, we must learn to use and erase our language at the same time.

In the last few pages, we have seen Heidegger and Derrida engaged in the process of this curious practice. Derrida in particular is acutely aware that it is a question of strategy. It is the strategy of using the only available language while not subscribing to its premises, or "operat[ing] according to the vocabulary of the very thing that one delimits" (MP 18, SP 147). For Hegel, as Hyppolite remarks, "philosophical discourse" contains "its own criticism within itself" (SC 336, 158). And Derrida describing the strategy "of a discourse which borrows from a heritage the resources necessary for the deconstruction of that heritage itself," remarks similarly, "language bears within itself the necessity of its own critique" (ED 416, SC 254). The remark becomes clearer in the light of writing "sous rature": "At each step I was obliged to proceed by ellipses, corrections and corrections of corrections, letting go of each concept at the very moment that I needed to use it, etc."[14]

---

14 Jacques Derrida, "La différance," *Bulletin de la société française de philosophie* 62(3) (1968): 103. This remark occurs in the discussion following the lecture and is neither reprinted in MP nor translated in SP.

There is some similarity between this strategy and what Levi-Strauss calls *bricolage* in *La pensée sauvage*.[15] Derrida himself remarks:

> Levi-Strauss will always remain faithful to this double intention: to preserve as an instrument that whose truth-value he criticizes, conserving [. . .] all these old concepts, while at the same time exposing [. . .] their limits, treating them as tools which can still be of use. No longer is any truth-value [or rigorous meaning] attributed to them; there is a readiness to abandon them if necessary if other instruments should appear more useful. In the meantime, their relative efficacy is exploited, and they are employed to destroy the old machinery to which they belong and of which they themselves are pieces. Thus it is that the language of the human sciences criticizes *itself*. (ED 417; SC 255, 254)

One distinction between Levi-Strauss and Derrida is clear enough. Levi-Strauss's anthropologist seems free to pick his tool; Derrida's philosopher knows that there is no tool that does not belong to the metaphysical box, and proceeds from there. But there is yet another difference, a difference that we must mark as we outline Derridean strategy.

Levi-Strauss contrasts the *bricoleur* to the engineer. ("The 'bricoleur' has no precise equivalent in English. He is a man who undertakes odd jobs and is a Jack of all trades or is a kind of professional do-it-yourself man, but [. . .] he is of a different standing from, for instance, the English 'odd job man' or handyman."[16]) The discourse of anthropology and the other sciences of man must be *bricolage*: the discourses of formal logic, and the pure sciences, one presumes, can be those of engineering. The engineer's "instrument" is "specially adapted to a specific technical

---

15 Claude Lévi-Strauss, *La Pensée sauvage* (Paris: Plon, 1962); translated into English as *The Savage Mind* (Chicago: University of Illinois Press, 1966).
16 Lévi-Strauss, *La Pensée sauvage*; *The Savage Mind*, p. 17

need"; the *bricoleur* makes do with things that were meant perhaps for other ends.[17] The anthropologist must tinker because, at least as Levi-Strauss argues in *Le cru et le cuit*, it is in fact impossible for him to master the whole field. Derrida, by an important contrast, suggests that the field is *theoretically,* not merely empirically, unknowable (ED 419 f., SC 259 f.). Not even in an ideal universe of an empirically reduced number of possibilities would the projected "end" of knowledge ever coincide with its "means." Such a coincidence—"engineering"—is an impossible dream of plenitude. The reason for *bricolage* is that there can be nothing else. No engineer can make the "means"—the sign—and the "end"—meaning—become self-identical. Sign will always lead to sign, one substituting the other (playfully, since "sign" is "under erasure") as signifier and signified in turn. Indeed, the notion of play is important here. Knowledge is not a systematic tracking down of a truth that is hidden but may be found. It is rather the field "of *freeplay,* that is to say, a field of infinite substitutions in the closure of a finite ensemble" (ED 423, SC 260).

For Derrida, then, the concept of the "engineer" "questioning the universe" is, like Hegel's father-text encompassing the son-preface, or Heidegger's Being as transcendental signified, "a theological idea," an idea that we *need* to fulfill our desire for plenitude and authority. He remarks that Levi Strauss, like Heidegger, is afflicted with nostalgia:

> [One . . .] perceives in his work a sort of ethic of presence, an ethic of nostalgia for origins, an ethic of archaic and natural innocence, of a purity of presence and self-presence in speech—an ethic, nostalgia, and even remorse which he often presents as the motivation of the ethnological project when he moves toward archaic societies—exemplary societies in his eyes. These texts are well known. (ED 427, SC 264)

---

17 Lévi-Strauss, *La Pensée sauvage,* pp. 44 f.; *The Savage Mind,* pp. 16 f.

Derrida does not offer the obverse of this nostalgia. He does not see in the method of the so-called exact sciences an epistemological model of exactitude. All knowledge, whether one knows it or not, is a species of bricolage, with its eye on the myth of "engineering." But that myth is always totally other, leaving an originary trace within "bricolage." Like all "useful" words, "bricolage" must also be placed "under erasure." For it can only be defined by its difference from its opposite—"engineering." Yet that opposite, a metaphysical norm, can in fact never be present and thus, strictly speaking, there is no concept of "bricolage" (that which is not engineering). Yet the concept must be used-untenable but necessary. "From the moment that we cease to believe in such an engineer [. . .] as soon as it is admitted that every finite discourse is bound by a certain *bricolage*, [. . .] the very idea of *bricolage* is menaced and the difference in which it took on its meaning decomposes" (ED 418, SC 256). The possible and implicit hierarchical move, reminding us that bricolage as a model is "*pre*-scientific," low on a chain of teleologic development, here disappears. Derrida does not allow the possibility of seeing *bricolage* as a cruder, pre-scientific method of investigation, low on the evolutionary scale. One can now begin to understand a rather cryptic sentence in the *Grammatology*: "Without that track [of writing under erasure . . .], the ultra-transcendental text [*bricolage* under erasure] will so closely resemble the pre-critical text [*bricolage* plain and simple] as to be indistinguishable from it" (90, **61**).

This undoing yet preserving of the opposition between *bricolage* and engineering is an analogue for Derrida's attitude toward all oppositions—an attitude that "erases" (in this special sense) all oppositions. I shall come back to this gesture again and again in this Preface.

(As he develops the notion of the joyful yet laborious strategy of rewriting the old language—a language, incidentally, we must know well—Derrida mentions the "cloture" of metaphysics. We must know that we are within the "cloture" of metaphysics, even as we attempt to undo it.

It would be an historicist mistake to represent this "closure" of metaphysics as simply the temporal finishing-point of metaphysics. It is also the metaphysical desire to make the end coincide with the means, create an enclosure, make the definition coincide with the defined, the "father" with the "son"; within the logic of identity to balance the equation, close the circle. Our language reflects this desire. And so it is from within this language that we must attempt an "opening.")

[. . .]

V

Of Grammatology is the provisional origin of this Preface. But we have not kept track of the book's outline. We have considered instead the importance of erasure in Derrida; provided some ingredients for the computation of the intertextuality between Derrida, and Nietzsche, Heidegger, Freud, Husserl; given some indications of Derrida's view of Structuralism, especially of the metapsychological practice of Jacques Lacan; commented on the place of "writing" in Derrida's thought, hinted at the chain of its substitutions, given the recipe for deconstruction. Now that we begin the concluding movements of this repetitive preface, let us make *Of Grammatology* our provisional end.

Derrida situates *Of Grammatology* among his own texts thus:

Of Grammatology can be taken as a long essay articulated in two parts [. . .] between which one can stitch in *L'écriture et la différence*. The *Grammatology* often refers to it. In that case, the interpretation of Rousseau [Part II of *Of Grammatology*] would be the twelfth item of the collection. Conversely, one can insert *Of Grammatology* in the middle of *L'écriture et la différence*. Since six texts of the latter are anterior, in fact and in principle, to the publication [. . .] in *Critique*, of the articles announcing *Of Grammatology*; the five last, beginning with "Freud and the Scene of Writing" are engaged in the grammatological overture. (Pos F 12–13)

Although Derrida continues "[. . .] things don't let themselves be reconstituted so simply," this fable of fragmentation is not without interest. There is a certain stitched-togetherness in *Of Grammatology*, and a decided disjunction between the sweeping, summarizing, theoretical breadth of the first part, and the interpretative, slow, reader's pace of the second.

Part I is an expanded version of a two-part review of Madeleine V.-David's *Le débat sur les écritures et l'hiéroglyphe aux xvii° et xviii° siècles*, André Lerori-Gourhan's *Le geste et la parole*, and the papers of a colloquium entitled *L'écriture et la psychologie des peuples*.[18] Although the review articles contained most of the material of the entire Part I in their present order, it is in Chapter 3—"Of Grammatology as a Positive Science"—that their mark is most clearly felt. Each of the three books reviewed receives a section of the chapter. The first gives a summary of the moment when grammatology could historically have opened but did not, the moment of the decipherment of non-European scripts. The second investigates the possible physiological bases for the differentiation between writing and speech and genetic writing as the determinant of life. The third deals with the implications of varieties of "nonphonetic" writing. One cannot help wondering if all this overt interest in an account of writing in the narrow sense—rather than in the interpretation of texts—is not simply due to the regulating presence of books to be reviewed.

Indeed, in Part I and in the postscript to "Freud and the Scene of Writing," Derrida speaks most often of rewriting the "history of writing" in something suspiciously like the narrow sense—"an immense field where hitherto one has only done preparatory work" (ED 340). "Writing" so envisaged is on the brink of becoming a unique signifier, and Jacques Derrida's chief care. In his later work, the theoretical significance of the

---

18 *Critique* 223 (December 1965): 1017–42, hereafter cited in the text as Crit I; and *Critique* 224 (January 1966): 23–53, hereafter cited in the text as Crit II .

structure of writing and the grammatological opening remain intact. But he quietly drops the idea of being the authorized grammatological historian of writing in the narrow sense. "Writing" then takes its place on the chain of substitutions. In the *Grammatology*, then, we are at a specific and precarious moment in Derrida's career.

It is fascinating to study the changes and interpolations made in the text of the review articles as they were transformed into the book. (The text is genuinely enriched as the appropriate "difference"-s are changed to "differance"-s.) Most of the changes make the philosophical ground of the argument stronger. The superb discussion of the proper name (136–37, **89–90**) is a case in point. So is the long footnote on the psychoanalysis of writing (132–34, **333–34nn**), and the insertion of the remarks on the radical alterity necessarily inhabiting the sign. (69, **47**) So is the cautionary addition on page 125 (**84**). (The original version ran: "It [genetic script] is a liberation which makes for the appearing of the *grammè* as such and no doubt makes possible the emergence of 'writing' in the narrow sense." [Crit II. 46] In the *Grammatology* Derrida annuls the possibility of the *grammè* ever appearing as such. He adds the following parenthesis after "as such": "[that is to say according to a new structure of nonpresence]," and goes on to add the following sentences: "But one cannot think them [the structurations of this *grammè*] without the most general concept of the *grammè*. That is irreducible and impregnable.")

From our point of view, what is most interesting is that the theme of "sous rature" is given its development almost entirely in the book rather than in the articles. As I have mentioned above, Derrida never discusses "sous rature" at great length. But in the articles all we have is a *mention* of the practice (Crit I. 1029) as it is to be found on page 38 (**23**) of *Of Grammatology*. The use of the crossed lines on page 31 (**19**), the discussion of Heidegger's notion of Being between pages 31 and 38 (**19–23**), the putting of "experience" under erasure on page 89 (**60–61**), of the "past" on page 97 (**66–67**), and the "originarity of the trace" on page 110 (**75**) are all passages only found in the book.

On the other hand, and curiously enough, the argument for historical necessity seems also to have been emphasized as the review articles were turned into the first part of the book. The first tiny change—from "the phoneticization of writing dissimulated its own history while producing it" (Crit I. 1017) to "the phoneticization of writing *must* dissimulate its own history while producing it" (11, **3**)—sets the tone for all the small but weighty changes that will be made. They are not many, but they are unequivocal. Most of them, naturally enough, are confined to Chapter 1, "The End of the Book and the Beginning of Writing." The paragraph beginning "these disguises are not historical contingencies" (17, **7**; the article had only the first two sentences) is a representative example. The repression of writing, and its recognition today, are seen as historically necessary events. In a text where he elaborately launches a theory against teleological patternings of history and thought, where he delivers the notion of the play of necessity and contingency, why does Derrida fabricate so strong an argument for historical necessity? Why is the opening chapter—"The End of the Book and the Beginning of Writing"—full of a slightly embarrassing messianic promise? If we really do not believe in "epistemological cut-off points," or in the possibility of stepping out of the metaphysical enclosure by simply deciding to, or in the linearity of time, then with what seriousness can we declare a different "world to come," a world where the "values of sign, speech, and writing," will be made to tremble? (14, **5**) How reconcile ourselves with this break between the world of the past and the world of the future? It seems an empiricist betrayal of the structure of difference and postponement, and any deconstructive reading of Derrida will have to take this into account.

(We have seen that Derrida will not call grammatology a psychoanalysis of logocentrism. On page 20 [**9–10**] of the *Grammatology*, there is the merest hint of a psychoanalytical patterning of the history of writing that Derrida does not pursue: "This situation [the role of writing in the naming of the human element] has always already been announced. Why is it today in the process of making itself recognized *as such* and *after the fact* [*après coup*]"? Making itself recognized *as such*. Derrida makes an attempt on that page at answering that part of the question in terms of the development in ways and means of information retrieval, phonography, and cybernetics, all joining forces with anthropology and the history of writing—the sciences of man. But elsewhere in the book, as we have seen, he emphasizes that the situation can never be recognized *as such*, that we must surrender ourselves to being inscribed within the chain of future deconstructions and decipherings. It is therefore the *après coup* that seems more interesting here. That is the French word for Freud's "*Nachträglichkeit*"—translated into English as "deferred action." As we recall, at the time that a stimulus is received, it goes *either* into the perceptual system or into the Unconscious and produces a permanent trace. That particular trace might be energized into consciousness—as Freud reminds us over and over again, this topographical language must be used with caution—long afterward: *nachträglich, après coup*. But it never comes up *as such*; in fact, as Derrida argues, following Freud, the trace [*die Bahnung*] itself is primary. There is no "thing" there in the Unconscious but simply the possibility for this particular path to be energized. When the track is opened up, and we have the *après coup* perception of the originary trace, the impulse in the Unconscious is not exhausted. Unconscious impulses are indestructible. Now before the remarks about theoretical mathematics, information retrieval et *alia* on page 20 [**9–10**], Derrida slips in, immediately after the sentences we are examining, the following words: "This question would call forth an interminable analysis." "Interminable analysis." The words themselves recall Freud's late essay "Analysis Terminable and Interminable."[19] The impulses in the Unconscious are indestructible,

---

19 Sigmund Freud, "Die endliche und unendliche Analyse," in *Gesammelte Werke* (hereafter referred to as GW), BAND XVI, pp. 59–99; *The Standard Edition of the Complete Psychological Works of Sigmund Freud* (hereafter referred to as SE) (James

après coup they come up into consciousness interminably, and thus constitute the subject. A neurosis can never be analyzed to the full—the analysis would in fact, be interminable, if the practical analyst did not terminate it. Is the trace of the repression of writing in some indeterminate historical Unconscious "coming up" to our consciousness at the present historical moment, *après coup*? Derrida himself is clearly not willing to assume the responsibility for what might seem a psychoanalytic schema. This again is an undertaking for a future deconstructor. Yet there is, no doubt, a strong sympathy between Freud's notion of the theoretical impossibility of a full analysis and Derrida's polemic of the need for the perpetual renewal of the grammatological or deconstructive undertaking. In fact, that is what all of Derrida's work on "writing" has presented—although it seems to be receiving articulation today, variations of previous articulations have existed throughout history and the complex will have to be confronted perpetually as the language of confrontation, obeying our will to power, adapts to and is retrieved by logocentrism, or, as Freud would say, with a little help from Heidegger, as "the ego treats recovery[x] itself as a new danger[x] [GW XVI. 84, SE XXIII. 238; erasures mine]. It seems quite plausible, then, to ask: if "the Freudian discourse—its syntax or [. . .] its work" were delivered from "his necessarily metaphysical and traditional concepts" [ED 294], would one be able to decipher a psychoanalytic schema in the obstinate historical pattern of *Of Grammatology*?)

There is also the shadow of a geographical pattern that falls upon the first part of the book. The relationship between logocentrism and ethnocentrism is indirectly invoked in the very first sentence of the "Exergue." Yet, paradoxically, and almost by a reverse ethnocentrism, Derrida insists that logocentrism is a property of the *West*. He does this so frequently that a quotation would be superfluous. Although something of the

---

Strachey ed. and trans., with Anna Freud eds) (London: Hogarth, 1953–74), VOL. 23, pp. 209–53.

Chinese prejudice of the West is discussed in Part I, the *East* is never seriously studied or deconstructed in the Derridean text. Why then must it remain, recalling Hegel and Nietzsche in their most cartological humors, as the name of the limits of the text's knowledge?

The discussion of Lévi-Strauss in Part II, the only genuinely polemical and perhaps the least formally awkward section of the book, first appeared in 1966, as part of an issue on Lévi-Strauss of the *Cahiers pour l'analyse* (IV, September–October 1966).

Derrida chooses Lévi-Strauss as his subject because, "at once conserving and annulling inherited conceptual oppositions, this thought, like Saussure's, stands on a borderline: sometimes within an uncriticized conceptuality, sometimes putting a strain on the boundaries, and working toward deconstruction" (154, **105**). And he takes Lévi-Strauss to task for slackness of method, for sentimental ethnocentrism, for an oversimplified reading of Rousseau. He criticizes Lévi-Strauss for conceiving of writing only in the narrow sense, for seeing it as a scapegoat for all the exploitative evils of "civilization," and for conceiving of the violent Nambikwara as an innocent community "without writing." If the end of Part I seems too concerned with writing in the narrow sense, these chapters redeem themselves in that respect. For in them Derrida repeatedly moves us from writing in the narrow sense to writing in general—through such "systematic" statements as: "the genealogical relation and social classification are the stitched seam of arche-writing, condition of the (so-called oral) language, and of writing in the colloquial sense" (182, **125**) to such "poetic" ones as: "the *silva* [forest] is savage, the *via rupta* [path cut through] is written [. . .] it is difficult to imagine that access to the possibility of road maps is not access to writing" (158, **108**).

Perhaps the most interesting reason given for the impossibility of a community without writing is that the bestowing of the proper name, something no society can avoid, is itself inhabited by the structure of writing. For the phrase "proper name" signifies a classification, an institution carrying the trace of history, into which a certain sort of sign is made to fit. Thus the proper name, as soon as it is understood as such, is no longer fully unique and proper to the holder. The proper name is always already common by virtue of belonging to the category "proper." It is always already under erasure: "When within *conscious-ness,* the name *is called* proper, it is already classified and is obliterated in *being named*. It is already no more than a *so-called* proper name" (161, **109**). Lévi-Strauss knows this, as his discussion of proper names in *The Savage Mind* (pp. 226f., Eng. pp. 172f.) demonstrates. But, having nothing but a restricted concept of writing, he cannot relate the proper name to writing: "The essence or the energy of the *graphein* [. . . is] the originary effacement of the proper name" (159, **108**).

This argument does not only serve to undo the anthropoloigst's reverse ethnocentrism toward an "innocent community without writing." It points to the presence of writing in general in all the rami-fications of the "proper"—the own, the distinguishing characteristic, the literal, the exclusively clean. It is so pervasive a Derridean theme that I can do no more than mention it here. In a way, Derrida's chief concern might be summarized thus: to problematize the proper name and proper (literal) meaning, the proper in general.

The argument points also to the theme of the play of desire around the proper name: The narcissistic desire to make one's own "proper" name "common," to make it enter and be at one with the body of the mother-tongue; and, at the same time, the oedipal desire to preserve one's proper name, to see it as the analogon of the *name* of the father. Much of Derrida's recent work meditates on this play. I shall quote the beginning of *Glas*, where Hegel (the "proper" name) is invoked as the eagle (the "common" name) that the French pronunciation of his name—"aigle"—turns him into:

Who, he?

His name is so strange. From the eagle he draws his impe-rial or historical power. Those who still pronounce it as French,

and there are those, are silly only to a certain point: the resti-
tution [. . .] of the magisterial cold [. . .] of the eagle caught in
ice and frost [*gel*]. Let the emblemished philosopher be thus
congealed. (p. 7)

Pages 145 to 151 (**97–102**) are a theoretical "justification" of what
Derrida will come to call "intertextuality:" the interweaving of different
texts (literally "web"-s) in an act of criticism that refuses to think of
"influence" or "interrelationship" as simple historical phenomena.
Intertextuality becomes the most striking conceptual and typographical
signature in *Glas*. Pages 226 to 234 (**157–64**)—"The Exorbitant: Question of Method"—are, as I have suggested, a simple and moving expo-
sition of the method of deconstruction as understood by the early
Derrida.

Rousseau's place in Derrida's text is most importantly marked by
the former's use of the word "supplement": "Writing will appear to me
more and more," Derrida writes,

as another name for this structure of supplementarity. [. . .] It
does not suffice to say that Rousseau thinks the supplement
without thinking it, that he does not match his saying and his
meaning, his descriptions and his declarations. [. . .] Using the
word and describing the thing, Rousseau in a way displaces and
deforms the sign 'supplement,' the unity of the signifier and the
signified. [. . .] But these displacements and deformations are
regulated by the contradictory unity—itself supplementary—
of a desire. (348, **245**)

Of the issue of supplementarity itself, abundantly developed by
Derrida in this book, there is no need to speak. Of more interest to me
is the question, how does the word "supplement" signify Rousseau's
desire? Before I attempt to gauge Derrida's enigmatic answer to this
question, I shall digress and point at the rather endearing conservatism
of Chapter 3, Section I: "The Placé of the Essay."

There is a certain mark of superior academic scholarship in that section that seems out of joint with the theoretical spirit of the book. Here the philosopher who has written "The outside is[x] the inside" in Part I, speaks with perfect seriousness about internal and external evidence, and the thinker of "intertextuality" concerns himself with the relative dating of *The Essay on the Origin of Languages* and *The Discourse on Inequality*. This reader is happy that those marks of traditional scholarship were not unstitched. It is engrossing to watch the bold argument operating in the service of a conventional debate. For the burden of the proof lies on "the economy of pity"—the supplementarity of pity in both Rousseau texts—and intertextual practice does emerge as the two texts are woven together: "From one [text] to the other, an emphasis is displaced, a continuous sliding is in operation. [. . .] The Discourse wants to *mark the beginning*. [. . .] The Essay would make us *sense the beginnings*. [. . .] It seizes man [. . .] in that subtle transition from origin to genesis. [. . .] The description of pure nature in the Discourse made room within itself for such a transition. As always, it is the unseizable limit of the *almost*" (358, **253**). I do not believe that Derrida ever again devotes himself to this sort of textual scholarship. Here, too, the reading of *Of Grammatology* gives us the taste of a rather special early Derrida, the young scholar transforming the ground rules of scholarship.

The book ends with Rousseau's dream, the supplementary desire that I refer to above. Such an ending is a characteristic Derrida touch, criticism giving up the idiom of expository mastery in the end and taking on the idiom of the fabulist. "La pharmacie de Platon" ends with the scene of Plato in his pharmacy, "White Mythology" with the heliotrope stone. Examples can be multiplied.

Rousseau, that famous masturbator, has a philosophical wet dream: "Rousseau's dream consisted of making the supplement enter metaphysics by force" (444, **315**).

But is not that force precisely the energy of Derrida's own project? Is this not precisely the trick of writing, that dream-cum-truth, that breaches the metaphysical closure with an intrinsic yet supplementary violence? At the end of Derrida's book on Rousseau, Rousseau is set dreaming of Derrida. Perhaps the book does end with its author's signature.

It is customary at this point to say a few words about the problem of translation. Derrida's text certainly offers its share of "untranslatable" words. I have had my battles with "exergue" and "propre."[20] My special worry is "entamer." As we have seen, it is an important word in Derrida's vocabulary. It means both to break into and to begin. I have made do with "broach" or "breach," with the somewhat fanciful confidence that the shadow-word "breach" or "broach" will declare itself through it. With "entamer" as well as with other words and expressions, I have included the original in parenthesis whenever the wording and syntax of the French seemed to carry a special charge. To an extent, this particular problem informs the entire text. Denying the uniqueness of words, their substantiality, their transferability, their repeatability, *Of Grammatology* denies the possibility of translation. Not so paradoxically perhaps, each twist of phrase becomes at the same time "significant" and playful when language is manipulated for the purpose of putting signification into question, for deconstructing the binary opposition "signifier-signified." That playfulness I fear I have not been able remotely to capture. Even so simple a word as "de" carries a touch of play—hinting at both "of" and "from." (I have once resorted to "from/of," where the playfulness seemed to ask for special recognition [page 269].) But that sort of heavy-handedness cannot punctuate an entire text where "penser" (to think) carries within itself and points at "panser" (to dress a wound); for does not thinking seek forever to clamp a dressing over the gaping and violent wound of the impossibility of thought? The

---

20 For a cogent discussion of the problems relating to these two words as used by Derrida, see his "White Mythology: Metaphor in the Text of Philosophy," *New Literary History* 6(1) (Autumn 1974): 5.

translation of the title, suggesting "a piece of" as well as "about," I have retained against expert counsel.

I began this preface by informing my readers that Derrida's theory admitted—as it denied—a preface by questioning the absolute repeatability of the text. It is now time to acknowledge that his theory would likewise admit—as it denies—translation, by questioning the absolute privilege of the original. Any act of reading is besieged and delivered by the precariousness of intertextuality. And translation is, after all, one version of intertextuality.[21] If there are no unique words, if, as soon as a privileged concept-word emerges, it must be given over to the chain of substitutions and to the "common language," why should that act of substitution that is translation be suspect? If the proper name or sovereign status of the author is as much a barrier as a right of way, why should the translator's position be secondary? It must now be evident that, desiring to conserve the "original" (*De la grammatologie*) and seduced by the freedom of the absence of a sovereign text (not only is there no *Of Grammatology* before mine, but there have been as many translations of the text as readings, the text is infinitely translatable), translation itself is in a double bind.

And, from quite another point of view, most practically and rigorously speaking, both Derrida and I being very roughly bilingual—his English a cut above my French—where does French end and English begin?

I shall not launch my philosophy of translation here. Instead I give you a glimpse of Derrida's:

Within the limits of its possibility, or its *apparent* possibility, translation practices the difference between signified and signifier. But, if this difference is never pure, translation is even less so, and a notion of *transformation* must be substituted for

---

21 For a cogent discussion of translation and intertextuality, see Jeffrey Mehlman, "Portnoy in Paris," *Diacritics* 2(4) (Winter 1972): 21.

the notion of translation: a regulated transformation of one language by another, of one text by another. We shall not have and never have had to deal with some "transfer" of pure signifieds that the signifying instrument—or "vehicle"—would leave virgin and intact, from one language to another, or within one and the same language. (Pos 31)

"From one language to another, or within one and the same language." Translation is a version of the intertexuality that comes to bear also within the "same" language. Ergo . . .

Heidegger's deconstructive (or "destructive") method is often based on consideration of how the so-called content of philosophy is affected by the exigencies of translation. Derrida writes of this in "La différance" and "Ousia et grammè" (MP 3–29, SP 129–60; MP 31–78). In the latter example there is a double play: Heidegger laments the loss for philosophy when the lone latin "presence" was pressed into service to translate the many nuanced Greek words signifying philosophical shadings of the idea of presence. Derrida engages in the parallel lament—how translate the many nuanced Heideggerian German words signifying philosophical shadings of the idea of presence through the lone Romance "présence?" Derrida goes on to use the business of "mistranslations" as an effective deconstructive lever of his own. The most sustained example is "La pharmacie de Platon," where he appropriately asks: why have translators obliterated the word "*pharmakon*" by providing a collection of different words as its translated substitute?

And all said and done, that is the sort of reader I would hope for. A reader who would fasten upon my mistranslations, and with that leyerage deconstruct Derrida's text beyond what Derrida as controlling subject has directed in it.

VI

"The first part of this book, 'Writing before the Letter,' sketches in broad outlines *Now I insert my text within his and move you on, situating here* a theoretical matrix. It indicates certain significant historical moments, and proposes *My name*: certain critical concepts. *Gayatri Chakravorty Spivak*. These critical concepts are put to the test *the places of this work: Iowa City, (New Delhi–Dacca–Calcutta), Boston, Nice, Providence, Iowa City*, in the second part, 'Nature, Culture, Writing.' *Its time: July 1970– October 1975*. This part may be called illustrative . . . "

The Politics of Translation

(1992)*

The idea for this title comes from the British sociologist Michele Barrett's feeling that the politics of translation takes on a massive life of its own if you see language as the process of meaning-construction.[1]

In my view, language may be one of many elements that allow us to make sense of things, of ourselves. I am thinking, of course, of gestures, pauses, but also of chance, of the subindividual force-fields of being which click into place in different situations, swerve from the straight or true line of language-in-thought. Making sense of ourselves is what produces identity. If one feels that the production of identity as self-meaning, not just meaning, is as pluralized as a drop of water under a microscope, one is not always satisfied, outside of the ethicopolitical arena as such, with "generating" thoughts on one's own. (Assuming identity as origin may be unsatisfactory in the ethicopolitical arena as well, but consideration of that now would take us too far afield.) I have argued in "Feminism and Deconstruction, Again: Negotiations" that one of the ways of resisting capitalist multiculturalism's invitation to self-identity and compete is to give the name of "woman" to the unimaginable other.[2]

---

* First published in *Outside in the Teaching Machine* (New York: Routledge, 2009[1993]), pp. 200–225.
1 The first part of this essay is based on a conversation with Michele Barrett in the summer of 1990.
2 In Spivak, *Outside in the Teaching Machine*, pp. 134–57.

The same sort of impulse is at work here in a rather more tractable form. For one of the ways to get around the confines of one's "identity" as one produces expository prose is to work at someone else's title, as one works with a language that belongs to many others. This, after all, is one of the seductions of translating. It is a simple miming of the responsibility to the trace of the other in the self.

Responding, therefore, to Barrett with that freeing sense of responsibility, I can agree that it is not bodies of meaning that are transferred in translation. And from the ground of that agreement I want to consider the role played by language for the *agent*, the person who acts, even though intention is not fully present to itself. The task of the feminist translator is to consider language as a clue to the workings of gendered agency. The writer is written by her language, of course. But the writing of the writer writes agency in a way that might be different from that of the British woman/citizen within the history of British feminism, focused on the task of freeing herself from Britain's imperial past, its often racist present, as well as its "made in Britain" history of male domination.

Translation as Reading

How does the translator attend to the specificity of the language she translates? There is a way in which the rhetorical nature of every language disrupts its logical systematicity. If we emphasize the logical at the expense of these rhetorical interferences, we remain safe. "Safety" is the appropriate term here, because we are talking of risks, of violence to the translating medium.

I felt that I was taking those risks when I recently translated some eighteenth-century Bengali poetry. I quote a bit from my "Translator's Preface":

> I must overcome what I was taught in school: the highest mark
> for the most accurate collection of synonyms, strung together
> in the most proximate syntax. I must resist both the solemnity

of chaste Victorian poetic prose and the forced simplicity of "plain English," that have imposed themselves as the norm [. . .] Translation is the most intimate act of reading. I surrender to the text when I translate. These songs, sung day after day in family chorus before clear memory began, have a peculiar intimacy for me. Reading and surrendering take on new meanings in such a case. The translator earns permission to transgress from the trace of the other—before memory—in the closest places of the self.[3]

Yet language is not everything. It is only a vital clue to where the self loses its boundaries. The ways in which rhetoric or figuration disrupt logic themselves point at the possibility of random contingency, beside language, around language. Such a dissemination cannot be under our control. Yet in translation, where meaning hops into the spacy emptiness between two named historical languages, we get perilously close to it. By juggling the disruptive rhetoricity that breaks the surface in not necessarily connected ways, we feel the selvedges of the language-textile give way, fray into *frayages* or facilitations.[4] Although every act of reading or communication is a bit of this risky fraying which scrambles together somehow, our stake in agency keeps the fraying down to a minimum except in the communication and reading of and in love. (What is the place of "love" in the ethical? As we saw, Luce

---

3 Nirode Mazumdar, inspired by Ram Proshad, *Song of Kali: A Cycle of Images and Songs* (Gayatri Chakravorty Spivak trans.) (Calcutta: Seagull Books, 2000), p. 29.
4 "Facilitation" is the English translation of the Freudian term *Bahnung* (pathing) which is translated *frayage* in French. The dictionary meaning is: "Term used by Freud at a time when he was putting forward a neurological model of the functioning of the psychical apparatus (1895): the excitation, in passing from one neurone to another, runs into a certain resistance; where its passage results in a permanent reduction in this resistance, there is said to be facilitation; excitation will opt for a facilitated pathway in preference to one where no facilitation has occurred" (J.-B. Pontalis, *The Language of Psychoanalysis* [London: Hogarth Press, 1973], p. 157).

Irigaray has struggled with this question.) The task of the translator is to facilitate this love between the original and its shadow, a love that permits fraying, holds the agency of the translator and the demands of her imagined or actual audience at bay. The politics of translation from a non-European woman's text too often suppresses this possibility because the translator cannot engage with, or cares insufficiently for, the rhetoricity of the original. The simple possibility that something might not be meaningful is contained by the rhetorical system as the always possible menace of a space outside language. This is most eerily staged (and challenged) in the effort to communicate with other possible intelligent beings in space. (Absolute alterity or otherness is thus differed-deferred into another self who resembles us, however minimally, and with whom we can communicate.) But a more homely staging of it occurs across two earthly languages. The experience of contained alterity in an unknown language spoken in a different cultural milieu is uncanny.

Let us now think that, in that other language, rhetoric may be disrupting logic in the matter of the production of an agent, and indicating the founding violence of the silence at work within rhetoric. Logic allows us to jump from word to word by means of clearly indicated connections. Rhetoric must work in the silence between and around words in order to see what works and how much. The jagged relationship between rhetoric and logic, condition and effect of knowing, is a relationship by which a world is made for the agent, so that the agent can act in an ethical way, a political way, a day-to-day way; so that the agent can be alive, in a human way, in the world. Unless one can at least construct a model of this for the other language, there is no real translation.

Unfortunately it is only too easy to produce translations if this task is completely ignored. I myself see no choice between the quick and easy and slapdash way, and translating well and with difficulty. There is no reason why a responsible translation should take more time in the doing. The translator's preparation might take more time, and her love for the text might be a matter of a reading skill that takes patience. But the sheer material production of the text need not be slow.

Without a sense of the rhetoricity of language, a species of neocolonialist construction of the non-Western scene is afoot. No argument for convenience can be persuasive here. That is always the argument, it seems. This is where I travel from Barrett's enabling notion of the question of language in poststructuralism. Poststructuralism has shown some of us a staging of the agent within a three-tiered notion of language (as rhetoric, logic, silence). We must attempt to enter or direct that staging, as one directs a play, as an actor interprets a script. That takes a different kind of effort from taking translation to be a matter of synonym, syntax, and local color.

To be only critical, to defer action until the production of the Utopian translator, is impractical. Yet, when I hear Derrida, quite justifiably, point out the difficulties between French and English, even when he agrees to speak in English—"I must speak in a language that is not my own because that will be more just"—I want to claim the right to the same dignified complaint for a woman's text in Arabic or Vietnamese.[5]

It is more just to give access to the largest number of feminists. Therefore these texts must be made to speak English. It is more just to speak the language of the majority when through hospitality a large number of feminists give the foreign feminist the right to speak, in English. In the case of the third world foreigner, is the law of the majority that of decorum, the equitable law of democracy, or the "law" of the strongest? We might focus on this confusion. There is nothing necessarily meretricious about the Western feminist gaze. (The "naturalizing" of Jacques Lacan's sketching out of the psychic structure of the gaze in terms of group political behavior has always seemed to me a bit

---

5 Jacques Derrida, "The Force of Law: The 'Mystical Foundation of Authority'," in Drucilla Cornell, Michel Rosenfeld, and David Gray Carlson (eds), *Deconstruction and the Possibility of Justice* (New York: Routledge, 1992), p. 5.

shaky.) On the other hand, there is nothing essentially noble about the law of the majority either. It is merely the easiest way of being "democratic" with minorities. In the act of wholesale translation into English there can be a betrayal of the democratic ideal into the law of the strongest. This happens when all the literature of the third world gets translated into a sort of with-it translatese, so that the literature by a woman in Palestine begins to resemble, in the feel of its prose, something by a man in Taiwan. The rhetoricity of Chinese and Arabic! The cultural politics of high-growth, capitalist Asia Pacific, and devastated West Asia! Gender difference inscribed and inscribing in these differences!

For the student, this tedious translatese cannot compete with the spectacular stylistic experiments of a Monique Wittig or an Alice Walker.

Let us consider an example where attending to the author's stylistic experiments can produce a different text. Mahasweta Devi's "Stanadayini" is available in two versions.[6] Devi has expressed approval for the attention to her signature style in the version entitled "Breast-Giver." The alternative translation gives the title as "The Wet-Nurse," and thus neutralizes the author's irony in constructing an uncanny word; enough like "wet-nurse" to make that sense, and enough unlike to shock. It is as if the translator should decide to translate Dylan Thomas's famous title and opening line as "Do not go gently into that good night." The theme of treating the breast as organ of labor-power-as-commodity and the breast as metonymic part-object standing in for other-as-object— the way in which the story plays with Marx and Freud on the occasion of the woman's body—is lost even before you enter the story. In the text Mahasweta uses proverbs that are startling even in the Bengali. The translator of "The Wet-Nurse" leaves them out. She decides not to try

---

6 "The Wet-Nurse," in Kali for Women (eds), *Truth Takes: Stories by Indian Women* (London: Women's Press, 1987), pp. 1–50; "Breast-Giver," in Mahasweta Devi, *Breast Stories* (Gayatri Chakravorty Spivak trans.) (London: Seagull Books, 2018[1997]), pp. 34–69.

to translate these hard bits of earthy wisdom, contrasting with class-specific access to modernity, also represented in the story. In fact, if the two translations are read side by side, the loss of the rhetorical silences of the original can be felt from one to the other.

First, then, the translator must surrender to the text. She must solicit the text to show the limits of its language, because that rhetorical aspect will point at the silence of the absolute fraying of language that the text wards off, in its special manner. Some think this is just an ethereal way of talking about literature or philosophy. But no amount of tough talk can get around the fact that translation is the most intimate act of reading. Unless the translator has earned the right to become the intimate reader, she cannot surrender to the text, cannot respond to the special call of the text.

The presupposition that women have a natural or narrative-historical solidarity, that there is something in a woman or an undifferentiated women's story that speaks to another woman without benefit of language-learning, might stand against the translator's task of surrender. Paradoxically, it is not possible for us as ethical agents to imagine otherness or alterity maximally. We have to turn the other into something like the self in order to be ethical. To surrender in translation is more erotic than ethical. In that situation the good-willing attitude "she is just like me" is not very helpful. In so far as Michele Barrett is not like Gayatri Spivak, their friendship is more effective as a translation. In order to earn that right of friendship or surrender of identity, of knowing that the rhetoric of the text indicates the limits of language for you as long as you are with the text, you have to be in a different relationship with the language, not even only with the specific text.

Learning about translation on the job, I came to think that it would be a practical help if one's relationship with the language being translated was such that sometimes one preferred to speak in it about intimate things. This is no more than a practical suggestion, not a theoretical requirement, useful especially because a woman writer who is wittingly or unwittingly a "feminist"—and of course all woman writers are not "feminist" even in this broad sense—will relate to the three-part staging of (agency in) language in ways defined out as "private", since they might question the more public linguistic maneuvers.

Let us consider an example of lack of intimacy with the medium. In Sudhir Kakar's *The Inner World*, a song about Kali written by the late nineteenth-century monk Vivekananda is cited as part of the proof of the "archaic narcissism" of the Indian [sic] male.[7] (Devi makes the same point with a light touch, with reference to Krisna and Siva, tying it to sexism rather than narcissism and without psychoanalytic patter.)

From Kakar's description, it would not be possible to glimpse that "the disciple" who gives the account of the singular circumstances of Vivekananda's composition of the song was an Irishwoman who became a Ramakrishna nun, a white woman among male Indian monks and devotees.[8] In the account Kakar reads, the song is translated by this woman, whose training in intimacy with the original language is as pains- taking as one can hope for. There is a strong identification between Indian and Irish nationalists at this period; and Nivedita, as she was called, also embraced what she understood to be the Indian philosophical way of life as explained by Vivekananda, itself a peculiar, resistant consequence of the culture of imperialism, as has been pointed out by many. For a psychoanalyst like Kakar, this historical, philosophical, and indeed sexual text of translation should be the textile to weave

---

7 Sudhir Kakar, *The Inner World: A Psycho-analytic Study of Childhood and Society in India*, 2ND EDN (Delhi: Oxford University Press, 1981), p. 171ff. Part of this discussion in a slightly different form is included in my "Psychoanalysis in Left Field and Fieldworking: Examples to Fit the Title," in Michael Munchow and Sonu Shamdasani (eds), *Speculations after Freud: Psychoanalysis, Philosophy and Culture* (London: Routledge, 1994), pp. 41–76.

8 For a feminist attempt at understanding such figures, see Kumari Jayawardena, *The White Woman's Other Burden: Western Women and South Asia During British Rule* (London: Routledge, 1995).

with. Instead, the English version, "given" by the anonymous "disciple," serves as no more than the opaque exhibit providing evidence of the alien fact of narcissism. It is not the site of the exchange of language.

At the beginning of the passage quoted by Kakar, there is a reference to Ram Prasad (or Ram Proshad; 1718–85). Kakar provides a footnote: "Eighteenth century singer and poet whose songs of longing for the Mother are very popular in Bengal." I believe this footnote is also an indication of what I am calling the absence of intimacy.

Vivekananda is, among other things, an example of the peculiar reactive construction of a glorious "India" under the provocation of imperialism. The rejection of "patriotism" in favor of "Kali" reported in Kakar's passage is played out in this historical theater, as a choice of the cultural female sphere rather than the colonial male sphere.[9] It is undoubtedly "true" that for such a figure, Ram Proshad Sen provides a kind of ideal self. Sen had retired with a pension from a clerk's job with a rural landowner, when the English were already in Bengal but had not claimed territory officially. He was himself given some land by one of the great rural landowners the year after the battle that inaugurated the territorial enterprise of the East India Company. He died eight years before the Permanent Settlement would introduce a violent epistemic rupture.[10] In other words, Vivekananda and Ram Proshad are two related

---

9 See Partha Chatterjee, "Nationalism and the Woman Question," in Kunkum Sangari and Sudesh Vaid (eds), *Recasting Women: Essays in Colonial History* (New Brunswick: Rutgers University Press, 1990), pp. 233–53, for a detailed discussion of this gendering in Indian nationalism.

10 I mention these details because Ram Proshad's dates and his rural situation make his pattern of recognition of the outsider on the landscape significantly different from that of the colonially educated, urban, ex-Communist, deeply nationalist/internationalist Vivekananda. Indeed, the latter's mediation into a text such as Ram Proshad's through the rural-origin urban-bound visionary Rama Krishna, his *guru*, makes his use precisely a "citation," in the most robust sense— "translation" into a displaced discursive formation. The first version of this essay was written at speed in Cambridge and reproduces a "life-history" of Ram Proshad

moments of colonial discursivity translating the figure of Kali. The dynamic intricacy of that discursive textile is mocked by the useless footnote.

It would be idle here to enter the debate about the "identity" of Kali or indeed other goddesses in Hindu "polytheism." But simply to contextualize, let me add that it is Ram Proshad about whose poetry I wrote the "Translator's Preface" quoted earlier. He is by no means simply an archaic stage-prop in the disciple's account of Vivekananda's "crisis." Some more lines from my "Preface": "Ram Proshad played with his mother tongue, transvaluing the words that are heaviest with Sanskrit meaning. I have been unable to catch the utterly new but utterly gendered tone of affection- ate banter"—not only, not even largely, "longing"—"between the poet and Kali." Unless Nivedita mistranslated, it is the difference in tone between Ram Proshad's innovating playfulness and Vivekananda's high nationalist solemnity that, in spite of the turn from nationalism to the Mother, is historically significant. The politics of translation has shifted into the register of reactive nativism. And that change is expressed in the gendering of the poet's voice.

How do women in contemporary polytheism relate to this peculiar mother, certainly not the psychoanalytic bad mother whom Kakar derives from Max Weber's misreading, not even an organized punishing mother, but a child-mother who punishes with astringent violence and is also a moral and affective monitor?[11] Ordinary women, not saintly women.

Why take it for granted that the invocation of goddesses in a historically masculinist polytheist sphere is more feminist than Nietzsche or Derrida claiming woman as model? I think it is a Western and male-gendered suggestion that powerful women in the Sakta (Sakti or Kali-worshipping) tradition necessarily take Kali as a role model.

---

firmly entrenched in the Bengali imaginary. I have corrected the details in this version.

11 Max Weber, *The Religion of India: The Sociology of Hinduism and Buddhism* (Hans H. Gerth and Don Martindale trans) (Glencoe, IL: Free Press, 1958).

Mahasweta's Jashoda tells me more about the relationship between god-desses and strong ordinary women than the psychoanalyst. And here too the example of an intimate translation that goes respectfully "wrong" can be offered. The French wife of a Bengali artist translated some of Ram Proshad Sen's songs to accompany her husband's paintings based on the songs. Her translations are marred by the pervasive orien-talism ready at hand. Compare two passages, both translating the "same" Bengali. I have at least tried, if failed, to catch the unrelenting mockery of self and Kali in the original:

> Mind, why footloose from Mother?
> Mind mine, think power, for freedom's dower, bind bower
>   with love-rope
> In time, mind, you minded not your blasted lot.
> And Mother, daughter-like, bound up house-fence to dupe
>   her dense and devoted fellow.
> Oh you'll see at death how much Mum loves you
> A couple minutes' tears, and lashings of water, cowdung-pure.

Here is the French, translated by me into an English comparable in tone and vocabulary:

> Pourquoi as-tu, mon âme, délaissé les pieds de Mâ?
> O esprit, médite Shokti, tu obtiendras la délivrance.
> Attache-les ces pieds saints avec la corde de la dévotion.
> Au bon moment tu n'as rien vu, c'est bien là ton malheur.
> Pour se jouer de son fidèle, Elle m'est apparue
> Sous la forme de ma fille et m'a aidé a réparer ma clôture.
> C'est à la mort que tu comprendras l'amour de Mâ.
> Ici, on versera quelques larmes, puis on purifiera le lieu.

> Why have you, my soul [mon âme is, admittedly, less heavy in
>   French], left Ma's feet?
> O mind, meditate upon Shokti, you will obtain deliverance.
>   Bind those holy feet with the rope of devotion.

In good time you saw nothing, that is indeed your sorrow.
To play with her faithful one, She appeared to me
In the form of my daughter and helped me to repair my enclo-
     sure. It is at death that you will understand Ma's love.
Here, they will shed a few tears, then purify the place.

And here, the Bengali:

মন কেন মার চরণ-ছাড়া ।
ও মন, ভাব শক্তি, পাবে মুক্তি, বাঁধ দিয়া ভক্তি-দড়া ॥
সময় থাকতে, না দেখলে মন, কেমন তোমার কপালপোড়া ।
মা ভক্তে ছলিতে, তনয়া রূপেতে বাঁধেন আসি ঘরের বেড়া ॥
মায়ে যত ভালবাসে, বুঝা যাবে মৃত্যুশেষে,
মোলে দণ্ড-হুচার কান্নাকাটি, শেষে দিবে গোবরছড়া ।

I hope these examples demonstrate that depth of commitment to correct cultural politics, felt in the details of personal life, is sometimes not enough. The history of the language, the history of the author's moment, the history of the language-in-and-as translation, must figure in the weaving as well.

Mere reasonableness will allow rhetoricity to be appropriated, put in its place, situated, seen as only nice. Rhetoricity is put in its place that way because it disrupts. Women within male-dominated society, when they internalize sexism as normality, act out a scenario against feminism that is formally analogical to this. The relationship between logic and rhetoric, between grammar and rhetoric, is also a relationship between social logic, social reasonableness, and the disruptiveness of figuration in social practice. These are the first two parts of our three-part model. But then, rhetoric points at the possibility of randomness, of contingency as such, dissemination, the falling apart of language, the possibility that things might not always be semiotically organized. (My problem with Julia Kristeva and the "presemiotic" is that she seems to want to expand the empire of the meaningful by grasping at what language can only point at.) Cultures that might not have this specific three-part model will still have a dominant sphere in its traffic with language and contingency. Writers like Ifi Amadiume show us that, without thinking of this sphere as biologically determined, one still has to think in terms of spheres determined by definitions of secondary and primary sexual characteristics in such a way that the inhabitants of the other sphere are para-subjective, not fully subject.[12] The dominant groups' way of handing the three-part ontology of language has to be learned as well—if the subordinate ways of rusing with rhetoric are to be disclosed.

To decide whether you are prepared enough to start translating, then, it might help if you have graduated into speaking, by choice or preference, of intimate matters in the language of the original. I have worked my way back to my earlier point: I cannot see why the publishers' convenience or classroom convenience or time convenience for people who do not have the time to learn should organize the construction of the rest of the world for Western feminism. Five years ago, berated as unsisterly, I would think, "Well, you know one ought to be a bit more giving etc.," but then I asked myself again, "What am I giving, or giving up? To whom am I giving by assuring that you don't have to work that hard, just come and get it? What am I trying to promote?" People would say, you who have succeeded should not pretend to be a marginal. But surely by demanding higher standards of translation, I am not marginalizing myself or the language of the original?

I have learned through translating Mahasweta how this three-part structure works differently from English in my native language. And here another historical irony has become personally apparent to me. In the old days, it was most important for a colonial or postcolonial student of English to be as "indistinguishable" as possible from the native speaker of English. I think it is necessary for people in the third world

---

12 Ifi Amadiume, *Male Daughters, Female Husbands: Gender and Sex in an African Society* (London: Zed Books, 1987).

translation trade now to accept that the wheel has come around, that the genuinely bilingual postcolonial now has a bit of an advantage. But she does not have a real advantage as a translator if she is not strictly bilingual, if she merely speaks her native language. Her own native space is, after all, also class-organized. And that organization still often carries the traces of access to imperialism, often relates inversely to access to the vernacular as a public language. So here the requirement for intimacy brings a recognition of the public sphere as well. If we were thinking of translating Marianne Moore or Emily Dickinson, the standard for the translator could not be "anyone who can conduct a conversation in the language of the original (in this case English)." When applied to a third world language, the position is inherently ethnocentric. And then to present these translations to our unprepared students so that they can learn about women writing!

In my view, the translator from a third world language should be sufficiently in touch with what is going on in literary production in that language to be capable of distinguishing between good and bad writing by women, resistant and conformist writing by women.

She must be able to confront the idea that what seems resistant in the space of English may be reactionary in the space of the original language. Farida Akhter has argued that in Bangladesh the real work of the women's movement and of feminism is being undermined by talk of "gendering," mostly deployed by the women's development wings of transnational nongovernment organizations, in conjunction with some local academic feminist theorists.[13] One of her intuitions was that "gendering" could not be translated into Bengali. "Gendering" is an awkward new word in English as well. Akhter is profoundly involved in international feminism. And her base is third world. I could not

---

13 For background on Akhter, already somewhat dated for this interventionist in the history of the present, see Yayori Matsui, *Women's Asia* (London: Zed Books, 1989), Chap. 1. See also Farida Akhter, *Depopulating Bangladesh: Essays on the Politics of Fertility* (Dhaka: Narigrantha, 1992).

translate "gender" into the US feminist context for her. This misfiring of translation, between a superlative reader of the social text such as Akhter, and a careful translator like myself, speaking as friends, has added to my sense of the task of the translator.

Good and bad is a flexible standard, like all standards. Here another lesson of poststructuralism helps: these decisions of standards are made anyway. It is the attempt to justify them adequately that polices. That is why disciplinary preparation in school requires that you write examinations to prove these standards. Publishing houses routinely engage in materialist confusion of those standards. The translator must be able to fight that metropolitan materialism with a special kind of specialist's knowledge, not mere philosophical convictions.

In other words, the person who is translating must have a tough sense of the specific

terrain of the original, so that she can fight the racist assumption that all third world women's writing is good. I am often approached by women who would like to put Devi in with just Indian women writers. I am troubled by this, because "Indian women" is not a feminist category. (In "More on Power/Knowledge" I have argued that "epistemes"—ways of constructing objects of knowledge—should not have national names either.)[14] Sometimes Indian women writing means American women writing or British women writing, except for national *origin*. There is an ethno-cultural agenda, an obliteration of third world specificity as well as a denial of cultural citizenship, in calling them merely "Indian."

My initial point was that the task of the translator is to surrender herself to the linguistic rhetoricity of the original text. Although this point has larger political implications, we can say that the not unimportant minimal consequence of ignoring this task is the loss of "the literarity and textuality and sensuality of the writing" (Barrett's words). I have

---

14 In Spivak, *Outside in the Teaching Machine*, pp. 27–57.

worked my way to a second point, that the translator must be able to discriminate on the terrain of the original. Let us dwell on it a bit longer.

I choose Devi because she is unlike her scene. I have heard an English Shakespearean suggest that every bit of Shakespeare criticism coming from the subcontinent was by that virtue resistant. By such a judgment, we are also denied the right to be critical. It was of course bad to have put the place under subjugation, to have tried to make the place over with calculated restrictions. But that does not mean that everything that is coming out of that place after a negotiated independence nearly fifty years ago is necessarily right. The old anthropological supposition (and that is bad anthropology) that every person from a culture is nothing but a whole example of that culture is acted out in my colleague's suggestion. I remain interested in writers who are against the current, against the mainstream. I remain convinced that the interesting literary text might be precisely the text where you do not learn what the majority view of majority cultural representation or self-representation of a nation state might be. The translator has to make herself, in the case of third world women writing, almost better equipped than the translator who is dealing with the Western European languages, because of the fact that there is so much of the old colonial attitude, slightly displaced, at work in the translation racket. Poststructuralism can radicalize the field of preparation so that simply boning up on the language is not enough; there is also that special relationship to the staging of language as the production of agency that one must attend to. But the agenda of poststructuralism is mostly elsewhere, and the resistance to theory among metropolitan feminists would lead us into yet another narrative.

The understanding of the task of the translator and the practice of the craft are related but different. Let me summarize how I work. At first I translate at speed. If I stop to think about what is happening to the English, if I assume an audience, if I take the intending subject as more than a springboard, I cannot jump in, I cannot surrender. My relationship with Devi is easygoing. I am able to say to her: I surrender to you in your writing, not to you as intending subject. There, in friendship, is another kind of surrender. Surrendering to the text in this way means, most of the time, being literal. When I have produced a version this way, I revise. I revise not in terms of a possible audience, but by the protocols of the thing in front of me, in a sort of English. And I keep hoping that the student in the classroom will not be able to think that the text is just a purveyor of social realism if it is translated with an eye toward the dynamic staging of language mimed in the revision by the rules of the in-between discourse produced by a literalist surrender.

Vain hope, perhaps, for the accountability is different. When I translated Jacques Derrida's *De la grammatologie*, I was reviewed in a major journal for the first and last time. In the case of my translations of Devi, I have almost no fear of being accurately judged by my readership here. It makes the task more dangerous and more risky. And that for me is the real difference between translating Jacques Derrida and translating Mahasweta Devi, not merely the rather more artificial difference between deconstructive philosophy and political fiction.

The opposite argument is not neatly true. There is a large number of people in the third world who read the old imperial languages. People reading current feminist fiction in the European languages would probably read it in the appropriate imperial language. And the same goes for European philosophy. The act of translating into the third world language is often a political exercise of a different sort. I am looking forward, as of this writing, to lecturing in Bengali on deconstruction in front of a highly sophisticated audience, knowledgeable both in Bengali and in deconstruction (which they read in English and French and sometimes write about in Bengali), at Jadavpur University in Calcutta. It will be a kind of testing of the postcolonial translator, I think.[15]

---

15 I have given an account of this in Spivak, "Acting Bits/Identity Talk," *Critical Inquiry* 18(4) (Summer 1992): 770–803.

Democracy changes into the law of force in the case of translation from the third world and women even more because of their peculiar relationship to whatever you call the public/private divide. A neatly reversible argument would be possible if the particular Third World country had cornered the Industrial Revolution first and embarked on monopoly imperialist territorial capitalism as one of its consequences, and thus been able to impose a language as international norm. Something like that idiotic joke: if World War II had gone differently, the United States would be speaking Japanese. Such egalitarian reversible judgments are appropriate to counterfactual fantasy. Translation remains dependent upon the language skill of the majority. A prominent Belgian translation theorist solves the problem by suggesting that, rather than talk about the third world, where a lot of passion is involved, one should speak about the European Renaissance, since a great deal of wholesale cross-cultural translation from Greco-Roman antiquity was undertaken then. What one overlooks is the sheer authority ascribed to the originals in that historical phenomenon. The status of a language in the world is what one must consider when teasing out the politics of translation. Translatese in Bengali can be derided and criticized by large groups of anglophone and anglograph Bengalis. It is only in the hegemonic languages that the benevolent do not take the limits of their own often uninstructed good will into account. That phenomenon becomes hardest to fight because the individuals involved in it are genuinely benevolent and you are identified as a trouble-maker. This becomes particularly difficult when the metropolitan feminist, who is sometimes the assimilated postcolonial, invokes, indeed translates, a too quickly shared feminist notion of accessibility.

If you want to make the translated text accessible, try doing it for the person who wrote it. The problem comes clear then, for she is not within the same history of style. What is it that you are making accessible? The accessible level is the level of abstraction where the individual is already formed, where one can speak individual rights. When you hang out and with a language away from your own (*Mitwegsein*) so that you want to use that language by preference, sometimes, when you discuss something complicated, then you are on the way to making a dimension of the text accessible to the reader, with a light and easy touch, to which she does not accede in her everyday. If you are making anything else accessible, through a language quickly learned with an idea that you transfer content, then you are betraying the text and showing rather dubious politics.

How will women's solidarity be measured here? How will their common experience be reckoned if one cannot imagine the traffic in accessibility going both ways? I think that idea should be given a decent burial as ground knowledge, together with the idea of humanist universality. It is good to think that women have something in common, when one is approaching women with whom a relationship would not otherwise be possible. It is a great first step. But, if your interest is in learning if there is women's solidarity, how about stepping forth from this assumption, appropriate as a means to an end like local or global social work, and trying a second step? Rather than imagining that women automatically have something identifiable in common, why not say, humbly and practically, my first obligation in understanding solidarity is to learn her mother tongue. You will see immediately what the differences are. You will also feel the solidarity every day as you make the attempt to learn the language in which the other woman learned to recognize reality at her mother's knee. This is preparation for the intimacy of cultural translation. If you are going to bludgeon someone else by insisting on your version of solidarity, you have the obligation to try out this experiment and see how far your solidarity goes.

In other words, if you are interested in talking about the other, and/or in making a claim to be the other, it is crucial to learn other languages. This should be distinguished from the learned tradition of language acquisition for academic work. I am talking about the importance of language acquisition for the woman from a hegemonic monolinguist culture who makes everybody's life miserable by insisting on women's solidarity at her price. I am uncomfortable with notions of feminist solidarity which are celebrated when everybody involved is similarly produced. There are countless languages in which women all over the world have grown up and been female or feminist, and yet the languages we keep on learning by rote are the powerful European ones, sometimes the powerful Asian ones, least often the chief African ones. We are quite at home, and helpful, when large migrant populations are doing badly in the dominant countries, our own. The "other" languages are learned only by anthropologists who *must* produce knowledge across an epistemic divide. They are generally (though not invariably) not interested in the three-part structure we are discussing.

If we are discussing solidarity as a theoretical position, we must also remember that not all the world's women are literate. There are traditions and situations that remain obscure because we cannot share their linguistic constitution. It is from this angle that I have felt that learning languages might sharpen our own presuppositions about what it means to use the sign "woman." If we say that things should be accessible to us, who is this "us"? What does that sign mean?

Although I have used the examples of women all along, the arguments apply across the board. It is just that women's rhetoricity may be doubly obscured. I do not see the advantage of being completely focused on a single issue, although one must establish practical priorities. In the book where this chapter was first anthologized, the editors were concerned with poststructuralism and its effect on feminist theory. Where some poststructuralist thinking can be applied to the constitution of the agent in terms of the literary operations of language, women's texts might be operating differently because of the social differentiation between the sexes. Of course the point applies generally to the colonial context as well. When Ngũgĩ decided to write in Gikuyu, some thought he was bringing a private language into the public sphere. But what makes a language shared by many people in a community private? I was thinking about those so-called private languages when I was talking about language learning. But even within those private languages it is my conviction that there is a difference in the way in which the staging of language produces not only the sexed subject but the gendered agent, by a version of centering, persistently disrupted by rhetoricity, indicating contingency. Unless demonstrated otherwise, this for me remains the condition and effect of dominant and subordinate gendering. If that is so, then we have some reason to focus on women's texts. Let us use the word "woman" to name that space of parasubjects defined as such by the social inscription of primary and secondary sexual characteristics. Then we can cautiously begin to track a sort of commonality in being set apart, within the different rhetorical strategies of different languages. But even here, historical superiorities of class must be kept in mind. Bharati Mukherjee, Anita Desai, and Gayatri Spivak do not have the same rhetorical figuration of agency as an illiterate domestic servant.

Tracking commonality through responsible translation can lead us into areas of difference and different differentiations. This may also be important because, in the heritage of imperialism, the female legal subject bears the mark of a failure of Europeanization, by contrast with the female anthropological or literary subject from the area. For example, the division between the French and Islamic codes in modern Algeria is in terms of family, marriage, inheritance, legitimacy, and female social agency. These are differences that we must keep in mind. And we must honor the difference between ethnic minorities in the first world and majority populations of the third.

In conversation, Barrett had asked me if I now inclined more toward Foucault. This is indeed the case. In "Can the Subaltern Speak?" I took a rather strong critical line on Foucault's work, as part of a general critique of imperialism.[16] As I have indicated in "More on Power/

---

16 Spivak, "Can the Subaltern Speak?" in Larry Grossberg and Cary Nelson (eds), *Marxism and the Interpretation of Culture* (Urbana: University of Illinois Press, 1988), pp. 271–313.

Knowledge," I do, however, find, his concept of *pouvoir-savoir* immensely useful. Foucault has contributed to French this ordinary-language doublet (the ability to know [as]) to take its place quietly beside *vouloir-dire* (the wish to say— meaning to mean).

On the most mundane level, *pouvoir-savoir* is the shared skill which allows us to make (common) sense of things. It is certainly not only power/knowledge in the sense of *puissance/connaissance*. Those are aggregative institutions. The common way in which one makes sense of things, on the other hand, loses itself in the sub-individual.

Looking at *pouvoir-savoir* in terms of women, one of my focuses has been new immigrants and the change of mother tongue and *pouvoir-savoir* between mother and daughter. When the daughter talks reproductive rights and the mother talks protecting honor, is this the birth or death of translation?

Foucault is also interesting in his new notion of the ethics of the care for the self. In order to be able to get to the subject of ethics it may be necessary to look at the ways in which an individual in that culture is instructed to care for the self rather than the imperialism-specific secularist notion that the ethical subject is given as human. In a secularism which is structurally identical with Christianity laundered in the bleach of moral philosophy, the subject of ethics is faceless. Breaking out, Foucault was investigating other ways of making sense of how the subject becomes ethical. This is of interest because, given the connection between imperialism and secularism, there is almost no way of getting to alternative general voices except through religion. And if one does not look at religion as mechanisms of producing the ethical subject, one gets various kinds of "fundamentalism." Workers in cultural politics and its connections to a new ethical philosophy have to be interested in religion in the production of ethical subjects. There is much room for feminist work here because Western feminists have not so far been aware of religion as a cultural instrument rather than a mark of cultural difference. I am currently working on Hindu performative ethics with Professor Bimal Krishna Matilal. He is an enlightened male feminist. I am an active feminist. Helped by his learning and his openness I am learning to distinguish between ethical catalysts and ethical motors even as I learn to translate bits of the Sanskrit epic in a way different from all the accepted translations, because I rely not only on learning, not only on "good English," but on that three-part scheme of which I have so lengthily spoken. I hope the results will please readers. If we are going to look at an ethics that emerges from something other than the historically secularist ideal—at an ethics of sexual differences, at an ethics that can confront the emergence of fundamentalisms without apology or dismissal in the name of the Enlightenment—then *pouvoir-savoir* and the care for the self in Foucault can be illuminating. And these "other ways" bring us back to translation, in the general sense.

Translation in General

I want now to add two sections to what was generated from the initial conversation with Barrett. I will dwell on the politics of translation in a general sense, by way of three examples of "cultural translation" in English. I want to make the point that the lessons of translation in the narrow sense can reach much further.

First, J. M. Coetzee's *Foe*. This book represents the impropriety of the dominant's desire to give voice to the native. When Susan Barton, the eighteenth-century Englishwoman from *Roxana*, attempts to teach a muted Friday (from *Robinson Crusoe*) to read and write English, he draws an incomprehensible rebus on his slate and wipes it out, withholds it. You cannot translate from a position of monolinguist superiority. Coetzee as white creole translates *Robinson Crusoe* by representing Friday as the agent of a withholding.

Second, Toni Morrison's *Beloved*.[17] Let us look at the scene of the change of the mother tongue from mother to daughter. Strictly speaking,

---

17 Toni Morrison, *Beloved* (New York: Plume Books, 1987). Hereafter cited in text as B with page numbers included.

it is not a change, but a loss, for the narrative is not of immigration but of slavery. Sethe, the central character of the novel, remembers: "What Nan"—her mother's fellow-slave and friend—"told her she had forgotten, along with the language she told it in. The same language her ma'am spoke, and which would never come back. But the message—that was— and had been there all along" (B 62). The representation of this message, as it passes through the forgetfulness of death to Sethe's ghostly daughter Beloved, is of a withholding: "This is not a story to pass on" (B 275).

Between mother and daughter, a certain historical withholding intervenes. If the situation between the new immigrant mother and daughter provokes the question as to whether it is the birth or death of translation, here the author represents with violence a certain birth-in-death, a death-in-birth of a story that is not to translate or pass on. Strictly speaking, therefore, an aporia. And yet it is passed on, with the mark of untranslatability on it, in the bound book, *Beloved*, that we hold in our hands. Contrast this to the confidence in accessibility in the house of power, where history is waiting to be restored.

The scene of violence between mother and daughter (reported and passed on by the daughter Sethe to her daughter Denver, who carries the name of a white trash girl, in partial acknowledgment of women's solidarity in birthing) is, then, the condition of (im)possibility of *Beloved*.

She picked me up and carried me behind the smokehouse. Back there she opened up her dress front and lifted her breast and pointed under it. Right on her rib was a circle and a cross burnt right in the skin. She said, "This is your ma'am. This," and she pointed . . . "Yes, Ma'am," I said. . . . "But how will you know me? . . . Mark me, too," I said . . . "Did she?" asked Denver. "She slapped my face." "What for?" I didn't understand it then. Not till I had a mark of my own." (B 61)

This scene, of claiming the brand of the owner as "my own," to create, in this broken chain of marks owned by separate white male agents of property, an unbroken chain of rememory in (enslaved) daughters as agents of a history not to be passed on, is of necessity different from Friday's scene of withheld writing from the white woman wanting to create history by giving her "own" language. And the lesson is the (im)possibility of translation in the general sense. Rhetoric points at absolute contingency, not the sequentiality of time, not even the cycle of seasons, but only "weather." "By and by all trace is gone, and what is forgotten is not only the footprints but the water and what it is down there. The rest is weather. Not the breath of the disremembered and unaccounted for"—after the effacement of the trace, no project for restoring (women's?) history—"but wind in the eaves, or spring ice thawing too quickly. Just weather" (B 275).

With this invocation of contingency, where nature may be "the great body without organs of woman," we can align ourselves with Wilson Harris, the author of *The Guyana Quartet*, for whom trees are "the lungs of the globe,"[18] not merely the translation but the trans-substantiation of the species. What in more workaday language I have called the obligation of the translator to be able to juggle the rhetorical silences in the two languages, Harris puts this way, pointing at the need for translating the Carib's English:

> The Caribbean bone flute, made of human bone, is a seed in the soul of the Caribbean. It is a primitive technology that we can turn around [trans-version?]. Consuming our biases and prejudices in ourselves we other way—as a metonymic devouring of a bit of flesh.[19] The link of music with cannibalism is a sublime paradox. When the music of the bone flute opens the

---

18 Wilson Harris, *The Guyana Quartet* (London: Faber, 1975). These quotations are from Wilson Harris, "Cross-Cultural Crisis: Imagery, Language, and the Intuitive Imagination," Commonwealth Lectures, University of Cambridge, Lecture no. 2 (October 31, 1990).

19 Derrida traces the trajectory of the Hegelian and pre-Hegelian discourse of the fetish in *Glas*. The worshipper of the fetish eats human flesh. The worshipper of God feasts on the Eucharist. Harris transverses the fetish here through the native imagination.

doors, absences flow in, and the native imagination puts together the ingredients for quantum immediacy out of unpredictable resources.

The bone flute has been neglected by Caribbean writers, says Harris, because progressive realism is a charismatic way of writing prize-winning fiction. Progressive realism measures the bone. Progressive realism is the too-easy accessibility of translation as transfer of substance.

The progressive realism of the West dismissed the native imagination as the place of the fetish. Hegel was perhaps the greatest systematizer of this dismissal. And psychoanalytic cultural criticism in its present charismatic incarnation sometimes measures the bone with uncanny precision. It is perhaps not fortuitous that the passage below gives us an account of Hegel that is the exact opposite of Harris's vision. The paradox of the sublime and the bone here lead to non-language seen as inertia, where the structure of passage is mere logic. The authority of the supreme language makes translation impossible:

> The Sublime is therefore the paradox of an object which, in the very field of representation, provides a view, in a negative way, of the dimension of what is unrepresentable [. . .]. The bone, the skull, is thus an object which, by means of its *presence*, fills out the void, the impossibility of the signifying *representation* of the subject [. . .]. The proposition "Wealth is the Self" repeats at this level the proposition "The Spirit is a bone" [both propositions are Hegel's]: in both cases we are dealing with a proposition which is at first sight absurd, nonsensical, with an equation the terms of which are incompatible; in both cases we encounter the same logical structure of passage: the subject, totally lost in the medium of language (language of gesture and grimaces; language of flattery), finds its objective counterpart in the inertia of a non-language object (skull, money).[20]

20 Slavoj Žižek, *The Sublime Object of Ideology* (Jon Barnes trans.) (London: Verso, 1989), pp. 203, 208, 212.

Wilson Harris's vision is abstract, translating Morrison's "weather" into an oceanic version of quantum physics. But all three cultural translators cited in this section ask us to attend to the rhetoric which points to the limits of translation, in the Creole's, the slave-daughter's, the Carib's use of "English." Let us learn the lesson of translation from these brilliant inside/outsiders and translate it into the situation of other languages.

Reading as Translation

In conclusion, I want to show how the postcolonial as the outside/insider translates white theory as she reads, so that she can discriminate on the terrain of the original. She wants to use what is useful. Again, I hope this can pass on a lesson to the translator in the narrow sense.

"The link of music with cannibalism is a sublime paradox." I believe Wilson Harris is using "sublime" here with some degree of precision, indicating the undoing of the progressive Western subject as realist interpreter of history. Can a theoretical account of the aesthetic sublime in English discourse, ostensibly far from the bone flute, be of use? By way of answer, I will use my reading of Peter de Bolla's superb scholarly account of *The Discourse of the Sublime* as an example of sympathetic reading as translation, precisely not a surrender but a friendly learning Harris hails the (re)birth of the native imagination as not object (skull, money). can let the bone flute help us open ourselves rather than read it the by taking a distance.[21]

P. 4: "What was it to be a subject in the eighteenth century?" The reader-as-translator (RAT) is excited. The long eighteenth century in Britain is the account of the constitution and transformation of nation into empire. Shall we read that story? The book will at least touch on that issue, if only to swerve. And women will not be seen as touched in their agency formation by that change. The book's strong feminist

---

21 Peter de Bolla, *The Discourse of the Sublime: Readings in History, Aesthetics, and the Subject* (Oxford: Blackwell, 1989). Page numbers are given in my text.

sympathies relate to the Englishwoman only as gender victim. But the erudition of the text allows us to think that this sort of rhetorical reading might be the method to open up the question "What is it to be a postcolonial reader of English in the twentieth century?" The representative reader of *The Discourse of the Sublime* will be postcolonial. Has that law of the majority been observed, or the law of the strong?

On p. 72 RAT comes to a discussion of Burke on the sublime:

The internal resistance of Burke's text [...] restricts the full play of this trope [power . . . as a trope articulating the technologies of the sublime], thereby defeating a description of the sublime experience uniquely in terms of the enpowered [sic] subject. Put briefly, Burke, for a number of reasons, among which we must include political aims and ends, stops short of a discourse on the sublime, and in so doing he reinstates the ultimate power of an adjacent discourse, theology, which locates its own self-authenticating power grimly within the boundaries of godhead.

Was it also because Burke was deeply implicated in searching out the recesses of the mental theater of the English master in the colonies that he had some notion of different kinds of subject and therefore, like some Kurtz before Conrad, recoiled in horror before the sublimely empowered subject? Was it because, like some Kristeva before *Chinese Women*, Burke had tried to imagine the Begums of Oudh as legal subjects that he had put self-authentication elsewhere?[22] *The Discourse of the Sublime*, in noticing Burke's difference from the other discoursers on the sublime, opens doors for other RATs to engage in such scholarly speculations and thus exceed and expand the book.

---

22 References and discussion of "The Begums of Oudh" and "The Impeachment of Warren Hastings" are to be found in *The Writings and Speeches of Edmund Burke* (P. J. Marshall ed.) (Oxford: Clarendon, 1981), *Volume 5: India: Madras and Bengal*, pp. 410–12, 465–66, p. 470; and in *Volume 6: India: Launching of the Hastings Impeachment*, respectively.

Pp. 106, 111–12, 131: RAT comes to the English National Debt. British colonialism was a violent deconstruction of the hyphen between nation and state. In imperialism the nation was subl(im)ated into empire. Of this, no clue in *The Discourse*. The Bank of England is discussed. Its founding in 1696, and the transformation of letters of credit to the ancestor of the modern check, had something like a relationship with the fortunes of the East India Company and the founding of Calcutta in 1690. The *national* debt is in fact the site of a crisis-management, where the nation, sublime object as miraculating subject of ideology, changes the sign "debtor" into a catachresis or false metaphor by way of "an acceptance of a permanent discrepancy between the total circulating specie and the debt." The French War, certainly the immediate efficient cause, is soon woven into the vaster textile of crisis. *The Discourse* cannot see the nation covering for the colonial economy. As on the occasion of the race-specificity of gendering, so on the discourse of multinational capital, the argument is kept domestic, within England, European.[23] RAT snuffles off, disgruntled. She finds a kind of comfort in Mahasweta's livid figuration of the woman's body as body rather than attend to this history of the English body "as a disfigurative device in order to return to [it] its lost literality." Reading as translation has misfired here.

On p. 140 RAT comes to the elder Pitt. "Although his functionality is initially seen as demanded [. . .] by the incorporation of nation," it is not possible not at least to mention empire when speaking of Pitt's voice:

the voice of Pitt [. . .] works its doubled intervention into the spirit and character of the times; at once the supreme example of the private individual in the service of the state, and the private individual eradicated by the needs of a public, nationalist, commercial empire. In this sense the voice of Pitt becomes the

---

23 See Spivak, "Reading the Archives: The Rani of Sirmur," in Francis Barker (ed.), *Europe and Its Others*, VOL. 1 (Colchester: University of Essex, 1985), pp. 128–51.

most extreme example of the textualization of the body for the rest of the century.[24]

We have seen a literal case of the textualization of the surface of the body between slave mother and slave daughter in *Beloved,* where mother hits daughter to stop her thinking that the signs of that text can be passed on, a lesson learned *après-coup*, literally after the blow of the daughter's own branding. Should RAT expect an account of the passing on of the textualization of the interior of the body through the voice, a metonym for consciousness, from master father to master son? The younger Pitt took the first step to change the nationalist empire to the imperial nation with the India Act of 1784. Can *The Discourse of the Sublime* plot that sublime relay? Not yet. But here, too, an exceeding and expanding translation is possible.

Predictably, RAT finds a foothold in the rhetoricity of *The Discourse*. Chapter Ten begins: "The second part of this study has steadily examined how 'theory' sets out to legislate and control a practice, how it produces the excess which it cannot legislate, and removes from the center to the boundary its limit, limiting case".[25] This passage reads to a deconstructive RAT as an enabling self-description of the text, although within the limits of the book, it describes, not itself, but the object of its investigation. By the time the end of the book is reached, RAT feels that she has been written into the text:

> As a history of that refusal and resistance [this book] presents a record of its own coming into being as history, the history of the thought it wants to think differently, over there. It is, therefore, only appropriate that its conclusion should gesture towards the limit, risk the reinversion of the boundary by speaking from the other, refusing silence to what is unsaid.[26]

---

24 De Bolla, *The Discourse of the Sublime*, p. 182.
25 De Bolla, *The Discourse of the Sublime*, p. 230.
26 De Bolla, *The Discourse of the Sublime*, p. 324.

Beyond this "clamor for a kiss" of the other space, it is "just weather."

Under the figure of RAT (reader-as-translator), I have tried to limn the politics of a certain kind of clandestine postcolonial reading, using the master marks to put together a history. Thus we find out what books we can forage, and what we must set aside. I can use Peter de Bolla's *The Discourse on the Sublime* to open up dull histories of the colonial eighteenth century. Was Toni Morrison, a writer well-versed in contemporary literary theory, obliged to set aside Paul de Man's "The Purloined Ribbon"?[27]

> Eighteen seventy-four and white folks were still on the loose . . . Human blood cooked in a lynch fire was a whole other thing . . . But none of that had worn out his marrow . . . It was the ribbon . . . He thought it was a cardinal feather stuck to his boat. He tugged and what came loose in his hand was a red ribbon knotted around a curl of wet woolly hair, clinging still to its bit of scalp . . . He kept the ribbon; the skin smell nagged him. (B 180–81)

Morrison next invokes a language whose selvedge is so frayed that no *frayage* can facilitate full passage: "This time, although he couldn't cipher but one word, he believed he knew who spoke them. The people of the broken necks, of fire-cooked blood and black girls who had lost their ribbons" (B, 181). Did the explanation of promises and excuses in eighteenth-century Geneva not make it across into this "roar"? I will not check it out and measure the bone flute. I will simply dedicate these pages to the author of *Beloved*, in the name of translation.

---

27 Paul de Man, "The Purloined Ribbon," reprinted as "Excuses (*Confessions*)," in *Allegories of Reading* (New Haven, CT: Yale University Press, 1979), pp. 278–301.

CULTURES OF TRANSLATION

Translation as Culture

(2000)*

Oviedo[1]

In every possible sense, translation is necessary but impossible. Melanie Klein, the Viennese psychoanalyst whom the Bloomsbury Group killed with kindness, suggested that the work of translation is an incessant shuttle that is a "life."[2] The human infant grabs on to some one thing and then things. This grabbing (*begreifen*) of an outside indistinguishable from an inside constitutes an inside, going back and forth and coding everything into a sign-system by the thing(s) grasped. One can

---

* A version of "Translation as Culture" was published in Isabel Carrera Suarez, Aurora Garcia Fernanadez, M. S. Suarez Lafuente (eds), *Translating Cultures* (Oviedo-Hebden Bridge: KRK–Dangaroo Press, 1999), pp. 17–30. The present text was first published in *Parallax* 6(1) (2000): 13–24 [We would like to thank both Gayatri Chakravorty Spivak and Isabel Carrera Suarez for the opportunity of republishing this text.—Eds]

1 The year after my speech at Oviedo, I received the Translation Award from Sahitya Akademi, the National Academy of Letters in India, and delivered an acceptance speech in 1998. There is a certain continuity between the two events. In the former I question the metropolitan hybridist. In the latter I take the national identitarians to task. I have taken the liberty of appending my acceptance speech as the appropriate conclusion to this essay, which is thus in two sections, *Oviedo* and *New Delhi*.

2 What follows is my own interpretative digest of Melanie Klein, *Works*, VOLS 1–4 (New York: Free Press, 1984). Giving specific footnotes is therefore impossible. The details may also not resemble orthodox Kleinian psychoanalysis.

call this crude coding a "translation." In this never-ending weaving, violence translates into conscience and vice versa. From birth to death this "natural" machine, programming the mind perhaps as genetic instructions program the body (where does body stop and mind begin?), is partly metapsychological and therefore outside the grasp of the mind. Thus "nature" passes and repasses into "culture," in a work or shuttling site of violence (deprivation—evil—shocks the infant system-in-the-making more than satisfaction, some say *Paradiso* is the dullest of *The Divine Comedy*): the violent production of the precarious subject of reparation and responsibility. To plot this weave, the reader—in my estimation, Klein was more a reader than an analyst in the strict Freudian sense—translating the incessant translating shuttle into that which is read, must have the most intimate knowledge of the rules of representation and permissible narratives which make up the substance of a culture, and must also become responsible and accountable to the writing/translating presupposed original.

It is by way of Melanie Klein that I grasped a certain statement which comes to me from Australian Aboriginals. But before I go on to talk about it I want to say just a little bit more about Melanie Klein.

The subject in the shuttling described by Klein is something that will have happened, not something that definitely happens—because, first, it is not under the control of the *I* that we think of as the subject and because; second, there is such a thing as a world out there, however discursive. In this understanding of *translation* in Melanie Klein, therefore, the word *translation* itself loses its literal sense, it becomes a catachresis, a term I use not for obscurity, but because I find it indispensable.

Here is why I have to use the word *catachresis*. I was recently having a discussion with Dr. Aniruddha Das, a cell biologist. He is working on how cells recognize, how parasites recognize, what to attack in the body. I asked him why he used the word *recognize*, such a mindy word, a word that has to do with intellect and consciousness. Why use that word to describe something that goes on in the body, not really at all in the arena of what we recognize as mind? Wouldn't the word *affinity* do for these parasites "knowing" what to attack? He explained to me that no, indeed, the word *affinity* would not do, and why it is that precisely the word *recognize* had to be used. (I cannot reproduce the explanation but that does not matter for us at this moment.) He added that the words *recognition*, *recognize* lose their normal sense when used this way; there is no other word that can be used. Most people find this difficult to understand. And I started laughing. I said, yes, most people do find it difficult to understand, what you have just described is a catachrestic use of the word *recognition*. In other words, no other word will do, and yet it does not really give you the literal meaning in the history of the language, upon which a *correct* rather than catachrestic metaphoric use would be based.

In the sense that I am deriving from Klein, *translation* does indeed lose its mooring in a literal meaning. Translation in this general sense is not under the control of the subject who is translating. Indeed the human subject is something that will have happened as this shuttling translation, from inside to outside, from violence to conscience: the production of the ethical subject. This originary translation thus wrenches the sense of the English word *translation* outside of its making. One look at the dictionary will tell you the word comes from a Latin past participle (of *transferre* = to transfer). It is a done deal, precisely not a future anterior, something that will have happened without our knowledge, particularly without our control, the subject coming into being.

When so-called ethnophilosophies describe the embedded ethico-cultural subject being formed prior to the terrain of rational decision making, they are dismissed as fatalistic. But the insight, that the constitution of the subject in responsibility is a certain kind of translation, of a genealogical scripting, which is not under the control of the deliberative consciousness, is not something that just comes from Melanie Klein. What is interesting about Melanie Klein is that she does indeed want to touch responsibility-based ethical systems rather than just rights-based ethical systems and therefore she looks at the violent translation that constitutes the subject in responsibility. It is in this sense that the human infant, on the cusp of the natural and the cultural, is in translation, except the word translation loses its dictionary sense right there. Here, the body itself is a script—or perhaps one should say a ceaseless inscribing Instrument.

When a translator translates from a constituted language, whose system of inscription, and permissible narratives are "her own," this secondary act, translation in the narrow sense, as it were, is also a peculiar act of reparation—toward the language of the inside, a language in which we are "responsible," the guilt of seeing it as one language among many. Translation in the narrow sense is thus a reparation. I translate from my mother tongue. This originary *Schuldigsein*—being-indebted in the Kleinian sense—the guilt in seeing that one can treat one's mother tongue as one language among many—gives rise to a certain obligation for reparation. I'm a slow translator, and for me it is the shuttle between the exquisite guilt of finding the mother tongue or the substitute mother tongue when I translate from French—every "original" is a place-holder for the mother tongue—shuttle between that guilt, a displacement of some primordial *Schuldigsein*, and the reparation of reality-testing, where each of the languages becomes a guarantee of the other. Each is assumed to be or to possess the generality of a semiotic that can appropriate the singularity of the other's idiom by way of conscientious approximations.

Singularity and generality, idiom and semiosis, private and public grammars. It is as if the play of idiom in semioticity becomes a simulacrum, or case, of the ethical as such, as the unaccountable ethical structure of feeling is transcoded into a calculus of accountability. The idiom is singular to the tongue. It will not go over. The semiotic is the system which is generalizable. This element of transcoding is what locates the recognizable violence of the recognizably political within the general violence of culturing as incessant and shuttling translation, a point much harder to grasp without familiarity with the discourses of the gift.

I am not referring only to discourses of the gift à la Heiddeger, Levinas and Derrida as they underpin, let us say, Derrida's wonderful *Given Time*.[3] I also mean discourses of the gift as they are available in ethnophilosophies. In my own case, for example, it is the discourse of *matririn*. Unless one is familiar with the discourses of the gift it is harder to grasp the general violence of culturing as incessant and shuttling translation. Klein locates this in whatever single object first signifies pleasure/pain, good/bad, right/wrong and allows itself to be concatenated into signifying the unmotivated giver of the gift (of life). I grasp my responsibility to take from my mother tongue and give to the "target"-language through the ethical concept-metaphor of *matririn* (mother-debt)—a debt *to* the mother as well as a debt (that) the (place of the) mother *is*. For the father debt I can give you chapter and verse. I cannot provide a citation for *matririn*. The aphorism: *matririn* is not to be repaid, or cannot be repaid, was part of my childhood every day, as it is of my intellectual life now. The mother-debt is the gift of birth, as it is imaged to be, but also the accountable task of childrearing (literally *manush kora* = making human, in my mother tongue). One translates this gift-into-accountability as one attempts to repay what cannot be repaid, and should not be thought of as repayable.

For me, then, it is within this open-ended nature-culture frame that all recognizable violence of the recognizably political within the general violence of culturing can be located—in an element of transcoding as well as translating. I will stay with the element of transcoding in this first part, with the location of the recognizable violence of the recognizably political. I leave aside for the moment the other terrain of culture as translation, where recognition begins in differentiation.[4]

---

3 Jacques Derrida, *Given Time: I. Counterfeit Money* (Peggy Kamuf trans.) (Chicago: University of Chicago Press, 1992).
4 This more colloquial sense is where we locate Charles Taylor, *Multiculturalism and the Politics of Recognition* (Princeton, NJ: Princeton University Press, 1994).

Let us then speak of idioms and semiotic systems within this frame. I learnt this lesson of the violence of transcoding as translation, from a group that has stayed in place for more than thirty thousand years. That lesson was contained in the philosopheme—the smallest unit of philosophy: "lost our language," used by the Australian Aboriginals of the East Kimberley region. The expression "lost our language" does not mean that the persons involved do not know their aboriginal mother tongue. It means, in the words of a social worker, that "they have lost touch with their cultural base," they no longer compute with it, it is not their software. In the Kleinian metaphorics, it is not the condition and effect of their nature-culture shuttling. Therefore, what these inheritors of settler-colonial oppression ask for is, quite appropriately, mainstream education, insertion into civil society, and the inclusion of some information about their culture in the curriculum. Under the circumstances this is the only practical request. The concept-metaphor "language" is here standing in for that word which names the main instrument for the performance of the temporizing, of the shuttling outside-inside translation that is called life. What the Aboriginals are asking for, having lost generalizing control of the semioticity of their system, is hegemonic access to chunks of narrative and descriptions of practice, so that the representation of that instrumentality, as a cultural idiom rather than a semiotic, becomes available for performance as what is called theater, or art, or literature, or indeed culture, even theory. Given the rupture between the many languages of Aboriginality and the waves of migration and colonial adventure clustered around the Industrial Revolution narrative, demands for multilingual education here become risible. All we have is bilingualisms, bilateral arrangements between idioms understood as essentially or historically private, on the one side, and English on the other, understood as the semiotic as such. This is the political violence of translation as transcoding, the contemporary translation industry about which many of us write. It is not without significance that I cannot check the lexicality of this "loss of language" against any original.

Recently I found corroboration in what Lee Cataldi and Peggy Rockman Napaljarri have written about the Warlpiri people of Central North Australia:

> For Warlpiri people, the coming of the Europeans was "the end of the Jukurrpa" [. . .] simultaneously an account of the creation of the places in [their narrative], an account of the mythical but human behavior of the ancestral figures, and a mnemonic map of the country with its important, life-giving features for the purpose of instructing a younger listener [. . .]. Rosie Napurrurla and many others are very aware that the intrusion into their lives and land of the dominating, metropolitan culture of the West meant the end of the Jukurrpa as a world-view [I would call it a discursive practice], as a single, total explanation of the universe. It is apparent that many Warlpiri people are much more clearly aware of the nature of cultural conflict and the nature of the two cultures than Europeans are [and, I would add, than are some academic theorists]. Such awareness is the privilege of the loser in this kind of conflict.[5]

When we establish our reputations on transcoding such resistant located hybridity, distinct from the more commonly noticed migrant hybridity, we lose the privilege of the loser because we claim that privilege. The translators in Cataldi and Napaljarri's book placed their effort

---

5 Peggy Rockman Napaljarri and Lee Cataldi (trans), *Yimikirli: Warlpiri Dreamings and Histories* (San Francisco, CA: HarperCollins, 1994), pp. xvii, 20. The immense labor of thinking the relationship of this "mnemonic mapping" with "satellite positioning technology offer[ing] a definitive solution to this question, which some claim has troubled us from our origin: where am I?" must be undertaken without foregone conclusions. (Laura Kurgan and Xavier Costa [eds], *You Are Here: Architecture and Information Flows* [Barcelona: Museum of Contemporary Art, 1995], p. 121. The entire text, especially the visuals, should be studied with an "active" perusal of *Yimikirli*, which may now be impossible. The necessary yet impossible task of cultural translation is made possible and ruined by the march of history.)

within resources for a cultural performance of the second degree. They were not themselves constricted by the violence of this culture performing itself, as originary and catachrestic translation—the coming into being of the responsible subject as divined by Klein.

After spending three or four days with a Canadian artist, originally of Islamic roots, I asked her a question, we had got to know each other well. I want you to tell me, I said, when you confront a situation where you have to make a decision between right and wrong, do you turn to Islam for the ethical answer? I quite understand that you and I must join in undermining the demonizing and dehistoricizing of Islam that is current in North America today, but this is a different kind of question. It is the difference between a generalizable semiotics that writes our life, and a cultural idiom that we must honorably establish so that we can "perform" it as art. And she said, after a long time, I've never been asked this question, but the answer is no.

The translators of the Warlpiri texts place their effort as a resource for a cultural performance, an idiom, rather than the violence of culture turning over, in and as the human subject, as originary and catachrestic translation. I quote again:

> Although it is true that Warlpiri people no longer live within the logic and constraints of the world-view known as the Jukurrpa, it is also the case that, like other traditional Aboriginal people, they have succeeded in creating for themselves a way of life which is unique and distinctive, nothing like the European culture with which they have to live. We hope that something of the spirit of this social creation is communicated by the translations and the narratives in this book.[6]

Alas, we cannot discover how that tradition worked as a violent catachrestic translation shuttle of the outside-inside when it was indeed the semiosis of subject-making. The Industrial Revolution put paid to

---

6 Napaljarri and Cataldi, *Yimikirli*, p. xxii.

that anti-essentialism, that placing of subject-making in alterity. And therefore any mention of tradition is silenced with the remark that that is just essentialist golden-ageism. On the contrary, we mourn the loss of aboriginal culture as underived fictions that are the condition and effect of the subject's history merely because it is the founding crime of the world we live in. There is no question of unwriting or rewriting history here. The bad-faith hybridistic essentialism of discovering diasporic hybrids and offering that transcoding of the popular as in itself a radical gesture cannot bind that wound of history. I am certainly not interested in censoring work. What I am objecting to is the kind of silencing that is operated when the transcoding of diasporic cultures mingling becomes in itself a radical gesture. It's that claim to effortless resistance, short-circuiting efforts to translate where "languages have been lost," about which I feel dubious.

Cataldi and Napaljarri, our translators, inhabit an *aporia*, a catch. Some of their material "is derived from land-claim documents," already a site of transcoding a mnemonic geography into the semiosis of land as property. Their book appears in a series that believes in "the global interdependence of human hearts and minds," which can be double-talk for the financialization of the globe, "culturalization" of electronic capital, alibi for the contemporary new world order, post-Soviet exploitation. Their book appears in such a series, "printed on acid-free paper that meets the American National Standards Institute Z39.48 standard." What is the relationship between the scene of global ecology, and the appropriation of traditional knowledge as trade related intellectual property in the name of biopiracy coded as bioprospecting? What is the relationship between standardized environmentalism on the one hand, and traditional knowledge systems on the other? Mnemonic geography and satellite positioning technology? This is also a transcoding question. Just as we cannot content ourselves with collecting examples of diasporic hybridity, so also can we not just read books translating "other cultures." We must work at the screen if we are really interested in translation as a phenomenon rather than a mere convenience because we cannot learn every language in the world.

Precisely in the pages showing the most stunning Warlpiri paintings, there is an insert advertising 52 percent student rate savings on *TIME* magazine and a free stereo cassette player "for your spare time." The act of the insertion is the mechanical gesture of a subordinate employee or a machine, completely at odds with the apparent intent of the translators. The international book trade is a trade in keeping with the laws of world trade. It is the embedding network which moves books as objects on a circuit of destined errancy. At one end, the coming into being of the subject of reparation. At the other end, generalized commodity exchange. We translate somewhere in-between. Even as the translators consign this text of Warlpiri dreaming (Jukurrpa) to this exchange, they cannot grasp, because of the depredations of history, the way in which the totalizing dreaming was an operative anti-essentialist semiosis, the infant shuttling between inside and outside and reality testing, the shuttling of violence and conscience making the subject in responsibility emerge. This book is interesting because it shows that the Warlpiri are themselves aware of this. They point at contemporary social creation.

Some assume that subalterns (those cut off from cultural mobility) have nothing but idiom which the historian translates into systematicity. (Not Cataldi and Napaljarri, of course.) In November 1996, I was in a gathering of about twelve hundred Aboriginals in a settlement on the outskirts of Akarbaid village in western West Bengal. (These "Aboriginals" are the descendants of the population of the Indian subcontinent before Indo-European-speaking peoples started trickling into that landmass.) Mahasweta Devi, the woman whose fiction I translate, was also present. Toward evening she asked Lochan Sabar, an eighty-four-year-old Aboriginal, to "tell Gayatri about the time when you were involved in India's Independence Struggle."

The historians' collective Subaltern Studies Group has been engaged since the early 1980s in questioning the nationalist historiography of Indian Independence, suggesting that it ignores the continuous tradition of insurgency among peasants and Aboriginals. Here was I confronted by a man who was on the cusp of that binary opposition, between bourgeois nationalist historiography and the subaltern. This Lochan Sabar, himself an Aboriginal who had not left that way of life, had taken part in the Independence Struggle and was getting the pension of a freedom fighter. He begins telling his story, a story that has been told many times before. I alone do not know it in that company. He is using the word *Gandhi* from time to time. He has translated his experiences in the freedom struggle into an oral formulaic mode, which I could at that point recognize because I had read A. B. Lord as an undergraduate.[7] Mahasweta turns aside and tells me, "By the way, he's not referring to Mahatma Gandhi." Any person in the position of a bourgeois leader staging himself as subaltern is being given the name Gandhi. Gandhi after all was no subaltern; he staged himself as one, took off his suit—so any time that some charismatic intellectual populist leader is described, Lochan is using the word Gandhi. In terms of the way in which they mythicize, Gandhi has become a type word. This shakes me up. Next, whenever there comes a moment in his epic recounting when, what the academic subalternist historians describe as religion coming into crisis and becoming militancy, comes to pass, Lochan Sabar marks it with the exclamation *Bande Mataram*! [Praise to the Mother!], without catching it in the web of his narrative. Those of you who have seen Satyajit Ray's *The Home and the World* will remember this as the slogan of the freedom fighters.[8] These are the

---

7 Albert B. Lord, *The Singer of Tales* (New York: Atheneum, 1965).

8 The film is based on Rabindranath Tagore's novel *Ghare Baire*. In an essay on translation, it should be noticed that the English title is a mistranslation. It does not catch the delicacy of the threshold effect of the original, which is in the locative case, and might translate as "inside outside."

opening words, in Sanskrit, of the nineteenth-century nationalist song written by Bankim Chandra Chattopadhyay.

Sanskrit is the classical language of the Hindus. The very word means "refined" (as opposed to "natural," "raw"). The refinement of the original Indo-European speech traditions into that form would politically be exactly opposed to the culture of the Aboriginals. How shall one compute Lochan Sabar's negotiation with this?[9] Further, the Mother in the song is Bengal-cum-India. The Bharatiya Janata Party, the Hindu nationalist party in India, wants to claim it as the national anthem in place of the more secular one in actual use. Lochan is not aware of this; he is not Hindu, only an unlettered animist whose religious idiom is contaminated by Hindu folk practice. He is transforming the hegemonic nationalist account, Gandhi as well as Bankim, into the semiotic conventions of subaltern or Sabar telling. He is deflecting Bankim's own effort, related to the British ideology of restoring Bengal to its Hindu lineaments against the Muslim rule that the British had brought to an end. Bankim attempted to establish a Hindu Bengali nationalism which would gradually vanish into "Indian" nationalism. He denies the Islamic component of Bengali culture; the Aboriginals are nothing but children to him. Bankim's brother, Sanjib Chandra Chattopadhyay, had written the immortal sentence, memorized by every schoolchild in my day: "The savage has beauty in the forest, as does the child in its mother's arms." In the process, denying the lexicalized Arabic and Persian elements of Bengali, Bankim lexicalizes Sanskrit into Bengali as Lochan Sabar weaves his words into subaltern formula.

I can see both as generalizing, from idiom to semiosis, differently. Lochan's is not just an idiomatics, which the historian then transcodes

---

9 I have discussed the hospitality of the subordinated toward the dominant in Spivak, "Deconstruction and Cultural Studies: Arguments for a Deconstructive Cultural Studies," in Nicholas Royle (ed.), *Deconstructions: A User's Guide* (New York: Palgrave), pp. 14–43.

and makes available in the more general semiotic of a recognizable historiography. My friends, fellow subalternists, said "But, Gayatri, you say you won't transcode it because you have this kind of primitivistic piety toward the tribals, but nonetheless you are saying it, aren't you?"

Indeed, this too is a moment of destined errancy. Just as *Yimikirli* enters the international book trade, so does my anecdote. I would like to place them on a taxonomy with the docketing of every hybrid popular phenomenon as a radical gesture as such, and yet mark the difference.

There was a moment when another man, who didn't know what was going on, cried from the opening of the enclosure, "Lochan, sing, sing for us," and Lochan Sabar said loudly, with great dignity, "No, this is not a moment for singing. I am saying History." He himself was making a distinction between entertainment and knowledge.

I too am a translator, into English. Some say I have not grasped either Derrida's French or Mahasweta's Indian spirit. I seem now engaged in an even more foolhardy enterprise, to catch the translations from the other side. It was in that spirit that I began my speech with a quotation from the Warlpiris. And thus I end, with a quotation from Lochan Sabar. I embed them both in translation in the general sense, translation as catachresis, the making of the subject in reparation.

New Delhi

I am deeply honored that the Sahitya Akademi have decided to acknowledge my efforts to translate the fiction of Mahasweta Devi. I want to begin by thanking Mahasweta Devi for writing such spectacular prose. I want to thank my parents, Pares Chandra Chakravorty and Sivani Chakravorty for bringing me up in a household that was acutely conscious of the riches of Bangla. My father was a doctor. But we children were always reminded that my father's Bangla essay for his matriculation examination had been praised by Tagore himself.

And my mother? I could not possibly say enough about her on this particular occasion. Married at fourteen and with children coming at ages fifteen and twenty-three, this active and devoted wife and mother, delighted every instance with the sheer fact of being alive, studied in private and received her MA in Bengali literature from Calcutta University in 1937. She reads everything I write and never complains of the obscurity of my style. Without her constant support and interest, and indeed without the freedom she gave me in the fifties, herself a young widow then, to lead my life as my errant mind led me, I would not have been able to write these words for you today.

Samik Bandyopadhyay introduced me to Mahasweta Devi in 1979. Initially, I was altogether overwhelmed by her.

In 1981, I found myself in the curious position of being asked to write on deconstruction and on French feminism by two famous US journals, *Critical Inquiry* and *Yale French Studies* respectively. I cannot now remember why that position had then seemed to me absurd. At any rate, I proposed a translation of Mahasweta's short story "Draupadi" for *Critical Inquiry*, with the required essay on deconstruction plotted through a reading of the story.

When I look back upon that essay now, I am struck by its innocence. I had been away from home for twenty years then. I had the courage to acknowledge that there was something predatory about the nonresident Indian's obsession with India. Much has changed in my life since then, but that initial observation retains its truth. I should perhaps put it more tactfully today.

Why did I think translating Mahasweta would free me from being an expert on France in the US? I don't know. But this instrumentality disappeared in the doing. I discovered again, as I had when I had translated Jacques Derrida's *De la grammatologie* ten years earlier, that translation was the most intimate act of reading. Not only did Mahasweta Devi not remain Gayatri Spivak's way of freeing herself from France, but indeed the line between French and Bengali disappeared in the intimacy of translation. The verbal text is jealous of its linguistic signature but impatient of national identity. Translation flourishes by virtue of that paradox.

The line between French and Bengali disappeared for this translator in the intimacy of the act of translation. Mahasweta resonated, made a *dhvani*, with Derrida, and vice versa.[10] This has raised some ire, here and elsewhere. This is not the occasion for discussing unhappy things. But let me crave your indulgence for a moment and cite a couple of sentences, withholding theory, that I wrote in a letter to my editor Anjum Katyal of Seagull Books, when I submitted to her the manuscript of my translation of "Murti" and "Mohanpurer Rupkatha" by Mahasweta Devi:

> [In these two stories] the aporias between gendering on the one hand ("feudal"—transitional, and subaltern) and the ideology of national liberation (as tragedy and as farce) on the other are also worth contemplating. But I am a little burnt by the resistance to theory of the new economically restructured reader who would prefer her NRI neat, not shaken up with the ice of global politics and local experience. And so I let it rest.

That hard sentence at the end reflects my hurt and chagrin at the throwaway remark about Gayatri Chakravorty Spivak's "sermonizing" offered by the reviewer, in *India Today,* of *Imaginary Maps*, the very book that you have chosen to honour.[11]

I was hurt, of course. But I was chagrined because "sermonizing" was also the word used by Andrew Steer, then deputy director for the environment at the World Bank, in 1992, when I had suggested, at the European Parliament, that the World Bank re-examine its constant self-justificatory and fetishized use of the word *people*.

---

10 One of the most important concept-metaphors in Sanskrit aesthetics. Literally, "resonance."

11 Mahasweta Devi, *Imaginary Maps* (Gayatri Chakravorty Spivak trans.) (New York: Routledge, 1995).

At both Oviedo and New Delhi, my concern is for the constitution of the ethical subject—as life/translator (Klein), narrow-sense/translator, reader-as-translator.[12]

Why did I decide to gild Mahasweta's lily? Shri Namwar Singh, professor of Hindi at Jawaharlal Nehru University, who presided over the occasion, will remember that instructors at the Department of Modern Indian Literatures at Delhi University had asked me in 1987 why, when Bangla had Bankim and Tagore, I had chosen to speak on "Shikar," one of the stories included in *Imaginary Maps*. I am most grateful to the Jnanpith committee for correcting such errors.[13] My devotion to Mahasweta did not need national public recognition.

To ignore the narrative of action or text as ethical instantiation is to forget the task of translation upon which being-human is predicated. Translation is to transfer from one to the other. In Bangla, as in most North Indian languages, it is *anu-vada*—speaking after, *translatio* as *imitatio*. This relating to the other as the source of one's utterance *is* the ethical as being-for. All great literature as all specifically good action— any definition would beg the question here—celebrates this. To acknowledge this is not to "sermonize," one hopes.

Translation is thus not only necessary but unavoidable. And yet, as the text guards its secret, it is impossible. The ethical task is never quite performed. "Pterodactyl, Puran Sahay, and Pirtha," one of the tales included in *Imaginary Maps*, is the story of such an unavoidable impossibility. The Indian Aboriginal is kept apart or othered by the descendants of the old settlers, the ordinary "Indian." In the face of the radically other, the prehistoric pterodactyl, the Aboriginal and the settler are historically human together. The pterodactyl cannot be translated. But the

---

12 For reader-as-translator (RAT), please see Spivak, "Politics of Translation," in this volume, pp. 36–66.

13 The Jnanpith Award, instituted on 22 May 1961, is given for the best overall contribution to literature by any Indian citizen in any of the languages included in the VIII Schedule of the Indian Constitution. Mahasweta Devi won it in 1996.

Aboriginal and the settler Indian translate one another in silence and in the ethical relation.

This founding task of translation does not disappear by fetishizing the native language. Sometimes I read and hear that the subaltern can speak in their native languages. I wish I could be as self-assured as the intellectual, literary critic and historian, who assert this in English. No speech is speech if it is not heard. It is this act of hearing-to-respond that may be called the imperative to translate.

We often mistake this for helping people in trouble, or pressing people to pass good laws, even to insist on behalf of the other that the law be implemented. But the founding translation between people is a listening with care and patience, in the normality of the other, enough to notice that the other has already silently made that effort. This reveals the irreducible importance of idiom, which a standard language, however native, cannot annul.

And yet, in the interest of the primary education of the poorest, looking forward to the privative norms of democracy, a certain standard language must also be shared and practised. Here we attempt to annul the impossibility of translation, to deny provisionally Saussure's warning that historical change in language is inherited. The toughest problem here is translation from idiom to standard, an unfashionable thing among the elite progressives, without which the abstract structures of democracy cannot be comprehended. Paradoxically, here, idiomaticities must be attended to most carefully. I have recently discovered that there is no Bangla-to-Bangla dictionary for this level (the primary education of the poorest) and suitable to this task (translation from idiom to standard).[14] The speaker of some form of standard Bengali cannot hear the self-motivated subaltern Bengali unless organized by politically correct editing, which is equivalent to succor from above.

---

14 I understand that the West Bengal State Academy of Letters has since then issued a student dictionary. My own efforts are now halted in red tape.

It is not possible for us to change the quality of rote learning in the lowest sectors of society. But with an easy-to-use same-language dictionary, a spirit of independence and verification in the service of rule-governed behavior—essential ingredients for the daily maintenance of a democratic polity—can still be fostered. The United Nations, and non-governmental organizations in general, often speak triumphantly of the establishment of numbers of schools. We hardly ever hear follow-up reports, and we do not, of course, know what happens in those classrooms every day. But a dictionary, translating from idiom to standard even as it resists the necessary impossibility of translation, travels everywhere. It is only thus that subalternity may painstakingly translate itself into a hegemony that can make use of and exceed all the succor and resistance that we can organize from above. I have no doubt about this at all.

I am sorry I will not be with you when these words are read. I am writing them by the light of a hurricane lantern in a tiny room in Jonara, a settlement of a certain denotified tribe. In the next room is a number of male tribal adults, one of whom came willingly and learned so much from me in four hours of concentrated work that another, older, came a bit later and learned some and later asked me to prepare the other one so he can teach the adults until I come again. (My teacher-training work, which I do systematically in the morning, is with groups of children and their teachers.) Now a group of adult males are murmuring in the next room, poring over letters and words, one of them a student in the local high school who was, until now, separated from his elders because idiom cannot translate itself into standard.

In the afternoon, the only barely literate bride whom I had seen last year said to me in the presence of senior women, "I've forgotten everything." Her head was turned away from them toward me, her eyes shining with tears. Later she came to my door and wrote her name and address, the first ten numbers, the usual proof of literacy, and then, her message: "Mashi, come again."

How long will the men's enthusiasm and the woman's anguish last? I cannot know now. But what I am describing is rather different from the self-conscious rectitude of so-called adult-education classes. Let me translate for you the lines written for me, in the middle of our lesson and on his own, by the first man who came for his lesson today, knowing nothing but the Bangla alphabet: "*yele koto anando holo choley jabey abar kobey abey boley na.*"

This is Bangla tribal Creole that Mahasweta attempts to reproduce in her fiction and I cannot translate into English. My friend Sahan Sabar thought he was writing standard Bengali. I give witness to the attempt to translate which the sentence bears. I made two changes for him, assuring him that the first was just a variation. I did not change the most powerful mark of the Creole—the absence of the "you"—*tumi*—an absence only poetry or affect would produce in standard Bangla. This is how Sahan"s sentence would translate into standard English: "[You] came how much joy there was [you] will leave us doesn't say when [she] will return."

This subaltern gave me the gift of speech, already on the way to translation, because I had attended to his idiom, not because I helped him in distress. These Sabars, women and men, constantly translate for me, consciously, between their speech, their Creole, my Bangla. *They* do not immediately need an anthropological dictionary of the Kheria language. There are a couple of those in the Columbia University Library. Today as we speak to accept our awards for translating well from the twenty-one languages of India, I want to say, with particular emphasis, that what the largest part of the future electorate needs, in order to accede, in the longest run, to democracy, rather than have their votes bought and sold, is practical, simple same-language dictionaries that will help translate idiom into standard, in all these languages. I hope the Akademi will move toward the satisfaction of this need.

For myself, I cannot help but translate what I love, yet I resist translation into English; I never teach anything whose original I cannot read, and constantly modify printed translations, including my own. I think it is a bad idea to translate Gramsci and Kafka and Baudelaire into Indian languages from English. As a translator, then, I perform the contradiction, the counter-resistance, that is at the heart of love. And I thank you for rewarding what need not be rewarded, the pleasure of the text.

Translating into English

(2005)*

I'd like to begin with what should be an obvious point. That the trans-lator should make an attempt to grasp the writer's presuppositions. Translation is not just the stringing together of the most accurate syn-onyms by the most proximate syntax. Kant's "Religion within the Boundaries of Mere Reason" is written with the presupposition that mere (rather than pure) reason is a programmed structure, with in-built possibilities of misfiring, and nothing but calculation as a way of setting right.[1] Since the eighteenth century, English translators, not res-onating with Kant's philosophical presuppositions, have psychologized every noun, making Kant sound like a rational-choice, bourgeois Chris-tian gentleman.[2] Kant's insight could have taken on board today's major

---

* This work was first presented as a keynote on January 17, 2001, at the Sahitya Akademi (India's National Academy of Letters), New Delhi, at a conference of translators. Since India has at least twenty-two official languages, the internal trans-lators were not all knowledgeable about Derrida, Foucault, and Lacan, though Kant was known to some, and Marx, of course, to all.

   The present text was first published in Sandra Berman and Michael Wood (eds), *Nation, Language and the Ethics of Translation* (Princeton, NJ: Princeton University Press, 2005), pp. 93–110.

1 Immanuel Kant, "Religion within the Boundaries of Mere Reason," in *Religion and Rational Theology* (Allen W. Wood and George di Giovanni eds and trans) (Cambridge: Cambridge University Press, 1996), pp. 39–215.

2 It is not that translators since the eighteenth century have not been aware that problems exist. The best known is the *Willkür–Wille* distinction, which the great translator T. K. Abbott translated as "elective will" and "will" respectively, thus

problem: Can there be a secularism without an intuition of the transcendental, of something that is inscrutable because it cannot be accessed by mere reasoning? Kant's project, to protect the calculus of reason by way of the transcendental as one parergon among four, was counterintuitive to his English translator.[3]

I will add three more examples here to show the generality of the problem. In these, the lack of translators' sympathy stalled a possible use for each text, a use that relates to the limits of rational choice. This brings the examples into my chief concern: the responsibility of the translator into English. I hope some readers will care to follow the trajectory suggested by each.

When Marx wrote about the commensurability of all things, that it was "contentless and simple" (*inhaftslas rind einfach*), he was speaking as a materialist speaks of form.[4] Not as *form*, but as a thing without content generations of empiricist English translators have missed the point, not resonating with Marx's philosophical presuppositions,

---

coming close to the sense of the mere mechanical ability to select one thing rather than the other, preserved in the ordinary language associations of "whim" or "willfulness" attached to *Willkür*. This is why, as John R. Silber notes, Kant associates *Willkür* with heteronomy rather than autonomy. Silber seems to me to be correct in suggesting that "[t]he discovery and formulation of meanings for these terms was [. . .] one of Kant's foremost achievements in the *Religion* and in the *Metaphysic of Morals* [. . .]. The evolving complexity of Kant's theory of the will is missed by the English reader unless they can know when Kant is using '*Wille*' and when he is using '*Willkür*'" ("Introduction," in Immanuel Kant, *Religion within the Limits of Reason Alone* [Theodore M. Greene and Hoyt H. Hudson trans.] [New York: Harper & Row, 1960], p. lxxxiv).

3 "Parergon" is Kant's word, describing a task that is outside the limits of the work undertaken ("Religion within the Boundaries of Mere Reason," p. 96 and passim). It is to be noticed that these parerga belong not only to the work of mere reason but that of pure reason as well. To discuss this detail is beyond the scope of this essay.

4 Karl Marx, "Preface to the First Edition," in *Capital: A Critique of Political Economy*, VOL. 1 (Ben Fowkes trans.) (New York: Vintage, 1977), p. 90.

translated *inhaltslos* as "slight in content," and thus made nonsense out of the entire discussion of value. Marx's insight could have taken on board today's transformation of all things into data—telecommunication rendering information indistinguishable from capital. Marx's presuppositions, to control the inevitability of intelligible formalism in a materialist interest, sues counterintuitive to his English translators.

In his seminar on the gaze or glance, the eminent French psychoanalyst Jacques Loran presents the scopic or apparently objectisizing sweeping glance as something like a symptom. To show his students this, Lacan cannot use proof. It is the very production of proof in the patient that Lacan is opening up. He therefore uses the interesting coinage *apologue*—apology, excuse, but also something that is just a little off the side of the Logos. "I will tell you a little apologue," he says (*Je vais vous raconter une petite apologue*).[5] The naturalizing translator, thinking Lacan is just talking about people looking, translates this important sentence as "I will tell you a little story."

When the French historian Michel Foucault described the ground floor of power as set up with "irreducible over-againsts" (*irréductible vis à vis*), he was trying to avoid transcendentalizing the empirical.[6] Humanist English translators, unable to resonate with Foucault's philosophical presuppositions, have translated "vis-a-vis" as "opposite," given content to a nonformalist intuition of form, and turned the argument into the micropolitics of power, understood as ordinary language.

Grasping the writer's presuppositions as they inform his or her use of language, as they develop into a kind of singular code, is what Jacques Derrida, the French philosopher who has taught me a great deal, calls entering the protocols of a text—not the general laws of the language,

---

5 Jacques Lacan, "The Line and Light," in *The Four Fundamental Concepts of Psychoanalysis* (Alan Sheridan trans.) (New York: W. W. Norton, 1978), p. 95.

6 Michel Foucault, *The History of Sexuality*, VOL. 1 (Robert Hurley trans.) (New York: Vintage, 1980), p. 96.

but the laws specific to this text. And this is why it is my sense that translation is the most intimate act of reading.

I begin this way because I am a translator *into* English, not just from specific languages. Because of the growing power of English as a global lingua franca, the responsibility of the translator into English is increasingly complicated. And, although I chose my four opening examples in order to avoid cultural nationalism, it is of course true that the responsibility becomes altogether more grass when the original is not written in one of the languages of northwestern Europe.

For a variety of reasons, the market for quick translations from such languages is steadily on the rise. Since the mid-1970s, it has been enhanced by a spurious and hyperbolic admiration not unrelated to the growing strength of the so-called international civil society.[7] In the 1970s, extra-state collective action in Europe, Latin America, Asia, and Africa concerned itself with issues such as health, the environment, literacy, and the like. Although their relationship with the nation-state was conflictual, there was still a relationship. Gradually, with the advance of capitalist globalization, this emergent force was appropriated into the dominant. These earlier extra-state collectivities, which were basically nongovernmental entities, often with international solidarity, were now used to undermine the constitutionality (however precarious or utopian) of the state. Powerful international NGOs now control these extra-state circuits globally. Indigenous NGOs typically have a large component of foreign aid. This self-styled international civil society (since it is extra-state) has a large cultural component, especially directed toward gender issues. It is here that the demand for trans-

---

7 For an assessment of the limits of the international civil society, see Satendra Prasad, "Limits and Possibilities for Civil Society Led Re-democratization: The Fijian Constitutional Debates and Dilemma," *Prime* (2000): 3–28; for a somewhat unexamined encomium, see Homi K. Bhabha, "Democracy Derealized," in Okwui Enwezor (ed.), *Documenta 11, Platform 1: Democracy Unrealized* (Ostfildern-Ruit: Hatje Cantz, 2002), pp. 346–64.

lation—especially literary translation, a quick way to know a culture—has been on the rise. At this point, we translators into English should operate with great caution and humility.

Yet the opposite is often the case. Meenakshi Mulzherjee, the well-known feminist Bengali scholar of English literature, has spoken to me of a person—she did not mention the name—who has recently turned their hand to translating from the Bengali. Upon repeated questioning about their proficiency in Bengali, this would-be translator has given the same answer: "*bangla porte jani*" (I can read Bengali). We all know of such cases.

It is time now to mention the other obvious point: the translator must not only make an attempt to grasp the presuppositions of an author but also, and of course, inhabit, even if on loan, the many mansions, and many levels of the host language. *Bangla porte jani* is only to have gained entry into the outer room, right by the front gate.

I am at the moment engaged in translating Mahasweta Devi's novel *Chotti Munda ebong tar tir* published in 1980.[8] In the last paragraph that I translated, I made a choice of level when I came across the phrase *mohajoner kachhe hat pa bandha*—"Arms and legs in hock to the moneylender," I wrote. "In hock" is more in the global lingua franca than in the English that is one of the Indian languages. Sujit Mukherjee, the brilliant Indian translator from Bengali into English, and I, had a running conversation about such choices. But "mortgaged" would have been, in my judgement, an error of level, and would have missed the pun, "being tied up or trussed," present in the original. Not that "in hock" catches the pun. But "hock" is sufficiently confusing in its etymology to carry the promise of nuances. The translator must play such games.

---

8 The translation appeared in 2002. Mahasweta Devi, *Chotti Munda and His Arrow* (Oxford: Blackwell, 2003 / London: Seagull Books, 2015[2002]).

Lower down in the paragraph, I'm less satisfied with my treatment of the phrase *hoker kotha bollo na Chotti?* as "Didn't Chotti speak of 'rights'?" *Hok*, in Bengali, a *totshomo* or identical loan from the Arabic *al haq*, is not rights alone but a peculiar mix of rights and responsibilities that goes beyond the individual. Anyone who has read the opening of Mahasweta's novel knows that the text carries this presupposition. I have failed in this detail. Translation is as much a problem as a solution. I hope the book will be taught by someone who has enough sense of the language to mark this unavoidable failure.[9]

This for me is an important task of translation, especially from languages that are dying, some fast, some slow, for want of attention. In our particular circumstances, we translators from the languages of the global South should prepare our texts as metropolitan teaching texts because that, for better or for worse, is their destiny. Of course, this would make us unpopular, because the implicit assumption is all that "third world" texts need is a glossary. I myself prepare my translations in the distant and unlikely hope that my texts will fall into the hands of a teacher who knows Bengali well enough to love it, so that the students will know that the best way to read this text is to push through to the original. Of course not everyone will learn the language, but one might, or two! And the problem will be felt. I should add here that I have the same feeling for Aristotle and classical Greek, Hrotswitha von

---

9 I have discussed the ambivalence of *al haq* in Spivak, *Imperatives to Re-imagine the Planet* (Vienna: Passagen, 1999). Patrick Wolfe has an interesting comment about "hock" and "haq," an unwitting coupling on my part: "I have nothing to base this on, but I can't help feeling that your text isn't the first place that these words have met up. In English, 'hock' has to do with ransoming—opposing groups (men and women, tenants and landlords, etc.) mock-kidnapped each other (tying up and trussing were involved) at Easter time and dues had to be paid for their return. A fair amount of ransoming went on during the Crusades. A practice associated with Saracens, hence the Arabic loan-word? Wild and woolly, I may well be suffering from a William Jones complex, but no doubt there's a philologist somewhere who'd know" (private communication).

Gandersheim and Latin, Dante and Italian—and, of course, Kant and Marx and German, Lacan and Foucault and French. It is just that these latter texts have plenty of teaching editions and the languages are not ignored. I received a contemptuous notice, I think, if memory serves, from *Kirkus Reviews*, some years ago, for preparing a volume of fiction by Mahasweta Devi with a preface and an afterword.[10] Literature and philosophy do, of course, belong to different slots on a publisher's list, but I contrast this with the abundant praise I have received over the last twenty-seven years all over the world for providing just that apparatus for a volume of philosophical criticism by Jacques Derrida.[11]

In this spirit I will turn now to *Ashomoyer Noteboi* (Untimely Notebook) by Farhad Mazhar, the activist-poet from Bangladesh.[12] *Ashomoy* is an interesting word. *Dushhomoy* would be "bad times" of course. But Nietzsche's use of *Unzeitmäßig*, typically translated as "untimely," as in *Untimely Meditations*, gave me a way out.[13] And a notebook is a place where meditations are jotted down.

Mazhar thinks of himself as "untimely" quite as Nietzsche does, indeed quite as Nietzsche believes genuine cultural figures must be: "Virtue [. . .] always swims against the tide of history, whether by combating its passions as the most proximate stupid factuality of its existence or by dedicating itself to being honorable while the lie spins its

---

10 Mahasweta Devi, *Imaginary Maps* (Gayatri Chakravorty Spivak trans.) (New York: Routledge, 1995).

11 Jacques Derrida, *Of Grammatology* (Gayatri Chakravorty Spivak trans.) (Baltimore, MD: Johns Hopkins University Press, 1976).

12 Farhad Mazhar, *Ashomoyer Noteboi* (Dhaka: Protipokkho, 1994), p. 42; translation mine. I have discussed this poem in another context in Spivak, *A Critique of Postcolonial Reason: Toward the History of the Vanishing Present* (Cambridge, MA: Harvard University Press, 1999), pp. 362–63. I have underlined the words in English in the original.

13 Friedrich Nietzsche, *Untimely Meditations* (R. J. Hollingdale trans.) (Cambridge: Cambridge University Press, 1983).

glittering web around it."[14] He offers no alternatives: "The untimely thinker, which is how Nietzsche viewed himself, does not work directly towards the establishment of another culture, in which his arguments might become 'timely', rather, he is working 'against my age, and thereby influencing my age, and hopefully for the benefit of a future age.'"[15]

As Foucault suggests in "Nietzsche, Genealogy, History":

If genealogy in its turn poses the question of the land that saw our birth, of the language that we speak, or of the laws that govern us, it is to make visible the heterogeneous systems which, under the mask of our "we," forbids us all identity [. . .]. [Another] use of history [. . .] uncovers the violence of a position taken: taken against ignorant happiness, against the vigorous illusions by which humanity protects itself, taken in favor of all that is dangerous in research and disturbing in discoveries.[16]

In pursuit of heterogeneity, Mazhar goes clear out of culture into nature, undertaking impossible translations from the animal world in a recognizably Nietzschean mode. We recall that this is precisely where Derrida locates Nietzsche as philosopher of life:[17]

Now then notebook, will you get the Philip's
Prize this time? Try hard, try hard, by Allah's grace.
Caution

---

14 Nietzsche, *Untimely Meditations*, p. 106; translation modified. See also pp. 22, 55, 60, 95, 146, 206, 251.

15 Gianni Vattimo, *Nietzsche: An Introduction* (Nicholas Martin trans.) (London: Athlone, 2002), pp. 31–32.

16 Michel Foucault, "Nietzsche, Genealogy, History," in *Language, Counter-Memory, Practice: Selected Essays and Interviews* (Donald F. Bouchard ed.) (Ithaca, NY: Cornell University Press, 1977), pp. 162–63; translation modified.

17 Jacques Derrida, *Of Spirit: Heidegger and the Question* (Geoffrey Bennington and Rachel Bowlby trans) (Chicago: University of Chicago Press, 1989), pp. 54, 57n3.

I'm copying down how the grass
Crawls copying down how the jaguar grabs
I'm slipping, my foot's missed its hold
I'm copying clown the problems on the way along with the
    foot's heel
Caution caution
Earlier you had to tight standing on the other side of the
    barbed wire
Now on both sides: Right and left, top and bottom, in water
    and on land
    [. . .]
Go get your teeth fixed by the alligator
From the snake a rubber spine
Go suckle the breasts of the bat
Hey my untimely notebook, the times are bad
    chum
Must walk with eyes peeled on all sides my
    friend
            Be careful!!
            Caution!!!

In the previous stanza, he speaks of the woman Nurjahan who was
stoned to death because she was supposed to have slept with someone
other than her husband. I can commend Mazhar's feminism and work
out his spiritual link with the anything-but-feminist Nietzsche but I
cannot work out the words *murtad* and *dorra* in lines 2 and 3:

Untimely notebook, I'm giving a fatwa,
        you're murtad
I'll dorra you a hundred and one times
        you're shameless
I'll fix you in a hole and stone you to death
    In front of the whole village
        You to Chhatakchhara, to Kalikapur

Must go, this time to die
Seek out a torn sari or a pitcher
Shariat witness, Allah has bred girls
         For the village elders and the world's rich men
Shariat witness, the task of imam and mollah
         is to fulfill Allah's will
Go faith go money go reaction go progress go
Go Jamaat-e-Islami go imperialism go Subal
         go Sudam[18]
Go hand in hand twin brothers let's watch and
         be delighted . . .

I am unable to access *murtad* and *dorra* because they are *tatshomo* words from Arabic. I add an explanation of this word and the companion word *tadbhabo*—words that were known to every Bengali schoolchild when I went to high school in the early 1950s. I am not a Bengalist, merely a translator in love with the language. What I am about to give you is a generalist's sense of things. *Tat* in these two words signifies "that" or "it," and refers to Sanskrit, one of the classical languages of India, claimed by the Hindu majority. They are descriptive of two different kinds of words. *Tadbhabo* means "born of it." *Tatshomo* means "just like it." I am using these two words by shifting the shifter *tat*—that or it—to refer to Arabic as an important loan-source.

Through the centuries of the Mughal empire in India (1526–1857) and the corresponding Nawabate in Bengal, Bengali was enriched by many Arabic and especially Persian loan-words. Of course Bengali is derived from Sanskrit, which was by then "dead," so the relationship is altogether different. But learned and worldly Bengali gentlemen were proficient in Arabic, and especially Persian—the languages of the court and the law. The important entry of the British into India was by way

---

18 Friends of the Hindu god Krishna. Mazhar typically mingles the Hindu and Muslim elements of Bengali culture. More about this in the text.

of Bengal. It is at least the generalist's assumption that the British played the Bengali Hindus with promises of liberation from the Muslim empire. William Jones's discovery that Sanskrit, Greek, and Latin were related languages even gave the Hindus and the English a common claim to Aryanism, a claim to intertranslatability, as it were.[19] And, from the end of the eighteenth century, the fashioners of the new Bengali prose purged the language of the Arabic-Persian content until, in great blank verse poetry of Michael Madhusudan Dutt (1824–73) and the *Bangadarshan* (1872–76) magazine edited by the immensely influential novelist Bankim Chandra Chattopadhyay (1838–94), a grand and fully Sanskritized Bengali emerged. Its Arabic and Persian components became no more than local color. This was the language that became the vehicle of Bengali nationalism and subsequently of that brand of Indian nationalism that was expressed in Bengali. The medium was simplified, expanded, and diversified into the contemporary Bengali prose that is the refined edge of my mother tongue, which I learned in school, and which did not allow me to translate *murtad* and *dorra*.

A corresponding movement of purging the national language Hindi of its Arabic and Persian elements has been under way since independence in 1947. Such political dismemberments of language have become part of Partition Studies—as Serbian separates from Croatian, Czech from Slovak, and Cantonese is dismissed as a mere dialect of Han. The political production of internal translation requires a different type of analysis, which I will touch upon in my conclusion.

If the Arabic and Persian elements were purged out of Bengali, how do I encounter them as a translator today? I encounter them as part of a general movement in Bangladesh to restore these components. This

---

19 I have discussed this at greater length in *A Critique of Postcolonial Reason*. Homi K. Bhabha misses this important and substantive religion/caste point when he quotes Alexander Duff as relating English and the Brahmins as proof of the merely formal irreducibility of hybridity (Bhabha, "Commitment to Theory," in *The Location of Culture* [New York: Routledge, 1994], p. 33).

is not to be confused with an Islamization of the language, since there can be no question of transforming the Sanskrit base of Bengali. Indeed, Mazhar uses the Sanskrit-based vocabulary of Bengali with considerable flair. One may call this an attempt persistently to mend the breach of a partition that started—as I have indicated in my generalist tale—long before the named Partition of India in 1947. It is to restore a word-hoard that went underground.

What was created as East Pakistan in 1947 became independent as Bangladesh in 1971. Although there was an important political and military conflict that brought this about, it would not be incorrect to say that one strong factor of the mobilization of what was to become Bangladesh was the issue of language.[20] And indeed the naming of the new nation as Bangladesh was to shrink an older cartography. Bangladesh (Banglaland) is the name of the entire land area whose people use Bangla, or Bengali; or Bangla is the name of the language of the entire people of the land or *desh* called Bangladesh. Before the Independence-Partition of 1947, this would have been the entire British province of Bengal, including today's Indian state of West Bengal and the modern nation-state of Bangladesh, whose geographical descriptive could be East Bengal—in Bengali, Paschim and Purbo Banga. Banga is the ancient name of a tract of land somewhat larger than the British province of Bengal. Thus the proper name of a premodern area and kingdom, displaced into the name of a nawabate, translated into the colonial proper name of a province, expanded beyond a language area into the governmental abstraction of a presidency, is now modernized to designate not a language-area but a bounded nation-state metonymically claiming the whole. This may be seen as the celebration of partition, however benign. Since 1947, the Indian state of West Bengal (or Paschim Banga) is the western part of a place that does not exist. Unlike those who propose

---

20 For discussions of the Bangladeshi language movement, see *Chinta* 22–23 (March 15, 2000): 20–25.

solutions such as calling it merely Banga, so that it too can claim the whole, by a more ancient name, I propose no nominative solution. Such a solution would finalize partition by making official the historically asymmetrical name of the whole for each geographically asymmetrical part. Even that could be undone, of course; for each part could say we are each the whole, in different ways. In the long run, it would not matter a great deal, for named places do not, strictly speaking, exist as such, since there are re-namings. If there is history, there is the renaming of place. In this case as elsewhere, I am interested in the political mode of production of the collectively accepted existence of named places, whose "other names" linger on as archaic or residual, emergent as local alternative or opposition, always ready to emerge.[21]

If the establishment of a place named Bangladesh in a certain sense endorses the Partition of 1947, the language policy of the state, strangely enough, honors that other partition—the gradual banishment of the Arabic and Persian elements of the language that took place in the previous century—and thus paradoxically undoes the difference from West Bengal. The official language of the state of Bangladesh, over 90 percent Muslim, is as ferociously Sanskritized as anything to be found in Indian Bengali.

It is over against and all entwined in this tangle that the movement to restore the Arabic and Persian element of Bengali, away from its century-old ethnic cleansing, does its work. And it is because I grew up inside the tangle that, in spite of my love of Bengali, I could not translate *murtad* and *dorra*—though I could crack *ashomoyer* with Nietzsche.

I am only a translator, not a Bengalist. I can cite only two names in this movement: Akhtaruzzaman Ilias (1943–97), the author of *Chilekothar Sepai* and the fantastic *Khoabnama*; and Farhad Mazhar,

---

21 I have discussed this in terms of the name "Asia" in Spivak, "Our Asias—2001: How to Be a Continentalist," in *Other Asias* (Oxford: Blackwell, 2007), pp. 209–38.

whose poem I was about to translate when I launched into this lengthy digression.[22]

It may be claimed that these writers do a double bluff on the Sanskritized linguistic nationalism of Bangladesh.

At the meeting of the Sahitya Akadami I was immediately side-tracked into a translation of the word *huda* (about which more later) as an Arabic-origin Urdu word foreign to Bengali; and a learned etymologico-philosophical disquisition (a pale imitation of which I would be able to provide for Sanskrit-origin Bengali words) from a distinguished professor of Urdu from Kashmir. None of the Indian Bengalis could offer a translation.

Murtad and *dorra* can be translated as "apostate" and "whiplash." *Huda* so overwhelmed the discussion that they remained un-Englished at the Akademi meeting. I have withheld this information for so long because, as I was moving through various European and Asian countries, revising, I kept wondering how I would get to find the English equivalents! A chance encounter, someone reading Bengali web in Bangkok airport—must be Bangladeshi!—provided them at last.

It is my belief that unless the paleonymy of the language is felt in some rough historical or etymological way, the translator is unequal to her task. Strangely enough, I got this lesson at St. John's Diocesan Girls' High School in Calcutta, from Miss Nilima Pyne, a young Christian woman (we thought her ancient, of course) who had learned Sanskrit with heart and soul. She had quoted at us, when I was no more than eleven or twelve, that famous pair of Sanskrit tags, both meaning "there's a dry branch in the way." See if you can sense the complete dissonance in the two sets of sounds; be sure to mark the greater length of the

---

22 Akhtaruzzaman Ilias, *Chilekothar Sepai* (Dhaka: Dhaka University Press, 1995); *Khoabnama* (Dhaka: Maola Brothers, 1996), available in English as *Khwab Nama* (Arunava Sinha trans.) (New Delhi: Hamish Hamilton, 2021).

vowels in the second example. I have not followed accepted phonetic transliteration, but given the closest Englishing of the Sanskrit sounds:

a. shushkum kashthum tishthattugrey

b. neerasa taruvara poorata bhaati

Can you sense the completely different ring of the two sentences? If you don't have a sense of Sanskrit, which is rather different from "knowing" Sanskrit, you cannot, of course. Sound and sense play together to show that translation is not merely transfer of sense, for the two lines "mean the same thing." Sanskrit is not just a moment in Benveniste.[23]

This was not a lesson in translation. But it was such instruction that allowed us to understand, three or four years later, Shakespeare's play with "the same meaning," once in Latinate and once in "Anglo-Saxon" English, metaphorizing enormity in the enormousness of the encompassing ocean:

This my hand will rather
The multitudinous seas incarnadine,
Making the green one red.

We transfer content because we must, knowing it cannot be done, in translation as in all communication, yet differently. We transpose level and texture of language, because we must, knowing that idiom does not go over. It is this double bind that the best and most scrupulous translation hints at, by chance, perhaps. *Mimesis* hits *poiesis* by *tuchè*.[24] Translators from the languages of the global South into English have lost this striving. The loss is incalculable. Responsible translators from the languages of the global South into English therefore often translate

---

23 Emile Benveniste, *Indo-European Language and Society* (Elizabeth Palmer trans.) (London: Faber, 1973).

24 Aristotle, *Poetics* (Stephen Halliwell trans.), Loeb Classical Library (Cambridge, MA: Harvard University Press, 1995), p. 29.

in the shadow of the imminent death of the host language as they know it, in which they are nurtured.

Translating these two words in Mazhar, I was also suggesting that the burden of history and paleonymy are added to this double bind. Arrived here I often hear, not everybody can be so well prepared! Is there ever such a refusal of craftspersonly expertise for European-language translation? I suggest we pay no attention to such excuses and proceed to the next poem, where another kind of history is invoked.

This poem refers us not to Bengali in the history of the nation-state but in the internationality of Islam. As already mentioned, Bengali is not of Arabic-Persian origin. It is not taken seriously as a language of Islam. During the war that established Bangladesh, soldiers of the then West Pakistan regularly taunted East Pakistani soldiers and civilians as not "real" Muslims, no more than the force-converted dregs of Hinduism. (It may be worth mentioning here that Assia Djebar is most unusual in acknowledging Bengali among the non-Arabic Islamic languages: "Arabic sounds—Iranian, Afghan, Berber, or Bengali.")[25]

In this frame, Mazhar addresses Allah, as follows:

Bangla Is Not Yours

You've built the Bangla language with the crown of
          my head and the roof of my mouth
My epiglottis plays with the "ah" and the long "ee"
Breath by breath I test the "om" and my chest's beat
Heartstrings ring in the enchanted expanse of the consonant
Oh I like it so, lord, I like the Bangla language so much
I lick it clean, greedy, as if paradise fruit.
Are you envious? For in this tongue you never
Proclaimed yourself! Yet, all day I keep at it

---

25 Assia Djebar, "Overture," in *Women of Algiers in Their Apartment* (Marjolin de Jaeger trans.) (Charlottesville: University of Virginia Press, 1992).

Hammer and tongs so Queen Bangla in her own
Light and power stays ahead of each and all, my dearest lord.

Some ask today, So, Bangla, are you divine as well?
You too primordial? Allah's alphabet?

I'm glad Bangla's not yours, for if it were—
Her glory'd raise your price, for no reason at all.

Let us look at the last line. *Dānt* is one of those particularly untranslatable idiomatic words: airs and graces, swelled head, hype—you see the choice I've made: "raise your price." What is interesting is that this word has been coupled with *behuda,* another Arabic *tatshamo* word that I have translated "unreasonably." Let me first say that there is a common Sanskrit-origin word—*ajotha* (Sanskrit *ayathā*)—that would fit snugly here. *Behuda* points at itself, incomprehensible to "the common reader." I believe now that the word is in general use in Bangladesh. As I have already mentioned, I received a lecture on the Arabic word *huda* from my learned colleague from Kashmir. I could best grasp his meaning by turning it into the English familiar. "Reason" in "for no reason at all" is an ordinary language word. Yet "reason" is also a word of great philosophical weight. *Huda* has a comparable range. What reason is being invoked here to claim a language connected to Revelation by imagination rather than letter? This is a different argument from the right to worship in the vernacular, where, incidentally, content transfer must be taken for granted. I go everywhere in search of the "secular." I will come back to this later. Here is a hint that expanding religion beyond mere reason may bring with it a question of translating rather than recording the transcendental.

Attempting to make the reader walk with the translator translating the poet translating his language through the history of nation-states and of internationality toward the transcendental, I will cite three poems here with brief introductions.

First, "Lady Shalikh."

The *shalikh* is a household bird, with no claim to beauty or musical skill. Mazhar is invoking the simplicity of the malnourished rural Bangladeshi woman, not the famed beauties of Bengal. Mazhar is a feminist poet. (I cannot unpack this difficult sentence here.) What does it mean to make the common woman cry out to Allah, in desperate humility, as the poet had, in pride of language?

> In the garden of paradise a body-brown Shalikh
> Calls. O my life, did you hear on paradise branch
> Our kindhearted Shalikh calls with life and soul
> Calling her own words at Allah's Durbar.
>
> Can you hear, can you see, our Lord,
> Holding the knee of her yellow gam straight
> > On gandam branch
> Hacking her throat with her humble beak in weak
> Abject low tones our Begum Shalikh calls?
>
> What have we asked, dear Lord, our hopes are small
>
> Let our life's bird reside in paradise
> Even if a dark-skinned girl, snub-nosed, bandy-legged
> Eyes sunk with body's work, yet in Bengal
> A well-loved daughter, without her paradise lost—
> > Bird call, call with life and soul, even Allah's
> > > heart does melt.

The next poem refers to Rabindranath Tagore, who has already been mentioned as a master fashioner of modern, ethnically cleansed Bengali, a language that slides easily into English. Mazhar cannot disclaim his pervasive influence, but . . .

The Tagore Kid

Our sir Rabi is a huge big poet, white folks
Gave him the Nobel Prize to vet his literary might
Just right. His dad and gramps
Ran after the Brits and gathered in the loot
Became landowners by own claim
But family faults ne'er stopped
His verse—he's now the whole world's poet.

I salaam him, welcome him heartfelt.
Yet my soul, dear lord, is not inclined
To him. Rabindra had faults. His pen
Remembered many a lucky sage, saint, renouncer,
    and great man,
But never in wildest dream did the name of
Prophet Muhammad come in shape or hint
To his pen's point, so I can never forgive.

But dear lord of grace, you please forgive that boy,
    from Tagore clan.

In the last poem that I will cite, the poet addresses a figure within the Hindu tradition who was open to all others. Sri Rama Krishna Paramahansa (1836–86) as he was known, was also a poet of the transcendental, although his medium was not literary verbality. He was not an intellectual and therefore could not alter the course of public language. But if *poiesis* is a making of the other that goes past *mimesis*, Rama Krishna must be called a poet in the general sense. Islam took its place among his imaginings and his iterations of the self. Because these moves acknowledged the irreducibility of the imperative to translate rather than its denial for the sake of identity, here Mazhar responds as part of that which is translated, not an "original," but an other. Here translation surprises the poet as no displacement at all, perhaps; the mode is not declarative and introduces a picture of the poet dancing in the othered mode: "Have I moved, then?"

In Rama Krishna's name Mazhar undertakes yet another translation or transfer into the transcendental, a messenger from the human mystic to God himself—the most easily recognizable name of the transcendental as such. And yet it is a translation: the poet articulates a plea for polytheist worship (a hibiscus for Kali) to achieve felicity in Allah's acceptance. He daringly offers to transport the Hindu hibiscus to the austere Allah of Islam. In the present of the poem, the transfer is forever performed.

Sri Ram Paramhansa

Have you seen the red hibiscus? You told that flower
                    to bloom, in Bengal
So it does hang and bloom
Blood red—haemoglobin of blood
In petals perhaps, it glows in wood and plot.

I a hibiscus flower in your honor my lord
Will give into the hands of th' blessed one,
Sri Rama Krishna Paramhansadeb.
He'll give his little chuckle, gap-tooth glowing in laugh
And say "O my Sheikh's Boy, here you are, you've come?"

Have I moved, then? Nope, I didn't move
If going, I go the same way everywhere.
Entranced the lord of love dances in state
The sheikh boy dances equal, loving this lord.

By way of Kali when Paramhansa sends
Hibiscus to you lord, accept with love.

Ground-level countertheological Islam has managed such exchanges, perhaps not so spectacularly, wherever Islam has flourished. Today, when the great tradition of Islamic secularism is tarnished, it seems particularly important to allow poetry such as this to launch us on an imaginative journey that can be risked if reader and translator venture beyond the sanctioned ignorance that guards translation from the languages of the global South into English. The literature of Bangladesh does not appear prominently on the roster. Rokeya Sakhawat Hossain's *Sultana's Dream* and *The Secluded Ones* are resuscitated from time to time in an indifferent translation from the Feminist Press.[26] Otherwise it is the fashioners of that other Bengali and their descendants who get Englished. It is of course different with development material, but that is another story.

As writers like Mazhar attempt to enter the detheologized "religious," they question the premises of a superficial secularism. They are, in turn, incorrectly perceived as providing fuel for fundamentalists.

I started this essay with a reference to "Religion within the Boundaries of Mere Reason." I mentioned that a problem of translation does not allow us to see that in that text Kant considers with scrupulous honesty if secularism is possible without the possibility of thinking the transcendental. This task is absolutely crucial today. Those sanitized secularists who are hysterical at the mention of religion are quite out of touch with the world's peoples, and have buried their heads in the sand. Class-production has allowed them to rationalize and privatize the transcendental and they see this as the welcome telos of everybody everywhere. There is no time here to connect this with the enforcement of rights, and the policing of education by the self-selected moral entrepreneurs of the self-styled international civil society—with no social contract and no democratic accountability. I can only assert here that

---

26 Rokeya Sakhawat Hossain, "*Sultana's Dream*": *A Feminist Utopia, and Selections from "The Secluded Ones"* (Roushan Jahan ed. and trans.) (New York: Feminist Press, 1988).

the connection can and must be made. I hope I have been able at least to suggest that this state of the world has something to do with a failure of responsible translation, in the general and the narrow sense.

I have walked you through the hybridity of a single language. I want now to make a comment on the notion of hybridity that is the migrant's wish-fulfillment: irreducible cultural translation in any claim to identity. I wish translation could be so irreducibly taken for granted. The impossibility of translation is what puts its necessity in a double bind. It is an active site of conflict, not an irreducible guarantee. If we are thinking definitions, I should suggest the thinking of trace rather than of achieved translation: trace of the other, trace of history, even cultural traces—although heaven knows, culture continues to be a screen for ignoring discussions of class. If translation is a necessary impossibility, the thought of a trace looks like the possibility of an anterior presence, without guarantees. It is not a sign but a mark and therefore cannot signify an "original," as a translation presumably can, especially when assumed as definitively irreducible. I contrast a comfortable notion of a permissive hybridity to the thought of the trace because the former is associated, sometimes precisely by the assurance of cultural translation, with the sanitized secularism of a global enforcement politics. This permissive hybridity can also foster an unexamined culturalism that can indeed give support to fundamentalisms here and there. That bit of the migrant population that faces a repressive state as well as dominant racism becomes a confused metonym for this other, separate global face of hybridity as translation. If the European context brought us to the sense of problems in the global public sphere, the context of Bangladesh brought us to the question of secularism. In my last section I come back to what has always been one my chief concerns: translation as reading. I examine here the problems of entering the protocols of a text, when the text seems to give way. I move to a singular example where the aporia of exemplarity—that the singular example loses singularity by entering the category "example"—is cleanly resolved by the poet himself into no more than a reader's choice:

This book of poems, focused on a girlfriend, and dealing only with a plea for love is indeed a diary [. . .]. If you think only of me, this poetry is only a plea for love [. . .]. Yet, because any one part is applicable to many situations connected to love, social theory, politics, science and many other topics, therefore one should be able to find a successful realization of any kind of situation in the lives of any sort of reader, male or female.[27]

This book of poetry was first published in 1961 and then republished in 1962 under the title *Phire Esho Chaka* (Come Back, Wheel). The book was dedicated to Gayatri Chakravorty. (The Sanskrit *chakra* of the surname means wheel and is transformed into *chaka* is modern Bengali. A cunning translation.)[28] Chakravorty did not know the poet, although she had noticed the intensity of his gaze. She left Kolkata for the United States in 1961. She did not read the poems, although she knew of the book's fame, and that it was dedicated to her. Many of the poems lament her absence, his loneliness without a response. It is not clear that such lamentations, included in poetry, require "response" in the ordinary way. Must the lost object not remain lost for the poems to retain their exact verbal contour? If reading is a species of translation, here was a rather singular double bind of translation, for a singular reader, with a specific proper name. Gayatri Chakravorty, not having read the poems, did not have to live this double bind.

In 2002, some forty years after the publication of the book, a facsimile edition of the manuscript was published. This book, in the poet's impeccable hand, is entitled *Gayatrike* (To Gayatri). I was shown a review of this text by a colleague, and a woman in the family bought

---

27 Binoy Majumdar, "Foreword" in *Gayatrike* (Kolkata: Protibhash, 2002). Hereafter cited in text with page numbers.

28 I have just read Jacques Derrida, *Voyous: deux essais sur la raison* (Paris: Galilée, 2003). His luminous and anguished words on the wheel ("La roue libre," pp. 25–39) add greater poignancy to this singular narrative.

me a copy. I have now read these brilliant poems. There is no question of response, other than what you read here.

A face and body, a figure, is a cipher, to be deciphered, read. The figure cannot read itself. The poet's uncanny eye has deciphered Gayatri Chakravorty, prefigured predicaments that she would like to think she averted in ways that he had counselled in those unread poems. At a certain point, the poet advises a different way of living:

> Not success outside,
> But a selfsame flowering as unstiff as the body's sleep
> Is what lovers want . . .
> Go on, try opening by yourself, like a shell would,
> Fail, yet that bit of sand, the little sand that finds its way just in,
> Will little by little be pearl, the proper success,
>   Of movement.
> If you want a life as easy and all nature, like the sleeper's pose,
> Try breathing in the heart's interior fragrance. (8)

This reader would like to think that the prayer to be haunted by the ethical is kin to that advice.[29] Binoy Majumdar has been in and out of mental hospitals for the last forty years. What is it for such a man to write: "I will now be mad, at last by insane claws / Will prise out the angel's home address, the door" (30)? There are poems that delicately hint how "madness" must be managed, and poems that ask: "O time, where, at whose door shall I appear / With my armored charms, my naked ways" (85)?

There is no question of response. The occasion of these poems has been translated into the transcendental. The facsimile edition ends with poems marked "not to be included in the printed version." I do not know if they are to be found in the printed versions. The last one of

---

29 For my most recent understanding of this, please see the conclusion to "Bangalir Manansheelota," forthcoming in *Anushtup*.

them is the only straightforward narrative poem in the sequence. The others are written "according to the psychological process by which we dream (setting together scene after scene)" (Foreword). Indeed, Gayatri Chakravorty is called "Dream-Girl" a number of times.

It is not possible to write about these poems briefly. There is spare praise of auto-eroticism, praise of the austere comforts of poetry, despair at loss of skill, a tremendous effort to imagine the smallest creatures, and the uncaringness of star and sky, to frame human frailty and loss, and a brilliantly heterogeneous collection of addressees. Sometimes the imagery is a rarefied dream lexicon: nail, cave, delta, rain. I hope they will not be translated soon. At last I would like to translate them.

There are repeated references to oneself as a letter lying on the wrong threshold, destined to err, a plea to be called if some "social need" should arise:

Come and pick me up like torn bits of a letter
Put 'em together for curiosity's sake, read once and leave
As if to disappear, leaving them like a slant look. (16)

There are reprimands to the frivolous girl, references to the future laughing at her sudden death (36), cryptic judgments such as the following, where nothing in the poems allows us to decide if Dream-Girl is among the exceptions or the rule: "In very few women is there a supplement placed" (3). I have been unable to catch the specificity of *ramani*—one of a handful of common words for woman—that carries the charge of *ramana*—the joy of sex. I have also been unable to catch the pun in *krorepatra* (translated "supplement")—literally "lapleaf." What does the pun mean? This poet is uncharitable to women who merely breed and copulate.

It is this particular ambivalence in the poems that seems exciting for this translator to access, as she makes the mistake of thinking the named subject is she. Thus the ambivalence seems to offer a codicil to that bit in J. M. Coetzee's *Waiting for the Barbarians* that she had so liked: How does the other see me? Identity's last secret. Coetzee describes the Magistrate describing his deciphering effort thus: "So I continue to swoop and circle around the irreducible figure of the girl, casting one net of meaning after another over her . . . . What does she see? The protecting wings of a guardian albatross or the black shape of a coward crow afraid to strike while its prey yet breathes?"[30]

I am the figure of the girl, the translator thinks, making that easy mistake, and this book offers what the poet sees as he casts his net. I come up both ways, albatross and crow. This is a lesson: to enter the protocols of a text one must other its characters.

In the last poem in the facsimile edition, in and out of the book, since it is not meant to be included in the printed version, Gayatri Chakravorty or "my divine mistress" is translated into a declarative narrative of transcendental alterity. Response stops here, in the representation of response without end:

> I've grasped it surely, life on earth is done;
> I'm straight in heaven's kingdom, earth's body's shed.
> These heavenly kingdoms are indeed our home, and we
> Are just two spirits—Dream-Girl and I—this pair
> Divinely live in heaven's kingdom now. I see,
> That she's still that familiar youthful form,
> And stands with a greeting smile upon her lips.
> My divine mistress. I too have by desire kept a body,
> Even in heaven—healthful, like Dream-Girl's,
> As tall as she, no glasses, eyesight good,
> I am to her taste, a good-looking young man.
> Smiling she speaks up—You're done, you've come at last,
> Now for the bliss of peace, fulfillment, thrill

---

30 J. M. Coetzee, *Waiting for the Barbarians* (New York: Penguin, 1980), p. 81.

In body and mind, in deep immeasurable kind,
Everything just so, as we would like it. Come.
Next, in a clasp so deep, and deeper still a kiss,
She promises that she will spend with me,
An eternity of shared conjugal life. (85)

What is it to be an "original" of a translation? This is what teaches me again the lesson of the trace. For a name is not a signifier but a mark, on the way to a trace. Binoy Majumdar makes Gayatri Chakravorty a hybrid, but not by the assurance of some irreducible cultural translation. The name as mark is caught between the place under erasure—crossed out but visible, on the handwritten title page—and its generalization as "my divine mistress": *amar ishwari*.[31]

On the flyleaf of this book I find notice of something that no critic has spoken of so far, a prose book, presumably, entitled *Ishwarir Swarachita Nibandha*—An Essay or Essays Composed by the Divine Mistress Herself. The book was out of print, I heard, but about to be printed again. How shall I be encountered by myself in that text, where I think the poet has attempted to access Gayatri Chakravorty's thinking? Here is an allegory of translation, turned inside out.

This task remains. And it remains to try that second way of reading, impersonal or diverse situations connected to social theory, politics, science. I am back where I began. I must get around the seduction of a text that seems to be addressed to myself, more than most texts, and enter the author's presuppositions, where my youthful proper name is obliterated in the concerns of general readers, equally welcome.[32] As I

---

31 I am using Derridian language here. The editor of the facsimile edition thinks there is some connection between Binoy's perceptive glance and my "spreading Derrida," as she puts it (Kankabati Dutta, "À Propos"). Perhaps there's something there, but she has got her dates wrong. I started teaching Derrida (and Lacan, and Foucault) in the 1960s, not the 1980s.

32 I was in Kolkata for two nights recently, after this essay was submitted to the editors. It was the time of the justly celebrated Kolkata Book Fair. There seemed to

do so, I must of course remember that those presuppositions have a history and a geography, and that I am a translator into English.

---

be a Binoy Majumdar revival. I acquired the slim "Complete Works." I read this, written in 1992, thirty-one years after book's publication, in a letter: "Gayatri Chakravorty was a student at Presidency College, and came First Class First in English in her BA, in 1960 or 1961 AD [actually 1959], thinking that she alone would understand my poems the book *To Gayatri* was addressed to her, and therefore I called the book *To Gayatri*, and I wrote in the book what I had to say to her" ("Patraboli," *Ishwarir Swarachito Nibandha o Anyanya* [Kolkata: Pratibhash, 1995], p. 3). But also this, in 1986, in an interview, twenty-five years later:

> I wanted to ask [says the interviewer]—were you in love with Gayatri?
>
> Hey, no—I only knew her for two or three days–she was a famously beautiful student of English literature at Presidency College—then she went off somewhere—to America or some place, I'm not sure.
>
> Then why write poems about her?
>
> One must write about someone, after all. Can one write forever about mango trees, jackfruit trees, and tuberoses?
>
> ("Phire Esho Chakar Nam Paribartan Shommondhe," *Kabyoshamogro*, VOL. 1 [Kolkata: Pratibhash, 1993], p. 162).

Binoy had in fact never exchanged a word with Gayatri.

[Translator's note: the three items in the last sentence seem exotic in English. They are the Bengali equivalent of: "apples and pears and red, red roses," let us say. I include these passages here in the interest of bibliographical detail. To think through their implications will take time.]

THE MOST INTIMATE ACT OF READING

Translator's Foreword to "Draupadi" by Mahasweta Devi

(1981)*

I translated this Bengali short story into English as much for the sake of its villain, Senanayak, as for its title character, Draupadi (or Dopdi). Because in Senanayak I find the closest approximation to the first-world scholar in search of the third world, I shall speak of him first.

On the level of the plot, Senanayak is the army officer who captures and degrades Draupadi. I will not go so far as to suggest that, in practice, the instruments of first-world life and investigation are complicit with such captures and such a degradation.[1] The approximation, I notice, relates to the author's careful presentation of Senanayak as a pluralist aesthete. In *theory*, Senanayak can identify with the enemy. But pluralist aesthetes of the first world are, willy-nilly, participants in the production of an exploitative society. Hence in *practice*, Senanayak must destroy the enemy, the menacing other. He follows the necessities and contingencies of what he sees as his historical moment. There is a convenient colloquial name for that as well: pragmatism. Thus his emotions at Dopdi's capture are mixed: sorrow (theory) and joy (practice). Correspondingly, we grieve for our third-world sisters; we grieve and rejoice that they must

* First published in *Critical Inquiry* 8(2) (1981): 381–402.
1 For elaborations upon such a suggestion, see Jean-François Lyotard, *The Postmodern Condition: A Report on Knowledge* (Minneapolis: University of Minnesota Press, 1984).

lose themselves and become as much like us as possible in order to be "free"; we congratulate ourselves on our specialists' knowledge of them. Indeed, like ours, Senanayak's project is interpretive: he looks to decipher Draupadi's song. For both sides of the rift within himself, he finds analogies in Western literature: Hochhuth's *The Deputy*, David Morell's *First Blood*. He will shed his guilt when the time comes. His self-image for that uncertain future is Prospero.

I have suggested elsewhere that, when we wander out of our own academic and first-world enclosure, we share something like a relationship with Senanayak's doublethink.[2] When we speak for ourselves, we urge with conviction: the personal is also political. For the rest of the world's women, the sense of whose personal micrology is difficult (though not impossible) for us to acquire, we fall back on a colonialist theory of most efficient information retrieval. We will not be able to speak to the women out there if we depend completely on conferences and anthologies by Western-trained informants. As I see their photographs in women's studies journals or on book jackets—indeed, as I look in the glass—it is Senanayak with his anti-Fascist paperbacks that I behold. In inextricably mingling historico-political specificity with the sexual differential in a literary discourse, Mahasweta Devi invites us to begin effacing that image.

My approach to the story has been influenced by "deconstructive practice." I clearly share an unease that would declare avant-garde theories of interpretation too elitist to cope with revolutionary feminist material. How, then, has the practice of deconstruction been helpful in this context?

---

2 See Gayatri Chakravorty Spivak, "Three Feminist Readings: McCullers, Drabble, Habermas," *Union Seminary Quarterly Review* 1–2 (Fall–Winter 1979–80): 15–34; and "French Feminism in an International Frame," in *In Other Worlds: Essays in Cultural Politics* (New York: Routledge, 1998), pp. 184–211.

The aspect of deconstructive practice that is best known in the United States is its tendency toward infinite regression.[3] The aspect that interests me most is, however, the recognition, within deconstructive practice, of provisional and intractable starting points in any investigative effort; its disclosure of complicities where a will to knowledge would create oppositions; its insistence that in disclosing complexities the critic-as-subject is herself complicit with the object of her critique; its emphasis upon "history" and upon the ethico-political as the "trace" of that complicity—the proof that we do not inhabit a clearly defined critical space free of such traces; and, finally, the acknowledgment that its own discourse can never be adequate to its example.[4] This is clearly not the place to elaborate each item upon this list. I should, however, point out that in my introductory paragraphs I have already situated the figure of Senanayak in terms of our own patterns of complicity. In what follows, the relationship between the tribal and classical characters of Draupadi, the status of Draupadi at the end of the story, and the reading of Senanayak's proper name might be seen as produced by the reading practice I have described. The complicity of law and transgression and the class deconstruction of the "gentlemen revolutionaries," although seemingly minor points in the interpretation of the story as such, take on greater importance in a political context.

---

3 This list represents a distillation of suggestions to be found in the work of Jacques Derrida: see, for example, "The Exorbitant Question of Method," in *Of Grammatology* (Gayatri Chakravorty Spivak trans.) (Baltimore, MD: Johns Hopkins University Press, 1976), pp. 157–64; "Limited Inc" (Samuel Weber trans.), *Glyph* 2 (1977): 162–254; "Où Commence et comment finit un corps enseignant," in Dominique Grisoni (ed.), *Politiques de la philosophie* (Paris: B. Grasset, 1976), pp. 55–97; and Spivak, "Revolutions That as Yet Have No Model: Derrida's 'Limited Inc,'" *Diacritics* 10 (December 1980): 29–49, and "Sex and History in Wordsworth's *The Prelude* (1805) IX–XIII," in *In Other Worlds*, pp. 46–76.

4 It is a sign of E. M. Forster's acute perception of India that *A Passage to India* contains a glimpse of such an exorbitant tribal in the figure of the punkha puller in the courtroom.

I cannot take this discussion of deconstruction far enough to show how Dopdi's song, incomprehensible yet trivial (it is in fact about beans of different colors), and exorbitant to the story, marks the place of that other that can be neither excluded nor recuperated.

"Draupadi" first appeared in *Agnigarbha* (Womb of Fire), a collection of loosely connected, short political narratives. As Mahasweta points out in her introduction to the collection, "Life is not mathematics and the human being is not made for the sake of politics. I want a change in the present social system and do not believe in mere party politics."[5]

Mahasweta Devi is a middle-class Bengali leftist intellectual in her fifties. She has a master's degree in English from Santiniketan, the famous experimental university established by Rabindranath Tagore. Her reputation as a novelist was already well established when, in the late 1970s, she published *Hajar Churashir Ma* (*Mother of 1084*). This novel remains within the dominant psychological idiom of the Bengali fiction of its time.[6] Yet in *Aranyer Adhikar* (The Rights or [Occupation] of the Forest), a serially published novel she was writing almost at the same time, a significant change is noticeable. It is a meticulously researched historical novel about the Munda Insurrection of 1899–1900. Here Mahasweta begins putting together a prose that is a collage of literary Bengali, bureaucratic Bengali, tribal Bengali, and the languages of the tribals.

Since the Bengali script is illegible except to the approximately 25 percent literate of the about 90 million speakers of Bengali, a large number of whom live in Bangladesh rather than in West Bengal, one

---

5 Mahasweta Devi, *Agnigarbha* (Kolkata: Karuna Prakashani, 1978), p. 8.

6 For a discussion of the relationship between academic degrees in English and the production of revolutionary literature, see Gayatri Chakravorty Spivak, "A Vulgar Inquiry into the Relationship between Academic Criticism and Literary Production in West Bengal," lecture delivered at the Annual Convention of the Modern Language Association, Houston, 1980.

cannot speak of the "Indian" reception of Mahasweta's work but only of its Bengali reception. Briefly, that reception can be described as a general recognition of excellence; skepticism regarding the content on the part of the bourgeois readership; some accusations of extremism from the electoral Left; and admiration and a sense of solidarity on the part of the non-electoral Left. Any extended reception study would consider that West Bengal has had a largely uninterrupted Left Front government of the united electoral Communist parties since 1967. Here suffice it to say that Mahasweta is certainly one of the most important writers writing in India today.

Any sense of Bengal as a "nation" is governed by the putative identity of the Bengali language.[7] (Meanwhile, Bengalis dispute if the purest Bengali is that of Nabadwip or South Calcutta, and many of the twenty-odd developed dialects are incomprehensible to the "general speaker.") In 1947, on the eve of its departure from India, the British government divided Bengal into West Bengal, which remained a part of India, and East Pakistan. Punjab was similarly divided into East Punjab (India) and West Pakistan. The two parts of Pakistan did not share ethnic or linguistic ties and were separated by nearly 1,100 miles. The division was made on the grounds of the concentration of Muslims in these two parts of the subcontinent. Yet the Punjabi Muslims felt themselves to be more "Arab" because they lived in the area where the first Muslim emperors of India had settled nearly 700 years ago and also because of their proximity to West Asia (the Middle East). The Bengali Muslims— no doubt in a class-differentiated way—felt themselves constituted by the culture of Bengal.

---

7 See Dinesh Chandra Sen, *History of Bengali Language and Literature* (Kolkata: University of Calcutta, 1911). A sense of Bengali literary nationalism can be gained from the (doubtless apocryphal) report that, upon returning from his first investigative tour of India, Macaulay remarked: "The British Crown presides over two great literatures: the English and the Bengali."

Bengal has had a strong presence of leftist intellectualism and struggle since the middle of the last century, before, in fact, the word "Left" entered our political shorthand.[8] As such, it is a source of considerable political irritation to the Central Government of India. (The individual state governments have a good deal more autonomy under the Indian constitution than is the case in the US.) Although officially India was, until recently, a socialist state with a mixed economy, historically it has reflected a spectrum of the Right, from military dictatorship to nationalist class benevolence. The word "democracy" becomes highly interpretable in the context of a largely illiterate, multilingual, heterogeneous, and unpoliticized electorate.

In the spring of 1967, there was a successful peasant rebellion in the Naxalbari area of the northern part of West Bengal. According to Marcus Franda, "unlike most other areas of West Bengal, where peasant movements are led almost solely by middle-class leadership from Kolkata, Naxalbari has spawned an indigenous agrarian reform leadership led by the lower classes" including tribal cultivators.[9] This peculiar coalition of peasant and intellectual sparked off a number of Naxalbaris all over India.[10] The target of these movements was the long-established oppression of the landless peasantry and itinerant farm worker, sustained through an unofficial government–landlord collusion that too easily circumvented the law. Indeed, one might say that legislation seemed to have an eye to its own future circumvention.

---

8 See Gautam Chattopadhyay, *Communism and Bengal's Freedom Movement* (New Delhi: People's Publishing House, 1970).

9 Marcus F. Franda, *Radical Politics in West Bengal* (Cambridge, MA: MIT Press, 1971), p. 153. I am grateful to Michael Ryan for having located this accessible account of the Naxalbari movement. There now exists an excellent study by Sumanta Banerjee, *India's Simmering Revolution: The Naxalite Uprising* (London: Zed Books, 1984).

10 See Samar Sen, Debabrata Panda, and Ashish Lahiri (eds), *Naxalbari and After: A Frontier Anthology*, VOL. 2 (Kolkata: Kathashilpa, 1978).

It is worth remarking that this coalition of peasant and intellectual—with long histories of apprenticeship precisely on the side of the intellectual—has been recuperated in the West by both ends of the polarity that constitutes a "political spectrum." Bernard-Henri Lévy, the ex-Maoist French "New Philosopher," has implicitly compared it to the May 1968 "revolution" in France, where the students joined the workers.[11] In France, however, the student identity of the movement had remained clear, and the student leadership had not brought with it sustained efforts to undo the privilege of the intellectual. On the other hand:

> [I]n much the same manner as many American college presidents have described the protest of American students, Indian political and social leaders have explained the Naxalites (supporters of Naxalbari) by referring to their sense of alienation and to the influence of writers like Marcuse and Sartre which has seemingly dominated the minds of young people throughout the world in the 1960s.[12]

It is against such recuperations that I would submit what I have called the theme of class deconstruction with reference to the young gentlemen revolutionaries in "Draupadi." Senanayak remains fixed within his class origins, which are similar to those of the gentlemen revolutionaries. Correspondingly, he is contained and judged fully within Mahasweta's story; by contrast, the gentlemen revolutionaries remain latent, underground. Even their leader's voice is only heard formulaically within Draupadi's solitude. I should like to think that it is because they are so persistently engaged in undoing class containment and the opposition between reading (book-learning) and doing, rather than keeping the two aesthetically forever separate, that they inhabit a world

---

11 See Bernard-Henri Lévy, *Bangla Desh: Nationalisme dans la révolution* (Paris: François Maspéro, 1973).

12 Franda, *Radical Politics in West Bengal*, pp. 163–64. See also p. 164n22.

whose authority and outline no text—including Mahasweta's—can encompass.

In 1970, the implicit hostility between East and West Pakistan flamed into armed struggle. In 1971, at a crucial moment in the struggle, the armed forces of the government of India were deployed, seemingly because these were alliances between the Naxalites of West Bengal and the freedom fighters of East Bengal (now Bangladesh). "If a guerrilla-style insurgency had persisted, their forces would undoubtedly have come to dominate the politics of the movement. It was this trend that the Indian authorities were determined to pre-empt by intervention." Taking advantage of the general atmosphere of jubilation at the defeat of West Pakistan, India's "principal national rival in South Asia"[13] (this was also the first time India had "won a war" in its millennial history), the Indian prime minister was able to crack down with exceptional severity on the Naxalites, destroying the rebellious sections of the rural population, most significantly the tribals, as well. The year 1971 is thus a point of reference in Senanayak's career.

This is the setting of "Draupadi." The story is a moment caught between two deconstructive formulas: on the one hand, a law that is fabricated with a view to its own transgression; on the other, the undoing of the binary opposition between the intellectual and the rural struggles. In order to grasp the minutiae of their relationship and involvement, one must enter a historical micrology that no foreword can provide.

Draupadi is the name of the central character. She is introduced to the reader between two uniforms and between two versions of her name. Dopdi and Draupadi. It is either that as a tribal she cannot pronounce her own Sanskrit name Draupadi, or the tribalized form, Dopdi, is the proper name of the ancient Draupadi. She is on a list of wanted

---

13 Lawrence Lifschultz, *Bangladesh: The Unfinished Revolution* (London: Zed Books, 1979), pp. 25, 26.

persons, yet her name is not on the list of appropriate names for tribal women.

The ancient Draupadi is perhaps the most celebrated heroine of the Indian epic Mahabharata. The Mahabharata and the Ramayana are the cultural credentials of the so-called Aryan civilization of India. The tribes predate the Aryan invasion. They have no right to heroic Sanskrit names. Neither the interdiction nor the significance of the name, however, must be taken too seriously. For this pious, domesticated Hindu name was given Dopdi at birth by her mistress, in the usual mood of benevolence felt by the oppressor's wife toward the tribal bond servant. It is the killing of this mistress's husband that sets going the events of the story.

And yet on the level of the text, this elusive and fortuitous name does play a role. To speculate upon this role, we might consider the Mahabharata itself in its colonialist function in the interest of the so-called Aryan invaders of India. It is an accretive epic, where the "sacred" geography of an ancient battle is slowly expanded by succeeding generations of poets so that the secular geography of the expanding Aryan colony can present itself as identical with it and thus justify itself.[14] The complexity of this vast and anonymous project makes it an incomparably more heterogeneous text than the Ramayana. Unlike the Ramayana, for example, the Mahabharata contains cases of various kinds of kinship structure and various styles of marriage. And in fact it is Draupadi who provides the only example of polyandry, not a common system of marriage in India. She is married to the five sons of the impotent Pandu. Within a patriarchal and patronymic context, she is exceptional, indeed "singular" in the sense of odd, unpaired, uncoupled.[15] Her

---

14 For my understanding of this aspect of the Mahabharata, I am indebted to Romila Thapar of Jawaharlal Nehru University, New Delhi.

15 I borrow this sense of singularity from Jacques Lacan, "Seminar on 'The Purloined Letter'" (Jeffrey Mehlman trans.), *Yale French Studies* 48 (1972): 53, 59.

husbands, since they are husbands rather than lovers, are *legitimately pluralized*. No acknowledgment of paternity can secure the Name of the Father for the child of such a mother. Mahasweta's story questions this "singularity" by placing Dopdi first in a comradely, activist, monogamous marriage and then in a situation of multiple rape.

In the epic, Draupadi's legitimized pluralization (as a wife among husbands) in singularity (as a possible mother or harlot) is used to demonstrate male glory. She provides the occasion for a violent transaction between men, the efficient cause of the crucial battle. Her eldest husband is about to lose her by default in a game of dice. He had staked all he owned, and "Draupadi belongs within that all" (Mahabharata 65:32). Her strange civil status seems to offer grounds for her predicament as well. "The Scriptures prescribed one husband for a woman; Draupadi is dependent on many husbands; therefore, she can be designated a prostitute. There is nothing improper in bringing her, clothed or unclothed, into the assembly" (65:35–36). The enemy chief begins to pull at Draupadi's sari. Draupadi silently prays to the incarnate Krishna. The Idea of Sustaining Law (Dharma) materializes itself as clothing, and as the king pulls and pulls at her sari, there seems to be more and more of it. Draupadi is infinitely clothed and cannot be publicly stripped. It is one of Krishna's miracles.

Mahasweta's story rewrites this episode. The men easily succeed in stripping Dopdi—in the narrative it is the culmination of her political punishment by the representatives of the law. She remains publicly naked at her own insistence. Rather than save her modesty through the implicit intervention of a benign and divine (in this case it would have been godlike) comrade, the story insists that this is the place where male leadership stops.

It would be a mistake, I think, to read the modern story as a refutation of the ancient. Dopdi is (as heroic as) Draupadi. She is also what Draupadi—written into the patriarchal and authoritative sacred text as proof of male power—could not be. Dopdi is at once a palimpsest and a contradiction.

There is nothing "historically implausible" about Dopdi's attitudes. When we first see her, she is thinking about washing her hair. She loves her husband and keeps political faith as an act of faith toward him. She adores her forefathers because they protected their women's honor. (It should be recalled that this is thought in the context of American soldiers breeding bastards.) It is when she crosses the sexual differential into the field of what could only happen to a woman that she emerges as the most powerful "subject," who, still using the language of sexual "honor," can derisively call herself "the object of your search," whom the author can describe as a terrifying superobject—"an unarmed target."

As a tribal, Dopdi is not romanticized by Mahasweta. The decision-makers among the revolutionaries are, again, "realistically," bourgeois young men and women who have oriented their book-learning to the land and thus begun the long process of undoing the opposition between book (theory or "outside") and spontaneity (practice or "inside"). Such fighters are the hardest to beat, for they are neither tribal nor gentlemen. A Bengali reader would pick them out by name among the characters: the one with the aliases who bit off his tongue, the ones who helped the couple escape the army cordon; the ones who neither smoke nor drink tea; and, above all, Arijit. His is a fashionable name, tinsel Sanskrit, with no allusive paleonymy and a meaning that fits the story a bit too well: victorious over enemies. Yet it *is* his voice that gives Dopdi the courage to save not herself but her comrades.

Of course, this voice of male authority also fades. Once Dopdi enters, in the final section of the story, the postscript area of lunar flux and sexual difference, she is in a place where she will finally act *for* herself in *not* "acting," in challenging the man to (en)counter her as unrecorded or misrecorded objective historical monument. The army officer is shown as unable to ask the authoritative ontological question: What is this? In fact, in the sentence describing Dopdi's final summons to the Sahib's tent, the agent is missing. I can be forgiven if I find in this an allegory of the woman's struggle within the revolution in a shifting historical moment.

As Mahasweta points out in an aside, the tribe in question is the Santhal, not to be confused with at least nine other Munda tribes that inhabit India. They are also not to be confused with the so-called untouchables, who, unlike the tribals, are Hindu, though probably of remote "non-Aryan" origin. In giving the name Harijan ("God's people") to the untouchables, Mahatma Gandhi had tried to concoct the sort of pride and sense of unity that the tribes seem to possess. Mahasweta has followed the Bengali practice of calling each so-called untouchable caste by the name of its menial and unclean task within the rigid structural functionalism of institutionalized Hinduism.[16] I have been unable to reproduce this in my translation.

Mahasweta uses another differentiation, almost on the level of caricature: the Sikh and the Bengali. (Sikhism was founded as a reformed religion by Guru Nanak in the late fifteenth century. Today the roughly nine million Sikhs of India live chiefly in East Punjab, at the other end of the vast Indo-Gangetic Plain from Bengal. The tall, muscular, turbanned and bearded Sikh, so unlike the slight and supposedly intellectual Bengali, is the stereotyped butt of jokes in the same way as the Polish community in North America or the Belgian in France.) Arjan Singh, the diabetic Sikh captain who falls back on the Granth-Sahib (the Sikh sacred book—I have translated it "Scripture") and the "five Ks"[17] of the Sikh religion, is presented as all brawn and no brains; and

---

16 As a result of the imposition of the capitalist mode of production and the Imperial Civil Service, and massive conversions of the lowest castes to Christianity, the invariable identity of caste and trade no longer holds. Here, too, there is the possibility of a taxonomy micrologically deconstructive of the caste–class opposition, functioning heterogeneously in terms of the social hierarchy.

17 The "five Ks" are *kes* (unshorn hair); *kachh* (drawers down to the knee); *karha* (iron bangle); *kirpan* (dagger); *kanga* (comb); to be worn by every Sikh, hence a mark of identity.

the wily, imaginative, corrupt Bengali Senanayak is, of course, the army officer full of a Keatsian negative capability.[18]

The entire energy of the story seems, in one reading, directed toward breaking the apparently clean gap between theory and practice in Senanayak. Such a clean break is not possible, of course. The theoretical production of negative capability is a practice; the practice of mowing down Naxalites brings with it a theory of the historical moment. The assumption of such a clean break in fact depends upon the assumption that the individual subject who theorizes and practices is in full control. At least in the history of the Indo-European tradition in general, such a sovereign subject is also the legal or legitimate subject, who is identical with his stable patronymic.[19] It might therefore be interesting that Senanayak is not given the differentiation of a first name and surname. His patronymic is identical with his function (not of course by the law of caste): the common noun means "army chief." In fact, there is the least hint of a doubt if it is a proper name or a common appellation. This may be a critique of the man's apparently self-adequate identity, which sustains his theory-practice juggling act. If so, it goes with what I see as the project of the story: to break this bonded identity with the wedge of an *unreasonable* fear. If our certitude of the efficient-information-retrieval and talk-to-the-accessible approach toward third-world women can be broken by the wedge of an unreasonable uncertainty, into a feeling that what we deem gain might spell loss and

---

18 If indeed the model for this character is Ranjit Gupta, the notorious Inspector General of Police of West Bengal between 1972 and 1976, the delicate textuality, in the interest of a political position, of Senanayak's delineation in the story takes us far beyond the limits of a reference à *clef*. I am grateful to Michael Ryan for suggesting the possibility of such a reference.

19 The relationship between phallocentrism, the patriarchy, and clean binary oppositions is a pervasive theme in Derrida's critique of the metaphysics of presence. See Gayatri Chakravorty Spivak, "Unmaking and Making in *To the Lighthouse*," in *In Other Worlds*, pp. 41–62.

that our practice should be forged accordingly, then we would share the textual effect of "Draupadi" with Senanayak.

The italicized words in the translation are in English in the original. It is to be noticed that the fighting words on both sides are in English. Nation-state politics combined with multinational economies produce war. The language of war—offense *and* defense—is international. English is standing in here for that nameless and heterogeneous world language. The peculiarities of usage belong to being obliged to cope with English under political and social pressure for a few centuries. Where, indeed, is there a "pure" language? Given the nature of the struggle, there is nothing bizarre in "Comrade Dopdi."[20] It is part of the undoing of opposites—intellectual–rural, tribalist–internationalist— that is the wavering constitution of "the underground," "the wrong side" of the law. On the right side of the law, such deconstructions, breaking down national distinctions, are operated through the encroachment of king-emperor or capital.

The only exception is the word "sahib." An Urdu word meaning "friend," it came to mean, almost exclusively in Bengali, "white man." It is a colonial word and is used today to mean "boss." I thought of Kipling as I wrote "Burra Sahib" for Senanayak.

In the matter of "translation" between Bengali and English it is again Dopdi who occupies a curious middle space. She is the only one who uses the word "kounter" (the "n" is no more than a nasalization of the diphthong "ou"). As Mahasweta explains, it is an abbreviation for "killed by police in an encounter," the code description for death by police torture. Dopdi does not understand English, but she understands

---

20 "My dearest Sati, through the walls and the miles that separate us I can hear you saying, 'In Sawan it will be two years since Comrade left us.' The other women will nod. It is you who have taught them the meaning of Comrade" (Mary Tyler, "Letter to a Former Cell-Mate," in Sen et al., *Naxalbari and After*, VOL. 1, p. 307). See also Mary Tyler, *My Years in an Indian Prison* (Harmondsworth: Penguin, 1978).

this formula and the word. In her use of it at the end, it comes mysteriously close to the "proper" English usage. It is the menacing appeal of the objectified subject to its politico-sexual enemy—the provisionally silenced master of the subject-object dialectic—to encounter— "kounter"—her. What is it to "use" a language "correctly" without "knowing" it?

We cannot answer because we, with Senanayak, are in the opposite situation. Although we are told of specialists, the meaning of Dopdi's song remains undisclosed in the text. The educated Bengali does not know the languages of the tribes, and no political coercion obliges him to "know" it. What one might falsely think of as a political "privilege"— knowing English properly—stands in the way of a deconstructive practice of language: using it "correctly" through a political displacement, or operating the language of the other side.

It follows that I have had the usual "translator's problems" only with the peculiar Bengali spoken by the tribals. In general, we educated Bengalis have the same racist attitude toward it as the late Peter Sellers had toward our English. It would have been embarrassing to have used some version of the language of D. H. Lawrence's "common people" or Faulkner's Blacks. Again, the specificity is micrological. I have used "straight English," whatever that may be.

Translator's Afterword to *Chotti Munda and His Arrow* by Mahasweta Devi

(2003)*

There is an air of festivity around the last stages of the production of this book. Mahasweta Devi herself, the book's editor Anjum Katyal, the publisher of Seagull Books, Naveen Kishore, become general dogsbody, and me, all pulling together to make the book ready for the Calcutta Book Fair! This afterword will be necessarily brief.

"I had but that one arrow," says Chotti at the end of the novel. What is the magic of Dhani Munda"'s magic arrow? Nothing but practice, repeats Chotti, attention to detail, focusing on the prey, caught in that ethnical glance that undoes the distinction between love and its opposite. That confusing practice—*adhyan*, in Sanskritic Bengali—*is* magic. That is the trick of teaching as infinite relay, the very spine of historical change. I have no doubt that related words will be found in the world's languages. Here I note the uncanny resemblance with the Sioux ghost dance.[1]

---

* First published in Mahasweta Devi, *Chotti Munda and His Arrow* (Gayatri Chakravorty Spivak trans.) (Oxford: Blackwell, 2003), pp. 289–92 / (London: Seagull Books, 2015[2002]), pp. 333–36.

[1] I learned of this first from the unabridged edition of James Mooney, *The Ghost-Dance Religion and the Sioux Outbreak of 1890* (Glorieta, NM: Rio Grande Press, 1973). For the animation of the ghost dance in 1970s activism, the text is, of course, Dee Alexander Brown, *Bury My Hearth at Wounded Knee: An Indian History of the American West* (New York: Holt, Rinehart & Winston, 1971), a book Mahasweta came to love long after she wrote *Chotti Munda*.

The ghost is not the abstraction of the spirit, it has a ghostly body. And magic in *Chotti* is not the mere irrationality of the epiphenomenal; it carries the sweat of target practice. Through the ghost dance as through arrow practice, the ancestors are touched and asked for a way to cope with a future that seems to overwhelm the present. That last scene of the book, fixed in the freeze frame of a dance: Chotti on one side, SDO on the other, and in-between a thousand bows upraised in space. And a warning announced in many upraised hands is where Chotti finds the open end of the redemptive solution by memorating Dhani Munda: Chotti gives an innocent smile and says, "I'll show ya." Then says fast in the language of the Mundas, "Dhani Munda! I'm raisin' yer name an' shootin' yer arrer today. To stay true, meself to meself." The novel's suspended conclusion looks forward to the possibility of the magic coming alive again.

Chotti Munda repeatedly dramatizes subaltern solidarity: Munda, Oraon, and the Hindu outcastes must work together. Today such a solidarity has a name: Dalit. The seduction of an identitarianism in the name of the Dalit can learn a lesson here. With a degree of regret, Chotti accepts that cultural identity must be—to take an altogether inappropriate metaphor that is easy for the reader to understand—museumized:

> Chotti returns home but the clouds don't lift from his mind.
> The day is coming. Mundas will not be able to live with their
> identity. In all national development work they will have to be
> one with those who, like Chhanag, are the oppressed of the
> land, and work as field hands, as sweated workers for contrac-
> tor or trader. Then there'll be a shirt on his body, perhaps shoes
> on his feet. Then the "Munda" identity will live only at festivals
> —in social exchange.

Between the performative of ritual transformed into performance and the power of a haunting magic anchored in practice the text charts the remote possibility of a resistant subalternity.

When in a conversation, Mahasweta proposes subaltern solidarity as resistance to globalization, I am not ready to situate the remark as benevolent Luddism. World trade and the trade-related measures of "development" are altogether dependent upon detail, and much of this detail is still located in large aboriginal, subaltern and sub-proletarian areas. More than the visible disruption of large-scale international meetings, as in Seattle (November 30–December 3, 1999), Naples (March 15–17, 2001), Genoa (July 20–21, 2001) or indeed the material destruction of the temple of World Trade (September 11, 2001), subaltern disruption in detail can throw the global machinery of world trade out of joint. I am not suggesting that *Chotti Munda* is predicting this in 1980. I am suggesting that the novel can prefigure this for the canny activist reader.

In 2000, mourning the passing of old Harlem, I had written: "How does one figure the cutting edge of the vanishing present?" I said nothing when Mahasweta spoke as follows during our conversation: "I had such a great *asthirata* in me, such a restlessness; an *udbeg*, this anxiety: I have to write, somehow I have to document this period which I have experienced because it is going away, it is vanishing." I said nothing, but I was filled with elation to think that, already at the end of the 1970s, Mahasweta had been driven by a kindred urge. Such resonances dictate the impulse to translate.

The last word, woman. If Chotti memorates Dhani at the end of the novel, at his own end Dhani memorates Sali, Birsa Munda's companion, and Pariwa, her son, adopted by him as his own. I want Mahasweta to unpack that proper name, Sali, which holds the names of the women who came out with axe, sword, and stick to fight in the Ulgulan:

> Gaya with a sword, Maki, his wife, with a long *lathi*, their little son with a *bulwa*, grandson Ramu, 14 years, with a bow and two arrows, the two daughters-in-law with a *dauli* and a *tangi* respectively and the three daughters, Thigi, Nagi and Lembu with a *lathi*, a sword and a *tangi* respectively . . . we [Gaya and

I] rolled into a corner . . . I on top . . . I was hammered from behind by one of the ladies . . . I thought at the time it was with an axe . . . but Sub-Inspector Iltaf Hussain tells me it was Gaya's wife, the most ferocious harridan of the lot, with a *lathi*: it was probably this old dame who flung the axe at the Sub-Inspector . . . I may add that at least two of the women had small babies in their left arms while brandishing arms with their right.[2]

Mahasweta's answer is illuminating: "I will write, about Laro"—her informant in the Gua shooting—"Laro is someone I know, I will write about her. And about women participating, those were again tribals brought from the Chhotanagpur Plateau, settled in Sunderbans, who took part in Tebhaga." I begin from what I know, says this soldier.

I have followed Mahasweta Devi for over twenty years. I have seen, again and again, how her fiction overflows her plans. I will look forward to fighting women, whatever their names, and look forward to translating their story.

Columbia University
January 6, 2002

---

2 Report of Deputy Commissioner Streatfield, cited in K. S. Singh, *Birsa Munda and His Movement (1872–1901)* (Calcutta: Seagull Books, 2002) pp. 107–08.

NECESSARY, YET IMPOSSIBLE

Questioned on Translation: Adrift

(2001)*

I gave you "Afterword" to read, and you sent me questions. At first reading, three questions stand out. Let me think around them. You ask me if I see myself as a cultural broker? How about Esperanto-style stuff? How about translation of discursive formations?

Cultural Broker

I believe becoming a cultural broker has been an unintended consequence of my translating Mahasweta Devi, but surely not Jacques Derrida? And what "culture" does Mahasweta represent?

"Describe some of your own experiences as a translator," you tell me. Now I feel as I did when I took my first written exam for my driver's license in 1967. How can these questions be answered as they are posed, I worried. I provided philosophically unassailable answers. I failed the exam. In other words, I had failed in the task of (low-level) epistemic translation, from the subject of the Iowa Department of Motor Vehicles to a young academic reading Derrida. I am failing again to translate from the subject of a colleague interested in me as a translator and my stereotype of myself, unavailable to me as "translator." Do I have "experiences" specifically as a translator? "Describe the importance of this work to your theoretical reflections," you say. Do you know I never

---

* First published in *Public Culture* 13(1) (2001): 13–22.

reflect theoretically; unless you count my "timed backups" from time to time, asking myself precisely what it is that I've been up to.

I'm in such a moment now, asking myself what roles my work as a translator plays in such thinking. As my example of the driver's license written test indicates, I think all reading is translation, that mistake or errancy is part of the game of reading. I made up a RAT at one point, reader-as-translator.[1] It could be that when we forget this, and read to identify, at worst to see our own face in the mirror of the text, we lose respect for the other as placeholder for the origin(al). So of course one keeps the faith. Do I believe "infidelity to the original," you ask. Yes, yes, not because it's possible, but because one must try. About "Breast-Giver," Mahasweta has said a number of times that she feels she is reading her own Bengali. And I won't teach anything if I can't strain toward that fidelity. In the case of texts "not written in English," such teaching turns out to be translation work, day in day out. I invite my undergraduates to think the shift between *eleos*, which is translated "pity" in Aristotle and "mercy" in the great Christian hymn "Kyrie eleison"—Greek-to-Greek, when there was not yet an English to pass through—so that they don't think the only way to "understand" anything is by way of their mother tongue, the dominant world language that has no history.[2]

With my graduate students, for over twenty years now, a different Marx keeps emerging in the interstices of the English and that nineteenth-century moment in German. Yet what of the failure of high-level epistemic translation in so loving a friend and ally as Friedrich Engels? Tayeb Salih's *Season of Migration to the North* reveals a relief map when

---

1 See Spivak, "The Politics of Translation" in this volume, pp. 36–66.
2 Henry Staten's Nietzschean analysis of the change from acknowledging the hero to commiserating with the sinner is, in broad strokes, the actual change, of course (communication with author, February 29, 2000).

the deployment of Arabic is noted.[3] Where does one end? I have even suggested, learning from Melanie Klein, that becoming-human is an incessant economy of translation.[4] And yesterday you saw how, attempting to answer Bobby Hill's question about my thinking about Manbhum, the old off-the-map name for the tract of land where the Aboriginals are in western West Bengal—I couldn't get my tongue around the fact that I'm never in English there. What does this mean? That suddenly "fidelity to an original" stops translation for me? Yet Manbhum is not an aboriginal name, just "land of honor" in Sanskrit, no trouble translating that at all.

"What stands out comparatively in my experience of translating Derrida and Devi?" That I was never allowed to translate any Derrida again, whereas the call to translate Devi becomes more and more urgent.

Esperanto

You think that my notion of "transnational literacy" might be useful "to examine the history of universal language movements." That fascinates me. Would such examinations be positive, or negative, or neutral, or not necessarily any of those? The last, I hope. For that idea of mine, which I first named in "Teaching for the Times" almost a decade ago, has to do with the uneven relationship of different nation-states with the agencies of universalization.[5] "Nation-state" is as vague as is "universalization," of course. But once you start keeping tabs on these incessant

---

3 Tayeb Salih, *Season of Migration to the North* (Boulder, CO: Lynne Rienner, 1997).

4 Spivak, "Translation as Culture" in this volume, pp. 69–88.

5 Gayatri Chakravorty Spivak, "Teaching for the Times," in Anne McClintock, Aamir Mufti, and Ella Shohat (eds), *Dangerous Liaisons: Gender, Nation, and Postcolonial Perspectives* (Minneapolis: University of Minnesota Press, 1997), 468–90. The piece was first presented in 1991 at the annual convention of the Midwestern Modern Language Association.

geopolitico-economic interrelations (the cloud of electronic economic movements remaining increasingly intractable), you discover that the "nation-state" is still a good abstract category for transnational discrimination. Thus my questions would always be: Who needs and leads the movement for universalization? Who celebrates it? In what interest? Why? There's never a satisfactory answer to these questions, but learning to ask them is required. This learning to ask is "literacy" in the articulation of the names of nation-states that assemble and disassemble a universal meta-message that is the incessantly written but never readable synonym for the "globe" standing in for the "universe."

Let me mention that in my recent Wellek Library lectures I have opened up the single name "Asia" and called for "transnational literacy" in Asian American studies.[6] In the context of translation, however, I draw your attention to the last sentence of the last paragraph, just to show that, for me, literacy is a Barthesian homology. Nation-states are to geopolitics as letters are to an alphabetical articulation; rather like Roland Barthes's notion of the "homological hypothesis" required to describe the relationship between narrative and the sentence: "Structurally, narrative shares the characteristics of the sentence without ever being reducible to the simple sum of its sentences."[7] I am not as pervasively influenced by Barthes as I am by Derrida. Two texts marked me: "Introduction to the Structural Analysis of Narratives" and the "Introduction" to *S/Z*.[8] I was a young assistant professor, moving into the euphoria of teaching comp. lit., when these texts came out. I read them as RAT, of course. What moved me in the first was the imperfect translation of structural linguistics into a homology that Barthes hesitated

---

6 Gayatri Chakravorty Spivak, "Planet-Think/Continent-Think," the Wellek Library Lecture delivered at the Critical Theory Institute, University of California–Irvine, May 25, 2000.

7 Roland Barthes, "Introduction to the Structural Analysis of Narratives," in *Image-Music-Text* (Stephen Heath trans.) (New York: Hill and Wang, 1997), p. 84.

8 Roland Barthes, *S/Z* (Richard Miller trans.) (New York: Hill and Wang, 1974).

to call a "theory." And in the second, that reading and writing had become allegorical figures for the agent and the subject, the psychological and the metapsychological, the personal and the impersonal, memory and history. It is in that sort of homological impulse that I had first spoken of literacy, not in any particular reference to print culture: "We not only should work mightily to take up the pen in our own hands but should also attempt to pick up the *qalam* [Arabic, "pen"] offered us in uneven decolonization and [. . .] to figure forth the world's broken and shifting alphabet."[9]

I wonder how the general trend toward uniformity of communication will be negotiated in terms of the multiplicity of languages? I continue to think, perhaps hope, that the view from this end seems more uniform than things really are. I cling to Ferdinand de Saussure's wise words, as reported by his students: "In language [. . .] everyone participates at all times, and that is why it is constantly being influenced by all. This capital fact suffices to show the impossibility of revolution" —meaning planned reforms like Esperanto, of course.[10] Has this changed because of electronic communication? Will slow speech perish, and, with it, rich speech and translatable differences?[11] I can't know. Yet I feel compelled to think that proud and confident declarations of rupture are always foolish. My argument about restricted permeability means that no one will ever translate into Fulani or Maya-Quiché without some particularly egregious agenda.[12]

---

9 Spivak, "Teaching for the Times," p. 487.

10 Ferdinand de Saussure, *Course in General Linguistics* (Wade Baskin trans.) (New York: Philosophical Library, 1959), p. 74.

11 Paper transactions are defective for electronic capitalism. Does it follow that they are therefore defective for thought and affect? Are we all, as Marx would say, "subjects of capital"? Is this cultural conservatism? These questions haunt me.

12 Gayatri Chakravorty Spivak, "Crossing Borders," in *Death of a Discipline* (New York: Columbia University Press, 2003), pp. 1–23.

You know my view about the impatience of human rights interventions. That, too, is a failure of translation, after all. The patience and the respect required to weave the discourse of the subjectship of human rights on to the right-to-responsibility conflict-resolution systems historically available to the so-called beneficiary group, invariably stagnant under earlier regimes, is always lacking. And that weaving—that invisible mending, that copying and pasting—is also a user "translation." In the absence of this particular brand of transnational literacy, rather different from knowing the lines of geopolitical maneuverings, human rights can become a nasty little weapon, working in the interest of the manifest destiny of the United States as the last best asylum for all.

You may say I'm making "translation" too big a figure. Perhaps so. But capitalism, in order to be itself, will always need buyers and sellers and a necessary translation between the two categories; the stock market will need winners and losers. Money does not grow by itself; it needs banks and the stock exchange, to manipulate the winner-loser dyad, done electronically today, and much of virtual money not needing to be realized at all. This entire mechanism works on coding that famous difference between laborpower given and wages returned as nonexistent. This machinal pattern is the figure of the disavowal of the failure of the translation of work into pay. It is a mistake to read this personally as some conspiracy theory. Socialist planning can happen when the translation is acknowledged and the irreducible difference in capital—industrial (mutatis mutandis commercial and finance)—is used for redistribution, "surplus labor and surplus product [. . .] reduced, to the degree needed, [. . .] on the one hand to form an insurance and reserve fund, on the other hand for the constant expansion of reproduction to the degree determined by social need."[13] If this utopian project succeeded, international socialism would be strategic globalization.

---

13 Karl Marx, *Capital: A Critique of Political Economy*, VOL. 3 (David Fernbach trans.) (New York: Vintage, 1981), p. 1016.

In our current style of globalization, this cannot happen. Its condition and effect may be the restricted permeability of cultural and linguistic translation that we have been talking about. To ignore restricted permeability in a triumphalist celebration of globality is to iterate the inevitability of unification as task. "Transnational literacy" can become a ground of its persistent critique—but only with effort, not by itself.

Colonialism as Discursive Translation

I will now cite a bit from a piece I wrote for a forthcoming volume of *Subaltern Studies*. What I am looking at there is two different kinds of failure of discursive translation. Let us start from an ad hoc Foucauldian definition: that a discursive formation is the reduced bunch of possible propositions that make up an "age." If this is so, then the construction and translation of something called "Greece" gave us something called "Europe," you will agree? Even the *Dialectic of Enlightenment*, such a perceptive book, precomprehends this (necessarily failed) translation.[14]

What I am going to quote is a reading of Jon Elster reading Homer to describe a definitive virtue of the European Enlightenment. In my view, one misfiring of the translation between the high Enlightenment and its colonial betrayal is reflected in the understanding of consensual rule-governed behavior—as in road crossing, defensive driving, chosen disease-preventive measures and, of course, all expectation of civic responsibility—as "fear." It would be a mistake, I think, to imagine that there are "cultures" proper to the Enlightenment where such voluntary self-restraint is "natural." Yet the sociopolitical restraints—"rule of law," "civil society," et cetera—that allow the myth of such *self*-restraint to flourish give way where a space for celebrating the failure of the Enlightenment contains a tendency toward a particular violence: the response to a coding of self-restraint as "fear."

---

14 Max Horkheimer and Theodor W. Adorno, *Dialectic of Enlightenment* (John Cumming trans.) (New York: Herder and Herder, 1972).

This voluntary self-restraint can be located in the ethical declaration of Ulysses faced with the Sirens that is given the lie by this dialectic of "fear" and the special space of violence: "You must bind me with harsh bonds, that I may remain fast where I am."[15] For an Elster, this "imperfect rationality" is what "takes care both of reason and of passion": "Man [*sic*] often is not rational, and rather exhibits *weakness* of *will*. Even when not rational, man knows that he is irrational and can *bind himself* to protect himself against the irrationality. This second-best or imperfect rationality takes care both of reason and of passion."[16] Elster's brilliant and complex discussion remains confined to the level playing field of European history. For him "culture" (never necessary to name, except altogether incidentally as "internalization of parental norms" [103]) is by default continuous with the politics and economics of the state.

It is unreasonable to expect Elster to conceive of the misfiring of a translation from Enlightenment to colony. Yet it is precisely that "imperfect rationality" that is given the lie by the rejection of it as "fear" in the special space of violence in antisystemic postcoloniality. The only loss entailed by imperfect rationality that Elster can imagine is loss of a sense of adventure: "This second-best or imperfect rationality takes care both of reason and of passion. What is lost, perhaps, is the sense of adventure" (103). (Thus he reveals, rather more than incidentally, that the European philosopher is susceptible to the coding of voluntary self-restraint as "fear," the espousal of which would be a denial of "adventurousness.") Yet, of course, Elster does know that "the crucial notion of the constituent assembly [. . .] as a real historical assembly

---

15 Homer, *The Odyssey*, VOL. 1 (A. T. Murray trans.) (Cambridge, MA: Harvard University Press, 1995), 12.160–61 (p. 461).

16 Jon Elster, *Ulysses and the Sirens: Studies in Rationality and Irrationality* (Cambridge: Cambridge University Press, 1979), 111; emphasis in the original. The rest of the quotations, all confined to these three paragraphs, are indicated in the text by page number alone.

seeking to bind its successors [. . .] is the closest analogy in society to the state of mind of Ulysses setting out on that dramatic part of his journey" (103). Further, "in modern democracies a number of institutions can be interpreted as devices for precommitment. [. . .] The central bank can be seen as the repository of reason against the short-term claim of passion" (90).

Elster also knows that the scene of Ulysses and the Sirens has something to do with "character-formation" (78). Using the language of agency, we can say that here the I speaks in its own name—not as the subject of affect, but as the agent of knowledge: I will hear and know; I will willingly allow myself to be bound. Delayed gratification—upstream even from knowledge (although never fully; the revelation, by the *Gedankenschnelle* of global circulating capital, that the circuits of capital are also circuits of knowledge/information, is as much a repetition as a rupture)—is indeed the motor of the self-determination of capital from the fault of a weak European feudalism: the dialectics of Enlightenment.[17] It should be mentioned that the Sirens in the epic are not elaborated in the clichés of the seductive female. They speak clearly, in tones of proclamation; they offer fuller knowledge (*pleiona eidos*); and they claim knowledge of the entire events of the Homeric epic. Ulysses thinks he hears the truth and wants to hear felicitously, by stopping. His past—Circe's advice against the Sirens and his rehearsal of it to his mates—and his future (getting home) "know" this as a lie. Ulysses is not "afraid" of the Sirens. He prevents himself from being absorbed by the present, attends to it in the frame of its passing, in a robust mistrust of the intending subject. He attends to the future anterior—in Elster's words, the "past future" (67).

---

17 The argument from weak European feudalism is taken from Samir Amin, *Unequal Development: An Essay on the Social Formations of Peripheral Capitalism* (Brian Pearce trans.) (New York: Monthly Review Press, 1976), and is developed in Chapter 1 of my book *A Critique of Postcolonial Reason: Toward a History of the Vanishing Present* (Cambridge, MA: Harvard University Press, 1999).

When this species of binding in the Enlightenment (the smooth, historical translation of "Greece" into "Europe" is Elster's) is understood in postcoloniality as mere "fear," there is a failure of translation, to be sure. When so understood, it is fear that is the subject, "fear" that is the metonym for the coercive training of colonialism, epistemic violation (mind-fucking). The subject is not "I," with desires relatively uncoercively rearranged in the violence of birth, not violation.

"Fear is not," is the sentence, not "I have no fear." In this instantiation, Ulysses is derouted and goes to his death in the violent perjury of the Sirens. Yet the mythos is still of a return to an original home. "History"—whatever that means—has uncoupled that mythos from the wife who is spinning there for whose sake the seductresses must be known but avoided.[18] The classic patriarchal story of Ulysses the imperfect rationalist loosely covers the lineament of capitalist civil society—of which one of the most assiduous agents today is global feminism, acting as the chief instrument of a self-declared "international civil society" that shares the impatience of human rights actions from above that I described earlier.

To hope that the absence of fear will have once again displaced itself, perhaps, as responsibility rather than the pride of conscience, Subaltern Studies studies the subaltern as writer of an impossible historical possibility, not only as an object of a new disciplinary opening. Surely that can be taken on board by the word "separation," in what Dipesh Chakrabarty has so accurately described as the consequence of a "rejection." Following Ranajit Guha's *rejection* of Eric Hobsbawm's category "pre-political," Chakrabarty writes that this gesture by Guha "is radical in that it fundamentally pluralizes the history of power in global

---

18 In Homer, Odysseus is managed by women acting in the interest of Zeus and Poseidon. He is let go by the nymph Calypso at the behest of Athene. Circe warns him of the Sirens. It is the Sirens—heraldic proclaimers of lie as truth, double guardians of the paradox, the very mode of fiction—who are never imagined as selved others.

modernity and *separates* it from any universal history of capital."[19] As I have been suggesting, the Odyssean delayed gratification is the motor of capital. The story of responsibility, as it is inscribed in different cultural formations, may be many stories, separate from this big, self-centered one.

The real point may be that Elster himself is also, and rather obviously, mistranslating. Circe, in Odysseus's reported account, gives him the formula for safe listening, with the preventive preservative, if he should *want* to hear: "if you yourself have a will to listen" [*atar autos akouemen ai k'ethelestha*]. Odysseus further reports his misreporting of Circe's ruse to his mates, specifically calling it what the translator calls a "rehearsal." In that telling, the "if" has been transformed into a command: "me alone she bade listen to their voice" [*oion em' enogei op' akouemen*]—intention tied to intent to obey.[20]

Thus the character of Odysseus is distinguished from his sailors. The sailors do not hear. Without this difference, there is no Odysseus. I have been told by a number of people that Elster, not being a literary critic, was not thinking of the text but only of "the story." I note the disciplinary difference, but also note that the story itself is bicameral, at least. Odysseus "transfers" or "translates" Circe's conditional to imperative, which constitutes him as the exception, the hero. In spite of what Elster suggests in his reading of the "story" (though not in the logic of his examples, central banking, and so on), no "man" can bind "himself" alone. He needs a collective, which must be separated from the experiment of imperfect rationality and which will provide the structure of mechanical facilitation and enforcement—thus, the "translation" of

---

19 Dipesh Chakrabarty, "A Small History of Subaltern Studies," in Henry Schwarz and Sangeeta Ray (eds), *A Companion to Postcolonial Studies* (Oxford: Blackwell, 2000), p. 475; emphasis mine. I have no idea if Chakrabarty had this in mind, of course.

20 Homer, *The Odyssey*, 12.49 (p. 452), 12.160 (p. 460).

laborpower (sailors) to knowledgepower (Odysseus) and the translation denied (man binds himself).[21] In Elster's repetition of the gesture of (the idea of) "Europe" as (a translation of) "Greece," there is this epistemic failure of translation. But unlike me at my driver's test, Elster will not fail. Failed translations like his will still drive the world. Nothing succeeds like success, to give it its cliché accolade.

***

Let me access some of your other questions, briefly.

1. I think translation is defined by its difference from the original, straining at identity. The management of this difference as identity is the varied politics of the situation of translation. Hence, I use the words that you have noted, although you do not provide the contexts, without which I cannot write in detail: "fraying," the pathbreaking of politics as difference-as-identity; "rhetoricity," difference from logic made transparent upon accessing the logical "original"; "disarticulation," suppressed to make the original more "articulate." All this is rather more banal than Walter Benjamin's "The Task of the Translator," but Benjamin belongs to the textuality of its time.[22]

2. The only way to get rid of *translatese* is to feel the authority as well as the fragility of the "original," by way of resonance with its irreducible idiomaticity. This can only be explained by looking at actual cases, and I have done rather a lot of that here and there.

3. I hesitate to proceed now into the mysterious thicket of "subaltern language communities," which you also invoke. In fact, I think I will end here, for the sake of saving time. "Transference," and "choosing the

---

21 This point has been developed as a Marxist analysis of telecommunication in Spivak, "Planet-Think/Continent-Think."

22 Walter Benjamin, "The Task of the Translator" (Harry Zohn trans.), in *Selected Writings, Volume 1: 1913–1926* (Marcus Bullock and Michael W. Jennings eds) (Cambridge, MA: Harvard University Press, 1996), pp. 253–63.

tongue," the burden of your other questions, such complexities! I hope we'll have a chance to engage with those, soon. This seems like the beginning of work, not the end of a conversation.

Necessary, Yet Impossible

(2018)*

Some years ago, I described the necessity of translation as follows. There is a more complex description, for those who are interested, which can be found in the journal *Parallax*:

> [T]here is a language we learn first, mixed with the prephe-nomenal [before we appear as a collection of changeful forms of appearance], which stamps the metapsychological [not available to our psychology or mental movements] circuits of "lingual memory" [abstract activatable "memory" as in a computer, within the history of the language, in other words before the generating of a personal memory. Let me read the sentence again.] The child invents a language, beginning by bestowing signification upon a part-object [bottle, breast, finger] (Melanie Klein). The parents "learn" this language. Because they [themselves] speak a named language, the child's language gets inserted into the named language which has a history before the child's birth, which will continue to produce a history after the child's death. As the child begins to navigate this language, he/she is beginning to access the entire interior network of the language, all its possibility of articulations, for which the best metaphor that can be found is—especially in the age of computers—"memory." By comparison, "cultural memory" is

---

* Lecture delivered at the India Habitat Centre, New Delhi, February 22, 2018.

a crude concept of narrative rememorization that attempts to privatize the historical record. [. . .] All languages are originary in this special way and establishes the reflexivity of language as habit, which some twentieth-century theorists of language think of as transcendental. Here the child is translating no locatable content but the very moves of languaging. [. . .] This is not to make an opposition between the natural spontaneity of the emergence of "my languaged place" and the artificial effortfulness of learning foreign languages. Rather, it is to emphasize the metapsychological and telecommunicative nature of the subject's being encountered by the languaging of place. If we entertain the spontaneous/artificial opposition, we will possibly value our own place over all others and thus defeat the ethical [. . .] impulse, a sense of equivalence among languages, rather than a comparison of historico-civilizational content. Étienne Balibar has suggested that equivalence blurs differences, whereas equality requires them. Precisely because civil war may be the allegoric name for an extreme form of untranslatability, it is that "blurring" that we need when we think the pre-phenomenal metapsychological translation of languaging as the condition of possibility of the human. It is necessary for us to keep the *pranbaichitra*—the biological diversity of the outside of the human—out of this.[1]

Melanie Klein, the literalist Jewish daughter of a Basque father, thought of the uterine as an originary original, and the violence of birth as a death into what we now know as the anthropocene.

Lacan describes the pre-subjective drive falling upon the "anatomical trace of a margin or border;"—every word here is full of meaning—"lips, enclosure of the teeth, rim of the anus, penile fissure, vagina,

---

1 Expanded version of "Translation as Culture," included in this volume, pp. 69–88. Last sentence slightly changed.

fissure of eyelid, indeed hollow of the ear. [. . .] Respiratory erogeneity [. . .] comes into play through spasms."[2] In other words, border-thinking is an undecided and primary constituent of our perception of reality itself, where reason is fashioned out of what precedes it. It is of no interest to me if this account is correct and therefore an instrument of cure. The literary critic learns from the singular and unverifiable. Lacan's imagining of the contaminating relationship between the unspeculable work of the drives—unspeculable because you cannot produce its reflection—since the subject has not been started yet—pre-phenomenal, metapsychological—and the normative deviation of fantasy takes us forward into the contrary emergence of a "real." I do not wish to write of perversions, Lacan writes in effect, I would rather deal with fantasy. The normative deviation of fantasy sets the norm by mistakenly establishing the unspeculable as specular and the result of that speculation as a repetition of the same; it is the realm of desire. A necessary translation into the "real." An origin without guarantees. Lacan's famous sentence: "The dog goes meow and the cat goes woof-woof."

> But the synchronic structure is more hidden, and it is this that carries us to the origin. It is metaphor insofar as the first attribution constitutes itself in it—that promulgates "the dog goes meow, the cat goes woof-woof," by which, in one fell swoop, the child, by disconnecting the thing from its cry, raises the sign to the function of the signifier and reality to the sophistics of signification, and by way of a contempt for verisimilitude, opens the diversity of objectifications to verify, of the same thing. (805, **682**)

---

2 Jacques Lacan, *Ecrits* (Bruce Fink trans.) (New York: W. W. Norton, 2006), p. 817, **692**. Henceforth the references to the passages from Lacan will have the French and the English, respectively, cited in the text with page numbers. Translation has always been modified.

I read such passages as poetic intuitions about translation at the origin, where the relationship with a presumed original is a necessary normative deviation without guarantees.

This, then, is my point one: translation is necessary. For my point two, the impossibility of translation, I will refer back to the written exchange between Naveen Kishore and me from which Naveen quoted in his introduction: "*I woke up this morning leaning slightly towards the italicization of my way of being,*" Naveen wrote. "*Aslant. At tangents to the world I am increasingly finding hard to decipher.*"

For me—I responded—aslant is the queer as such, not derived from the straight, which is the most powerful grounding error. The straight is useful but fragile; it keeps all else at bay. The angle of slant is called "imagination"—it is a separator, I wrote, as much as a bringer-together as in the German *Einbildungskraft*. [I was on the Suri Express, an evening train taking me to Kolkata from my five village schools, after a week of deeply instructive but punishing work, and therefore my references here are to the folks in those villages I had just left behind.] I will not, for example—I wrote to Naveen on that moving train—be able to touch my (obviously heterogeneous but still not) students, teachers, co-workers, supervisors, companions, women (yes, a separate category, obviously heterogeneous but still not), unacknowledgeable LGBTQs (heterogeneous but abbreviatable in a set of Latin alphabet capitals), until I know what word or words takes or take the slant for them. I know the gentlemanly ভদ্রলোকী words. In this context, I slightly prefer Tagore's কোথাও আমার হারিয়ে যাবার নেই মানা, মনে মনে to D. L. Roy's কল্পনা কবি-কথন—both class-continuous with the English word carrying the Romantic load.

মন—cognate with "mind" and even with the anthropological "mana"—can slip downward. I have often quoted my illiterate friend Nimai Lohar: মন করে উড়িবার তরে বিধি দেয় না পাখা—mind makes as if to fly, fate/law gives no wings. In Berlin I compared *bidhi* to Cordelia's "bond:"

CORDELIA. Unhappy that I am, I cannot heave
My heart into my mouth. I love your majesty
According to my bond; no more nor less.

KING LEAR. How, how, Cordelia? Mend your speech a little,
Lest you may mar your fortunes.

মন করে উড়িবার তরে বিধি দেয় না পাখা

The impossibility of the flight into translating the untranslatable—
bidhi or bond.

So, caught in the double bind between a necessity of being-in-translation, underived from anything but the effect of an original, before the coming-together of the subject, the gendered space before our proper-ing or propriation, we decide anyway, break the double bind, claim agency through some kind of institutional validation. The oldest validating institution all the world over, before all other socialization kicks in, is reproductive heteronormativity. I will not touch upon it here for lack of time. Since we are here readers, writers, teachers, and that rare phenomenon, an independent publisher, facilitating teaching and writing, I will place a claim to the agency to translate within the authority to publish without entering the space of the "original."

Translation as task, then. My example is Gramsci.

Edward Said and Ranajit Guha, indeed all the Indian subalternists, read Gramsci from this English translation. Therefore, Yashadatta Alone was right in suggesting—I am quoting from memory so I may not be exactly correct—that to be focused on the subaltern is to be focused on class, and thus move away from the consideration of the situation of the Dalit. Although I do think that even the Dalit movement should consider the effects upon it of upward class mobility, I understand that simply to focus on class is to take it away from the real problem. You notice that Gramsci, beginning from slavery, really wanted to find out how one could relate to and relate the subaltern outside of class.

I want the Dalit movement to take Gramsci from his prison cell into their critical Gramsci and give us a Gramsci that is not the Gramsci in the current English translation, or the Gramsci of the extraordinary intellectual agenda that is subaltern studies. The entire Notebook 25 of Gramsci is being translated by Joseph Buttegieg. But remember, even that translation needs to be checked. And don't tell me, you don't have the time to touch Gramsci's plans for an active future, that could not be fulfilled because death claimed him. Incidentally, it was really also rather peculiar that in the very powerful essay in the very first volume of subaltern studies, Ranajit Guha did not mention caste at all. I am sure he had his reasons and I will ask him when I see him next. But I remain puzzled.

In closing, I want to touch on the decolonization of the mind, a phrase learned from Ngũgĩ wa Thiong'o, the Kenyan American writer who will be with us tomorrow—the argument as unusual and brave in 1981 as it is today. Ngũgĩ's general point, which I cite from memory and therefore perhaps incorrectly, was that African first languages were not just private languages. The imperial languages and African lingua francas should continue to be used for general administrative and political purposes, but the first languages should be acknowledged as public by way of the public practice of shared theatre and, finally, novels. Bilingual in Gikuyu and English, Ngũgĩ "translated" his texts, to instruct a wider and different audience into flexing the imagination. I say this last thing because I find these signals embedded in the English translation as I teach his texts.

In our time, in postcolonial countries, decolonizing the mind in translation practices has mostly not yet been activated or achieved. We tend to translate from translations into imperial languages. I believe my old friend Ackbar Abbas has a theory that, since postcolonials would otherwise read the text from the imperial language which they would understand at best imperfectly, it is not illogical in the postcolonial situation to translate texts translated into the imperial language into the local language from that imperial-language translation rather than from the original. I think such theories accept the past of colonization not as changeful history but as unchanging inevitability.

I know that we must not translate from English translations and thus forget the most important task of the translator toward the original, to be haunted by its ghost, to imagine it as first language, to be forgiven for the death of its phonic substance, its sound body, allow its ghost to flourish. Do not tell me your university does not have language departments. Mine didn't either. In globality, there are one million ways of deep-learning languages. If you don't have the money to do it at French and German institutes in your capital city, find it somewhere. I am talking about the person who loves the text enough to want to translate it, not every student or reader. S/he goes toward the original, which is the only key to the social formations within the space where the texts were produced.

This last bit is taken from my lecture at Jamia Milia Islamia yesterday (see "What Is It, Then, to Translate?" in this volume), addressed to a particular friend who would like to translate Mahasweta Devi into Arabic, and therefore I am urging him to want to enter Bengali and be haunted by its ghost. For, translation's first contribution is to kill the phonic and phonetic—and therefore sociocultural?—existence of the text. We walk under the shadow of that loss.

In order to push my Syrian friend into it, I declaimed some very well-known lines and their excellent translation yesterday, and I think I will do it again. If you were there yesterday, just bear with it because that stuff is certainly worth repeating. So, here goes:

Here is the opening of a famous poem *Meghnadbadh Kabya* (The Slaying of Meghnad) that Sankha Ghosh and I will include in a series of bilingual Bengali texts on the model of the Loeb Classical Library of European Antiquity, that has lasted 150 years.

সম্মুখে সমরে পড়ি, বীর-চূড়ামণি
বীরবাহু, চলি যবে গেলা যমপুরে
অকালে, কহ, হে দেবি অমৃতভাষিণি,
কোন্ বীরবরে বরি সেনাপতি-পদে,
পাঠাইলা রণে পুনঃ রক্ষঃকুলনিধি
রাঘববারি ?

Now here is the extraordinary translation by Clinton Seeley, Euro-American, who has loved Bengali well enough to be able to tackle this difficult task, and in spite of the magnificence of his literalist translation echoing or attempting to echo as much as possible the grandeur of the Bengali, especially the fantastic proper names, you will hear the corpse of the original sending out its ghost on the translation:

When in face-to-face combat Vīrabāhu, crown-gem of
warriors, fell and went before his time to Yama's city—
speak, O goddess of ambrosial speech—which best of warriors
did the foe of Rāghava, treasure-trove among that clan
of Rākṣasas, designate commander, then send fresh
to the battle?

This is why the translator must inhabit the original, taking the idea of the right to an original positive law.

I summarize, then. Where translation is necessary, we are produced. Where translation is impossible, we surrender actively to the impossibility to make our practice stronger. Where translation is a task, we forget the first two and hunker down to be as responsible to the original as possible. In this translating, we must not translate from the imperial language translations of other texts. I speak to the many translators present in the audience. Don't let English help you avoid intellectual labor learning to love the language of the underived original. Necessary and impossible. Claim it as a task. Get yourself invited to an adventure.

What Is It, Then, to Translate?

(2018)*

As you know, as you just heard, my title is "What Is It, Then, to Translate?" I want to open with the position implicit in the assumption that it is possible to translate. I want to open with the right to an original. Whenever we speak of a "right," we are speaking of something like constitutions. The idea of rights is conceptual. The human being is much larger than concepts. That is why, the fact of an original language is simply a fact for anyone who can give and take in a language. All human beings learn the language or a mixture of languages in their parent's arms, or their caregiver's arms, or, under extreme politics, sometimes even in displaced persons' camps. Whatever that may be, no human being can be separated from an ability to make meaning associated with the time before reason has begun.

When we consider things from the perspective of social power, it is perfectly possible to deny a language the status of the original. Today is the 21st of February. It is the anniversary of a major event where the right to an original was claimed in blood in what is now Bangladesh, in 1952.

Students and bystanders, among them a child, were killed and injured by police as they claimed the right to their language. This was not just a claim to an original but a claim to constitutionality itself—to

---

* Lecture delivered at the Department of English, Jamia Millia Islamia Central University, New Delhi, February 21, 2018.

be the language of governance, of civil society, and of the juridico-legal. As the citizens' desires, wishes, and needs are translated by the state into policy, and themselves into resistance if necessary, it must be in the meaning-articulation of Bangla, said the student activists of 1948–52. Urdu and Bangla were both established as state languages for what was then East Pakistan on 21st of February 1956 and this was indeed related to the subsequent movement of establishing an independent nation-state, also with considerable bloodshed and war-rape in the name of the language.

FIGURE 1. Woman under a tree at the rehabilitation center, January 1973. *Photograph and courtesy: Gayatri Chakravorty Spivak.*

Today, speaking about translation, let us all remember the 21st of February 1952, when the claim to an original, altogether related to the possibility of authoritative and definitive translations, also claimed the blood of the claimants.

I want to move now to a situation where the claim to public space—conceptual space, if you like—in the field of power is staged in a different way. It reflects the difference between colonialism and globalization. Not in the nation-state, but in the fringes of history, namely, among the very bottom layer of societies, where today, a particularly insidious kind of exploitation called "development"—whose synonyms, not translations (please mark the difference) are *bikash* or *unnayan*—is practiced. Often this is called sustainable development; but in fact some of us call this sustainable underdevelopment, because what is sustained is cost efficiency and profit maximization in the face of the minimum of environmental plausibility that can be maintained—therefore, sustainable underdevelopment.

When I asked what development meant for him, a student from a small new rural university in Nigeria said "Improvements in the standard of living. How to measure—once a person can afford two square meals a day, have access to clean and potable water, can send kids to schools." Health, in other words, education, and welfare. In order, supposedly, to secure this, I have suggested elsewhere, "development" is an insertion into the circuit of capital, without developing the subject of development, of capital's ethical, or even appropriate social, use. The development of the subject is apparently in the self-interest of the "underdeveloped," but the larger pattern is in the interest of developed capital. Development workers do not speak the local versions of language spoken by those who are being developed. The policymakers for development consider languages a problem. Especially in Africa.

Many first languages in Africa were not systematized by the missionaries. These are in use today, by underclass communities but also by highly educated folks, because of the appeal of the mother tongue, and by electoral candidates, who campaign in these languages and maybe provoke ethnic violence, typically before elections. There is tremendous dialectal continuity between these languages, and when there is not, there is an enviable level of multilingualism among adjacent subaltern communities. These communities write on the memory, and, you can say, only half-fancifully, they practice a prescientific digitization. In other words, the lessons of nineteenth- and twentieth-century linguistics—stabilizing the language by giving it a name; putting it in a box separating it from other languages; grammatizing; establishing orthography, vocabulary, and script, among other things; maybe establishing a historical moment—become symptomatic when confronted with these languages. These lessons depend on a limited concept of writing, whereas writing on memory as these unsystematized first languages do, creates a stream that today's digitization has exponentially enhanced.

Understandably, then, a certain vanguard of the discipline of linguistics is now investigating the ways in which these unwritten and unsystematized languages were taught or absorbed in the context of prevailing multilingualism. It should be mentioned that we are not speaking of languages that are going extinct and that many institutions are seeking to document and preserve. These attempts are altogether admirable, but they are not identical with the work that I am describing.

Now, suppose we acknowledge that the business of sustainable underdevelopment is today the greatest barrier to the creation of a level playing field. Much of the failure of this process, even when well intentioned, is due to the lack of the sort of responsibility enhanced by the teaching of literature as the cultivation of an imagination that can flex into another's space—in order to translate, the most intimate act of reading. It is not possible for the development lobby today to attend upon those who are to be developed—inserted into the circuit of capital without adequate subject formation—so that their desires can be rearranged into wanting the possibility of development in mind and body, regulated by themselves. We assume, however, that among development workers there are some who really do wish to touch the ones who are being developed.

Let us remind ourselves that the humanities are worldly, not global. Let us also remind ourselves that this distinction obliges the humanities to work through collectivities, not only through global networks (even as we also remember that this is a taxonomy, not a binary opposition).

We further remind ourselves that we draw a response from the other—act "response-ibility"—through language. And finally, on this list of self-reminders, let us remind ourselves that the subaltern, on the fringes of history, located in language, is not generalizable. Although this is not usually the case, we can indeed find some sincere people among health workers and agricultural workers. Typically, job descriptions for development workers do not include language requirements. And, also typically, the best-intentioned development workers may learn a well-established lingua franca such as Kiswahili or IsiZulu and feel that they are preparing themselves, unaware that to those who customarily use the unsystematized first languages, these lingua francas are themselves also languages of power.

Some of us are trying to push for the establishment of a language requirement into development job descriptions and for the creation of simple on-the-field techniques for those few well-meaning development workers to learn the unsystematized first languages of those who are being "developed," and thus to put digitalization into the service of the continuous and persistent destruction of subalternity and pass agency to the subaltern.

I am speaking, then, of agency for the condition of possibility of translation—the right to claim an original. My first example was from the play of colonialism and sub-colonialism in the aftermath of post-coloniality. My second example comes from contemporary globality, where the narratives of postcoloniality persist but are not dominant. Here the claim to constitutionality is so undone by precolonial structures of corruption and domination combined with the absolute technological superiority of the digital that our own resistant motives just would not suffice.

Having spoken of establishing the possibility of translation by constitutionally validating the "original," let us think specifically of the situation of translation.

Translation's first contribution is to kill the phonic and phonetic existence of the text. We walk under the shadow of that loss, whether we are thinking of poetry, or development. In the field of constitutionality and global governance, our real problem is elite synonym-hunting, incomprehensible to those who are being developed.

I have written at great length about the useless elite translations of the Universal Declaration of Human Rights, incomprehensible to the subaltern. Rather must we understand how we lexicalize the old imperial languages. *Ishkule jabar pathe poshtapisher pasher dokan theke duto penshil kinlam.* This is creolity. Some of us have given the name of creolization to the movement of history itself. It took a Buddha to choose creole so he could talk to the people—a political gesture that was destroyed almost immediately after his death. It took a Marcel Proust to write: "What is French but false Latin?" because he wanted to stand to defend the accent of Françoise, a maid servant.

But it is the situation within poetry that makes most tragic the deaths of the phonic body upon which translation exists. Here is the opening of a famous poem *Meghnadbadh Kabya* (The Slaying of Meghnad) that Sankha Ghosh and I will include in a series of bilingual Bengali texts on the model of the Loeb Classical Library of European Antiquity, that has lasted 150 years.

সম্মুখে সমরে পড়ি, বীর-চূড়ামণি
বীরবাহু, চলি যবে গেলা যমপুরে
অকালে, কহ, হে দেবি অমৃতভাষিণি,
কোন্ বীরবরে বরি সেনাপতি-পদে,
পাঠাইলা রণে পুনঃ রক্ষঃকুলনিধি
রাঘববারি ?

Now here is the extraordinary translation by Clinton Seeley, Euro-American, who has loved Bengali well enough to be able to tackle this difficult task, and in spite of the magnificence of his literalist translation echoing or attempting to echo as much as possible the grandeur of the

Bengali, especially the fantastic proper names, you will hear the corpse of the original sending out its ghost on the translation:

> When in face-to-face combat Vīrabāhu, crown-gem of
> warriors, fell and went before his time to Yama's city—
> speak, O goddess of ambrosial speech—which best of warriors
> did the foe of Rāghava, treasure-trove among that clan
> of Rākṣasas, designate commander, then send fresh
> to the battle?

This is why the translator must enter the spirit of the original, prepared to write much better than conceptual-constitutional, indeed taking the idea of right outside of positive law—underived right that belongs to the fact that both the language of the translator and the language of that which is translated are indeed first languages, each learned before reason begins. I am a teacher and student of comparative literature and I want to cite here from a piece that I wrote some time ago, because it brings my mother's virtue in front of you and shows how much she has affected what I am telling you today.

I am standing with my mother in Charles de Gaulle Airport in Paris. For a week we have fed our ears on academic French. Suddenly I hear an exchange in the harsh accents of upstate New York. I turn to my mother and say, in Bengali, roughly this: "Hard to listen to this stuff." And my mother: "Dear, a mother tongue." My mother, caught up as she was in the heyday of resistance to the Raj, still extended imaginative charity to English.

> I have told this story before and will say it again. Today I hold
> on to the fact that there is a language we learn first, mixed with
> the prephenomenal, which stamps the metapsychological cir-
> cuits of "lingual memory." The child invents a language, begin-
> ning by bestowing signification upon a part-object (Melanie
> Klein). The parents "learn" this language. Because they speak
> a named language, the child's language gets inserted into the

named language with a history before the child's birth, which will continue after its death. As the child begins to navigate this language, he/she is beginning to access the entire interior network of the language, all its possibility of articulations, for which the best metaphor that can be found is—especially in the age of computers—"memory." By comparison, "cultural memory" is a crude concept of narrative rememorization that attempts to privatize the historical record. Comparative literature imagines that each language may be activated in this special way and makes an effort to produce a simulacrum through the reflexivity of language as habit. Here we translate not the content but the very moves of languaging. We can provisionally call this peculiar form of translation before translation the "comparison" in comparative literature. This is not to make an opposition between the natural spontaneity of the emergence of "my languaged place" and the artificial effortfulness of learning foreign languages. Rather, it is to emphasize the metapsychological and telecommunicative nature of the subject's being encountered by the languaging of place. If we entertain the spontaneous/artificial opposition, we will possibly value our own place over all others and thus defeat the ethical comparativist impulse, a sense of equivalence among languages, rather than a comparison of historico-civilizational content. Étienne Balibar has suggested that equivalence blurs differences, whereas equality requires them. Precisely because civil war—started by the violence against the students on 21 February 1952, for example—may be the allegoric name for an extreme form of untranslatability, it is that "blurring" that comparative literature needs.[1]

---

1 Expanded version of "Translation as Culture," included in this volume, pp. 69–88. Last sentence slightly changed.

Our rethinking of comparativism starts, then, with the admission that as language, languages are equivalent, and that deep language learning must implode into a simulacrum of lingual memory. We must wait for this implosion, which we sense after the fact, or, perhaps, others sense in us, and we thus enter into a relationship with the language that is rather different from the position of a comparer, a charter of influence, who supposedly occupies a place above the linguistic traditions to be compared. When we rethink comparativism, we think of translation as an active practice rather than a crutch. I have often said that translation is the most intimate act of reading. Thus translation comes to inhabit the new politics of comparativism as reading itself, in the broadest possible sense.

My mother reminded me that English was a mother tongue. I went from that to understanding that all languages, when they are mother tongues or first languages, are learned before reason. I thought comparative literature should try to access the impossible limit over "foreign" language as it was learned before reason. A prayer to be haunted by its ghost. This is of course also the task of translation. A prayer to be haunted by the original as first language.

I believe my old friend Ackbar Abbas has a theory that, since postcolonials would otherwise read the text from the imperial language which they would understand at best imperfectly, it is not illogical in the postcolonial situation to translate texts translated into the imperial language into the local language from that imperial-language translation rather than from the original. I think such theories accept the past of colonization not as changeful history but as unchanging inevitability.

We must not translate from English translations and thus forget the most important task of the translator toward the original, to be haunted by its ghost, to imagine it as first language, to be forgiven for the death of its phonic substance, allow its ghost to flourish. Do not tell me your university does not have language departments. Mine didn't either. In globality, there are one million ways of deep-learning languages. If you don't have the money to do it at French and German institutes in your capital city, find it somewhere. I am talking about the person who loves the text enough to want to translate it, not every student or reader. S/he goes toward the original, which is the only key to the social formations within the space where the texts were produced.

Think again of the good development worker turning agency back to the subaltern. I quote Prof. Claire Bowern's formula for the worker confronted by an unwritten creole:

■ Figure out what type of language data workers need
  - Greetings
  - Basic/common vocabulary
  - Domain-specific vocabulary (e.g. health, construction)
  - Short sentences
  - Questions
  - Ways to address people appropriately
  - Provide a way for workers to learn the basics that doesn't rely on a lot of pre-analysis by linguists/creation of pedagogical materials
  - Web site where speakers can record pre-specified sentences.
  - 'Notebook' format where workers can record vocabulary, phrases, and sentences, and request translations.
  - Primarily mobile (i.e. record and upload from phones)
  - Online pooling/sharing data
  - Tips for language learning without guides (sort of like *Where There Is No Doctor* for language learning)
  - Make it easier for workers to practice with speakers
  - Examine the structural/social setups in field sites that make it easier to develop language skills:

- Down time
  - Time to socialize outside of work with locals
  - Immersion language acquisition settings?
  - Dedicated time to language learning before the assignment?
  - Language buddies?

And then, when the development worker wishes to translate this original so that it would feed into a statistic, these first steps are undone because the disciplinary formation of statisticians, even when they provide least corrupt statistics, is not one that can be amenable to the sort of auto-critique that such a task of translation would require. And, if you want to hear about the general run of development workers that gives you another story.

Invited by good middle-level global networking development leaders, I have attended many R&D—research and development— meetings all around the world, mostly in Africa. Whenever I encounter agricultural disciplinarians who work in the development field, basically providing good statistics—I ask them, individual group by individual group, never in public knowledge management sessions: Do you get to the people for whom you are providing developmental statistics? Yes, they say, and I ask, How? We collect the data, train research assistants, send them out into the field to validate the data and they come back to us having touched the people we are developing. So the data is pre-established and then validated. At this stage I always ask if there are ever any surprise. And I always get the answer "no."

Therefore, where social justice can be approached by giving agency back to the three continent subaltern—there is a barrier between that fragile workspace and the arena of the confident policymakers. I want to give you two examples.

One is an email I received from Dr. Ravi Kumar, not personally known to me, last week. Now you must understand that I respect this colleague. I simply think that the arena which seduces them do not allow them with the translation work of social justice that I have been trying hard to describe so far. Here is the email:

I just returned from the 6th edition of the World Government Summit, Dubai where I was hired as an Interpreter for the Summit. The Summit was held in Dubai from February 11–13, 2018 where our Prime Minister Narendra Modi was invited as the Guest of Honor. This is an annual event conceptualized and hosted by the Government of United Arab Emirates.

I had the opportunity to interpret for some of the top leaders of the world such as Edouard Philippe, the Prime Minister of France; Prof. Klaus Schwab, Founder and Chair of World Economic Forum–Davos; Agnel Gurria, Secretary General, OECD; Princess Haya Bint Al Hussein, Chair of International Humanitarian City; Christine Lagarde, Managing Director of the IMF; Jim Yong Kim, President, world Bank; Richard Quest, CNN; Prof. Michio Kaku, Physicist and Futurist; Bill McDermott, CEO, SAP; Deepak Chopra, Public Speaker and Prominent Figure of New Age Movement; Maurice Levy, CEO Publicis; Dr. Tedros Adhanom, Director General, WHO; Roberto Azevedo, Director General of WTO; Audrey Azoulay, Director General of UNESCO; Sheikh Abdullah Bin Zayed al Nahyan, Chairman of the Education and Human Resources Council, UAE.

It is important to note that since its inception in 2013, this event has become one of the largest events in the Arab world and has emerged as the common platform for sharing knowledge with presence of representatives from government, futurism, technology, and innovation. It provides a platform for thought leadership and acts like a networking hub for policymakers, experts and pioneers in human development. It also showcases innovations, best practices and smart solutions to inspire creativity to tackle these future challenges.

This year the event hosted more than 4,000 delegates coming from 140 countries. The Summit was held in partnership with the International Monetary Fund (IMF), the World Bank, the World Economic Forum, the UN, the Organisation for Economic Co-operation and Development (OECD), the Abu Dhabi Fund for Development, the Dubai Municipality, and El Centro Latin americano de Adimistracion para el Desarollo.

Having the opportunity to provide Interpretation services at such a platform was a unique experience in itself. Not just [that] I found myself amidst such eminent dignitaries of the world, it was also a challenge to perform my duties as an Interpreter well. Since I regularly update myself on various subject matters, luckily my overall understanding of IT, Artificial intelligence, databank, Politics, Public Policy, Business, International Commerce, UNO and its functions, Law and current affairs helped me position myself well during interpreting. Thus, I was able to successfully carry out my interpreting task with ease. . . . [T]his summit was yet another occasion to challenge myself and learn new things during the rendering process. I returned to New Delhi, my workplace with a rich experience of what the future holds and what it is likely to look like.

[Author Ravi Kumar is a seasoned translator and interpreter for Hindi-English-Spanish and Founder of Modlingua Group.]

To educate the young into this digital saving of epistemological and imaginative labor is a kind of shrinking. Listen to its description:

Live Interpretation or Media Interpretation is another upcoming concept in the field of Interpretation. Professionally trained Interpreters capable of delivering quality services will certainly find themselves getting an edge over others in this niche area. I feel fortunate to have successfully conducted Intensive Live

Interpretation training for a selected few employees of Zee Media whom one shall see performing their duties as Live Interpreters on TV screens from next month. This will be the first time ever in the history of Indian media that live interpretation of news will be attempted. Modlingua wishes good luck to this first-generation of Live Media Interpreters to lead the pack and scale heights.

The successful completion of this training module is yet another lead taken by Modlingua, which has always been aiming at not just providing quality services to its clients all over the world but also to train and prepare a sound and competent next generation of linguists who can work in diverse fields with international standards of professionalism. We also wish to see other renowned media houses catching up on this novel concept thus, opening newer avenues for upcoming linguists.

Our Best wishes to the first generation of Media Interpreters in India.

Compare this to the live interpretation undertaken by the interpreters in the truth and reconciliation commissions in South Africa, Latin America, in the Balkans. Because they had to be translating immediately into the language of the aggressors and yet speak as if what was coming down in the immediate future of the translator's experience, what the victim would be saying, was part of the translator's lived past, so to do such stressful persuasive translation, took so much out of them that they dried out after short periods of time. No resemblance at all to these young people being described above.

And now here's one form letter to me, which once again shows how a temptation to meet award-winning people can take our focus away from the real task of translation. I am going through these in such detail because ambitious young people from so called "developing" countries get tempted by this and thus get habituated into being led away from working for thick social justice.

14 December 2017

Dear Gayatri Chakravorty Spivak,

On behalf of the hosts and the steering committee of Culture-Summit 2018, Abu Dhabi, it is our pleasure to invite you to attend the Summit as one of the featured participants in your capacity as a thought leader and influencer in the worlds of culture, media, public policy and international affairs. The event will take place in Abu Dhabi, United Arab Emirates from Sunday, 8 April to Thursday, 12 April 2018. CultureSummit is the world's first high-level summit that convenes leaders from the worlds of the arts, media, public policy and technology, to identify ways that culture can raise awareness, build bridges and promote positive change. Last year's inaugural event was attended by 450 delegates from 80 countries, including internationally acclaimed visual artist Idris Khan, Academy Award–winning composer and conductor Tan Dun, MacArthur Award–winning choreographer Liz Lerman, and representatives from Ministries of Culture from around the world. This year's programme, titled *Unexpected Collaborations: Forging New Connections Between Heritage and Innovation, Near and Far, Creativity and Purpose*, will focus on partnerships that are unique, different and that blend tradition and innovation. Workshops, presentations and performances throughout the event will engage participants in expanding on their ideas about the role of culture in improving our world. This year, a special portion of the programme will take place at the newly opened Louvre Abu Dhabi, with events and tours scheduled exclusively for participants of CultureSummit 2018. You can learn more about CultureSummit 2018 and the programme and objectives by visiting the website. . . . CultureSummit 2018 is hosted by the Department of Culture and Tourism–Abu

Dhabi, and is presented in collaboration with The Rothkopf Group, an interactive media and advisory firm specialising in international issues, and TCP Ventures, LLC, a producer of artistic endeavours and an advisory firm focused on cultural matters.

We invite you to join as a speaker in one or more of the sessions. We will be happy to work with you to find a role that will ensure your visit is worthwhile and rewarding. We hope that you will be able to attend this unique event where you can share your insight and expertise, as well as collaborate with other leading professionals in the fields of culture, technology and public policy. We kindly request your response by 18 January 2018. To RSVP . . .

Translation, as I said a bit ago, is the most intimate act of reading. If reading is understood as surrendering oneself into the other's space—the text's space—as much as possible, it is also a preparation for the ethical reflexes to act if the call to the ethical interrupts the epistemological preparation for imaginative flexibility. The imagination in training, flexing out, embraces the other in a critical intimacy which does not resemble the proclamation of interpretation that is the style of global capitalism.

To end on a positive note let me take you to Pramila Lohar's potato field, a veritable *seminarium*, for her whole group, belonging to the people I work with in the extreme west of Birbhum, is crazed now about old fertilizer, old seeds. Nothing imposed by me, a counter-colonialism, not self-declared decolonization. Because our work is so different from large-scale development, here constitutionality is once again indistinguishable from desire.

FIGURE 2. *Photograph and courtesy: Gayatri Chakravorty Spivak.*

There's a bit of land to cross before I get there, and a bit of water gathered. As I start to take off my sneakers, Suresh Roy, a co-worker, quickly builds a soft bridge, and I walk across. Let this effective bridge-building be a parable for us.

FIGURE 3. *Photograph and courtesy: Gayatri Chakravorty Spivak.*

Of course we must learn to market our skills, and make the best of our budgets. Racialized, colonized, gendered spaces should use digitized resources to access long-withheld information, not mistaking the tool for the performance. But I also hope that you will continue to build soft bridges with language, only to be washed away and built again, rather than put together global access circuits that change the desire to flex the imagination toward the other into lucrative digital alternatives for global policies of sustainable underdevelopment. Let me close with something I often quote, the only blog I ever wrote for the World Economic Forum:

> Normally our desire is to do things ourselves or for ourselves. In good literary teaching, the student is taught carefully to hang out in the space of the other—understand what s/he confronts in terms of the unknown person who wrote what s/he confronts. This is the secret of the ethical and the democratic. One has to stay with it, not follow easy steps so that one can say, "I have helped you." [. . .] The long-term implementation of our Covenant's values, in addition to persuading CEOs and heads of state, calls for the teaching of the humanities at all levels and in all places so that the desire for social justice [. . .] can inhabit souls long-term, not always susceptible to evaluation by checking statistically how each item on a list is institutionally fulfilled. Huge and detailed country-by-country statistical tables are no doubt useful, but, in terms of sustaining an improved world, we have to look at the fact that nations are not monolithic abstract averages, and that evaluations are remote factgathering which often do not reflect everyday reality. [Here I said a word about religion which I must skip in the interest of time. . . .] We teachers of the humanities—literature and philosophy—at our best train the imagination into knowing ourselves differently, and knowing the world differently, so that we want to work for social justice under sometimes very trying circumstances rather than have to be checked following enforcement.

Today the emphasis in education is acquiring digital speed. In order to be able to use the digital for social justice, the soul has to be trained slowly, and that is where literary training as I have described it comes into play. Recently, at the celebration of the Nigerian writer Chinua Achebe's life, the positive effect of his literary writings was repeatedly emphasized. With my experience of work in Africa, I was obliged to say that, below a certain class line, Nigerians had no idea who he was and what he wrote. The task therefore was to expand the circle of Nigerians who could not only read but also learn from the literary. [...] If we are thinking the world, we must—absolutely— remember the many languages that make meaning for its peoples. As a doctor working in Kenya who refuses to be a top-down health worker remarked: "The people will understand Swahili, but you can't speak to their heart unless you speak their language: 'I'm getting what you're saying, but I'm not taking it in.'" That *is* a basic human value: talking to the heart. If you think it is inconvenient, as it is, indeed, don't dream of improving the world.

(When the young Nigerian student from the rural university said, So we are trying to change what development stands for, Joseph Oduro-Frimpong, a colleague from Ghana, said as he was speaking on the phone to our group, Yes, we ourselves will then be developed. And I would like to emphasize that we must come down from the summit of global meetings focused on self-praise, name dropping, quantity rather than quality, and saving imaginative labor; and listen to develop ourselves, to change ourselves epistemologically, the way we think of ourselves as acting on and for others, we must pray to be haunted by the ghost of the others—no top-down philanthropy.)

Knowledge depends on cooking the soul with slow learning, not the instant soup of a one-size-fits-all toolkit. The world is not populated by humanoid drones. You cannot produce a toolkit for "a moral metric," or if you do, you will be disappointed.

What is it, then, to translate? Deep language learning of the original, straining to be haunted by it as it can be learned before reason. Effacing oneself, being as little as possible so the text speaks. Never to translate from an imperial language translation—never. Mahmoud, much of this is in the hope that you will take this seriously—not because I want it but because you do. I have spoken in the hope that one or two of the translating students and teachers here will have overheard our conversation. Thank you.

TEACHING, LEARNING, UNLEARNING TRANSLATION

Translation in the Undergraduate Curriculum

(2009)*

I have been a translator for over thirty years, translating different kinds of documents into English. At a recent MLA convention I spoke on a project of translating from the French into Bengali.[1] My experience as a translator convinces me that translation ought to be taught as a practice rather than embraced as a convenience with no footprint. I should also mention that I have been involved with a vision of globalizing comparative literature even longer than I have been a translator, unless you count my lost translation of Edmund Spenser's *Faerie Queene* into Bengali while I was preparing to take my punishing BA honors exam at the University of Calcutta in 1959.

It is taken for granted these days that the United States is a monolingual country. I will not go into the theoretical details of the monolingualism of the other here (Derrida). I will simply note that, living in New York, I am daily reminded that it is at least a bilingual city. If you keep your ears open on the streets, you can begin to hear the 170 languages that are spoken. The many languages prove that borders are becoming porous. The languages are not present in the kind of deep learning status that we can encourage at universities and colleges. But

---

* First published in *ADFL Bulletin* 41(2) (2009): 26–30.

1 My project is to translate Assia Djebar's *Loin de Médine* (Paris: Albin Michel, 1991) for Narigrantha Prabartana in Bangladesh.

then, as I said, we take it for granted that the United States is monolingual in English and, additionally, that speed is the essence of our brief as university teachers, speed producing results that can be ascertained.

Two things in my academic experience contradict these assumptions of monolingualism and speed. One, I have myself been an undergraduate in continuing education at Columbia for the last five years, learning Chinese. The extraordinary enthusiasm of the undergraduates as they go into the mysterious thickets of this language never ceases to amaze me. Two, I direct the Institute of Comparative Literature and Society at Columbia, which carries an undergraduate major, where all the students are ferocious language learners, often studying in great depth languages that certainly do not fall into the purview of commonly taught languages.

Therefore, I continue to cherish the conviction that translation ought to be taught as a practice. however, I must also listen to the wisdom of the times, which says US kids won't learn languages. I have been teaching History of Literary Criticism, in English translation, for a decade now or more. There was some initial objection to my teaching this course, because I'm not a trained classicist. But I think my colleagues have come to accept my pigheadedness, and I am allowed to teach the course from time to time. I am not going to give you a syllabus, because although the method is appropriate to our discussion, I devised the course not with a view to the teaching of languages but simply to make the students aware that texts, especially ancient texts, were sometimes written or composed before English came into being. To develop in students a historical sense, if you like.

Rather than speak theoretically, I present a specific sample course. The course is devised specifically for the possibility that students, especially undergraduate students, will become interested in learning languages if the teacher teaches through "problems in translation." The method is to introduce a language-conscious comparativist element into undergraduate teaching, using the strengths of traditional comparative literature. With the budget crunch and the consequent cut in the humanities budgets, the course is utopian. I have always had an obstinate disinclination to cut myself down to the size prescribed by circumstances where the humanities are considered expendable. It should also be said that perhaps this plan fits the more elite institutions of education. The reader will make the necessary calculations, without ignoring the ideas altogether.

I believe that globalizing the curriculum must be distinguished from culture wars and canon debates. a globalized world does not provide or endorse a pure non-Eurocentric gaze. Unless we include Europe in our attempt at a historical study of regionalist and world-system intuitions, teaching through problems in translation will exoticize and not offer a practical program, one that moves between the relatively familiar and the unfamiliar. This sample course will, I hope, point the way to what may be called cross-civilization courses. Unlike most courses of this type, it is primary-text-based. It covers a significant depth of time, with a transdisciplinary method that places the discussion of ethical systems at the center. The text-based nature of the course should reveal to students that we cannot access ethical systems without deep language-learning. I hope that it will provide the means for breaking down the opposition, now operative, between Western and other "major" cultures. The course I describe here focuses on the Mediterranean. Ideally, such courses will include material on cultures that have been excluded from the category of major, such as those of Southeast Asia.

Typically, students read the texts in English. The instructor, who knows the original language, teaches through attending to the problems of translation, on a level accessible to the young student who does not know the language. Given the global constituency of the New York classroom, there is usually a single student or group of students who can navigate the original better than the rest of the class. This difference creates patterns of sharing that are pedagogically useful. Typically the class is taught by guest professors for different languages. Postdoctoral fellows or graduate teaching assistants with special language skills can also be used.

The course is titled Ocean Rims: The Mediterranean. The assumption is that ocean rims are more interesting cultural units than continentally defined civilizations. The Mediterranean rim is especially fertile ground for developing this thematic. The course can also be taught with reference to the Indian Ocean rim, the Asian rim, Oceania, and the like. This series is particularly appropriate for undergraduate training in the context of the deleterious effects of the clash-of-civilizations concept. The description below is a general outline only; the designer is not a specialist of the area. Such a course needs a group of teachers who have different languages and who can think new thoughts in this innovative area.

The course idea of the Mediterranean may be found in Fernand Braudel's *Mediterranean and the Mediterranean World in the Age of Philip II*.[2] For the students the explanation of the task of the course will come from Polybius:

> Previously the doings of the world had been, so to say, dispersed [. . .] ; but ever since this date [220 BCE] history has been an organic whole, and the affairs of Italy and Libya [Africa] have been interlinked with those of Greece and Asia, all leading up to one end.[3]

The languages needed are Greek, Latin, Arabic, Middle French, French, and Turkish.

---

2 Fernand Braudel, *Mediterranean and the Mediterranean World in the Age of Philip II*, 2 VOLS (Siân Reynolds trans.) (New York: Harper & Row, 1972–73).
3 Polybius, *The Histories of Polybius* (W. R. Paton trans., F. W. Walbank and Christian Habicht revd.), Loeb Classical Library 128 (Cambridge, MA: Harvard University Press, 2010), pp. 8–9, 1.3.3–4.

Outline for Ocean Rims: The Mediterranean

WEEK 1

Selections from *The Odyssey*

Background reading: Jon Elster, *Ulysses and the Sirens*; Jacques Derrida, "Mochlos"; Richard Rand et al. (eds), *Logomachia*; François Hartog, *Memories of Odysseus*

The teacher should convey to undergraduates that *The Odyssey* is not only a text of classical European antiquity but also, and perhaps more important, a text of the ancient Mediterranean.

WEEK 2

Selections from Herodotus, *The Persian Wars* (440 BCE), outlining his sense of Egypt and Greece

Background reading: François Hartog, *Mirror of Herodotus*; Jean-François Breton, *Arabia Felix from the Time of the Queen of Sheba: Eighth Century B.C. to First Century A.D.* (Albert LaFarge trans.); Charles Freeman, *Egypt, Greece, and Rome: Civilizations of the Ancient Mediterranean*

WEEK 3

Selections from Polybius, *Histories* (200–118 BCE), Book 1

Background reading: Paul Cartledge et al. (eds), *Hellenistic Constructs: Essays in Culture, History, and Historiography*; Craige B. Champion, *Cultural Politics in Polybius's Histories*; Maria Eugenia Aubet, *The Phoenicians and the West: Politics, Colonies and Trade*; G. W. B. Huntingford, *The Periplus of the Erythraean Sea*; Arrian in A. Diller, *The Tradition of the Minor Greek Geographers* (pp. 102–46); O. A. W. Dilke, *Greek and Roman Maps* (pp. 130–44)

WEEK 4

Augustine, *Confessions* (397–401)

Background reading: selections from Derrida, "Circumfession"; J. E. Merdinger, *Rome and the African Church in the Time of Augustine*

WEEK 5

Selections from Abu Hayaan (987–1076)

Background reading: Gil Anidjar, "Our Place in Al-Andalus"; David Luscombe et al. (eds), *The New Cambridge Medieval History* (VOL. 4, PT. 1)

WEEK 6

La chanson de Roland (1040–1115)

Background reading: H. T. Norris, *Islam in the Balkans: Religion and Society between Europe and the Arab World*; Sharon Kinoshita, *Medieval Boundaries: Rethinking Difference in Old French Literature*; Donald J. Kagay and Joseph T. Snow (eds), *Medieval Iberia: Essays on the History and Literature of Medieval Spain*

WEEK 7

Selections from Ibn Khaldun (1332–1406), *Al-Muqaddima*

Background reading: selections from Antony Black, *History of Islamic Political Thought: From the Prophet to the Present*; Aziz al-Azmeh, *Ibn Khaldun in Modern Scholarship: A Study in Orientalism*; Yves Lacoste, *Ibn Khaldun: The Birth of History and the Past of the Third World*; Muhsin Mahdi, *Ibn Khaldun's Philosophy of History: A Study in the Philosophic Foundation of the Science of Culture*; Lenn E. Goodman, *Jewish and Islamic Philosophy: Crosspollinations in the Classic Age*; Louis Baeck, *Mediterranean Tradition in Economic Thought*; Barbara Freyer

Stowasser, *Religion and Political Development: Some Comparative Ideas on Ibn Khaldun and Machiavelli*

WEEK 8

Selections from Leo Africanus, *History and Description* (1526)

Background reading: Natalie Davis, *Trickster Travels*; Augustus St. John, *Lives of Celebrated Travellers*; selections from W. B. Yeats, *A Vision*; Tabish Khair (ed.), *Other Routes: 1500 Years of African and Asian Travel Writing*

WEEK 9

Evlia Celibi (1611–84), *Book of Travels*

Background reading: Charles Montesquieu, *The Persian Letters*; critical material from Alexander Pallis, *In the Days of the Janissaries*; introduction and selections from Robert Dankoff, *The Intimate Life of an Ottoman Statesman*; Caroline Finkel, *Osman's Dream*

WEEK 10

Assia Djebar, *Fantasia* (1993)

Background reading: Derrida, *The Other Heading*; Mohammed Arkoun, *The Unthought in Islamic Thought*; Marnia Lazreg, *Eloquence of Silence: Algerian Women in Question*

WEEK 11

Orhan Pamuk, *Istanbul* (2003)

Background reading: Henry Maguire, *Art and Eloquence in Byzantium*; Philip Whitting (ed.), Byzantium: *An Introduction*; Karen Barkey and Mark von Hagen (eds), *After Empire: Multiethnic Societies and Nation-Building: The Soviet Union and Russian, Ottoman, and Habsburg Empires*; H. C. Armstrong, *Gray Wolf*

In conclusion, I return to the course on the history of literary criticism that I mentioned and cite just one small example. In that course, I teach—incompetently, I must add—texts of Sanskrit aesthetics by Abhinavagupta and Anandavardhana.[4] Most of the examples in those texts are from Prakrit or "the natural language," as opposed to Sanskrit or "the refined language." This detail is lost on students if they think that the text as translated into English— and indeed Jeffrey Masson's translation is excellent—is where its footprint began. This opening up of the origin also relates to my long-standing interest in the work of Derrida. This connection can be shared with students without naming names or constructing a vocabulary. The important thing here is that, if the teacher can begin to welcome students into understanding why the examples come from Prakrit, the idea that creole follows the dominant language begins to waver. By the time, in the second part of the course, we come to Dante's *De vulgari eloquentia*, that ancient Sanskrit gesture begins to take on a completely different kind of value in terms of locating Dante also as simply another origin, especially the origin of European nationalism. Comparativists typically invoke Goethe and world literature—and this access to a world, celebrated by our brilliant colleague Pascale Casanova as a kind of beginning, can be questioned in the simple process of undergraduate teaching if the origin is attended to.[5] This questioning of course also relates to the reading of the Dhammapada, which is often included in "other cultures" courses— although not in my literary criticism course.[6] The fact that Gautama Buddha made the critical gesture of encouraging the texts of his preaching to be in the creole when, as a prince, he certainly had access to the

---

4 *The "Dhvanyaloka" of Anandavardhana with the "Locana" of Abhinavagupta* (Daniel H. H. Ingalls, Sr. ed. and trans., Jeffrey Moussaieff Masson and M. V. Patwardhan trans) (Cambridge, MA: Harvard University Press, 1990).

5 Johann Wolfgang von Goethe, *Conversations with Eckermann* (Washington, DC: Dunne, 1901), p. 175; Pascale Casanova, *The World Republic of Letters* (Malcolm DeBevoise trans.) (Cambridge, MA: Harvard University Press, 2007).

6 *Dhammapada* (Ananda Maitreya trans.) (Berkeley, CA: Parallax, 1995).

refined language, and the further fact that this gesture was undone within a century by translation into Sanskrit and Chinese are lost on students if problems of translation are not discussed.

Commenting on Casanova's work, I invoked that extraordinary page in Antonio Gramsci's *Prison Notebook* Number 29, where Gramsci talks about all historical grammar as comparative and indeed an account of struggle.[7] We should welcome our students into the struggle if they are going to become citizens of the world. Otherwise any notion of globalizing the curriculum becomes a too-speedy Americanizing of every bit of the globe that is useful to us.

---

7 Antonio Gramsci, *A Gramsci Reader: Selected Writings, 1916–1935* (David Forgacs ed.) (New York: New York University Press, 1988), p. 355.

Scattered Speculations on Translation Studies

(2012)*

What follows is the edited transcript of remarks made at the Translation Studies Research Symposium of the Nida School of Translation Studies in New York on September 14, 2011. I had a prepared speech for the occasion as well. The beginning of the speech is embedded toward the end of the remarks. I have taken the liberty of adding the rest of the speech at the end.

It is a great pleasure to be here. I like talking in the City. I live here. I am a New Yorker. Nobody is weird in New York. I am at home. It is here in my place of employment, a great university, that I am engaged in the losing battle of real (as opposed to sellable) institutional change. Like Anthony Pym, I too am against boycott politics as a substitute for activism. I have repeatedly taken a stand against boycott politics. I think what we have to recognize is that there is a double bind at work here. Like in most things, if you want not to be a follower of boycott politics, nothing changes. But at the same time you have to acknowledge that the idea that there are no national boundaries within scholarship is simply false.

The history of the difficulty with which scholars from the West Bank travel or sometimes do not travel to conferences is well known. I am a green card holder. My green card was stolen in Kosovo on May 20th, 2011. I am traveling now on a little stamp given to me by the

* First published in *Translation* 1 (Summer 2012): 63–75.

Homeland Security Office. This little stamp is valid until June 12th, 2012.[1] This is not really something that one can just ignore. When it is said that boycott politics is the only politics for academics today I write internationally to say, "sorry, I can't be there." But at the same time I think it is necessary not to simply declare that it does not put you in a minority of one. It puts you in a collectivity which ignores the double bind, transforms it into a binary opposition and goes either on this side or that.

We cannot simply say that boycotts are denying the freedom of scholars. That is to blame the victim. It is the usual way of breaking strikes: "If nurses strike the patients are hurt. If teachers strike the students are hurt." The real question—why is there a strike, or a boycott?—is not asked.

I gave a talk in Pecs, Hungary, which called itself borderless. On the way, I lost my passport for a few hours. Denmark couldn't give me anything. The Hungarian Consulate couldn't give me anything. The Indians couldn't give me anything because I hadn't the passport. I was reminded of Phil Ochs's fantastic song "I Declare the War Is Over," composed during the anti–Vietnam War movement. When he sang it the first time, this Texas boy, Phil Ochs, said: I'm now going to sing a futuristic song. And many years later, when Derrida started talking of politics in the mode of "to come," I thought about that half-educated boy from Texas, Phil Ochs, that it was his way of saying "to come"—it's a futuristic song.

This, then, is how one copes with double binds. Even as you say there are no borders; even as you say "I declare the war is over," the declarative is only in the mode of "to come." I would suggest that within the working of translation studies this is something that we might keep in mind. We are not in fact on an even playing field, first of all. Secondly, we are working with translation studies as a discipline. The first pages

---

1 I have now received a new green card.

of Lawrence Venuti's influential anthology we read that translation studies is now becoming a discipline. That's where critical scholars like me come in: on the question of disciplinarization.

I believe in disciplines. I think disciplines construct you epistemologically. Your sustained disciplinary production shows you how to construct an object for knowledge. I am not, therefore, simply against disciplines although, of course, I attend to Foucault's spectacular warnings. And I take the challenge of interdisciplinarity seriously. It's an easy word, but in fact it's hardly ever done successfully. The moment, however, you disciplinarize something, the laws that start to work are not the substantive laws of the action that is the content of the discipline—but the abstract laws of disciplinarization, which are institutional and old.

I was in Kosovo because I used to run a little group that looked into the disciplinarization of preservation. I dissolved it because the seductions of personal or group accomplishment were too great. Disciplinarization is a problem. I am not really in translation studies, women's studies, cultural studies, postcolonial studies—those newish subdisciplines. I'm not a translator. I happen to have translated stuff and written on translation when friends have requested me to do so. I'm not really a player in translation studies.

A philosopher only ever develops one idea. I'm not a philosopher, but if there is one idea that has always occupied me it's the idea of the necessity of vanguards. In the beginning I unfortunately mentioned the other end of vanguardism (the subaltern), and, unfortunately, since every upwardly mobile sector of a dominated group wanted to claim subalternity, I've never been able to shake that one off. But in fact what I was thinking about when I was younger was supplementing the vanguard, although I did not quite know it. This has in fact been my main thing right from the start. Therefore what I am looking at is how the translation vanguard legitimizes its powerful position by reversal.

I have earned the right to see how American theory operates, from the inside. I've lived here over fifty years; I've taught here fulltime for forty-seven years. Yet my passport and my active participation in the civil society of my citizenship make me try at least to speak from that other side. More or less three semesters worth of teaching work is done every year by me in India. I'm part of an eighty-six percent majority there that is often violent in deed and/or spirit.[2] It is therefore hard for me to be treated only as a minority other culture when the benevolent translators are speaking. Yet to be a native informant is also not a good idea. Just on May 19 (2012)—a detail I offer at the time of revision—the moderator for my lecture in Croatia chastised me because I did not offer a socialist analysis of why, in spite of many parliamentary left parties, there was so much illiteracy and poverty in India; since Croatians knew nothing about India! Once again, I was being asked to be a native informant! The occasion was called "subversive Festival." But the subversion was local to the Balkans—in Europe.

In the early 80s I left my passport in London and entered JFK without papers. The immigration officer sent me to her boss, who immediately gave me a temporary green card. I poured myself a glass of whiskey and called my mother. I said, "Ma, the entire crowd of passengers is still waiting out there and I got in first without papers." I used a Bengali proverb: "Ma, the lord of thought provides for the one who expects it" (*je khay chini takey jogay chintamoni*). My mother, a philosophical and ecumenical Hindu, a plain-living, high-thinking intellectual, quoted

---

2 In a rich field of documentation, see at least Tapan Basu, Pradip Datta, Sumit Sarkar, Tanika Sarkar, and Sambuddha Sen, *Khaki Shorts and Saffron Flags: A Critique of the Hindu Right* (New Delhi: Orient Longman, 1993); Parvis Ghassem-Fachandi, *Pogrom in Gujarat: Hindu Nationalism and Anti-Muslim Violence in India* (Princeton, NJ: Princeton University Press, 2012); Christophe Jaffrelot, *Hindu Nationalism: A Reader* (Princeton, NJ: Princeton University Press, 2007); Siddharth Varadarajan (ed.), *Gujarat: The Making of a Tragedy* (New Delhi: Penguin India, 2002).

Psalm 23 back at me: "The Lord is my Shepherd, I shall not want." She said, to be precise, *Shadaprobhu amar palok amar obhab hoibey na*.

Shadaprobhu is a word absent from old or modern Bengali except as a translation of "Lord" in the King James Bible. Readers of this essay will know that in the Hebrew Bible there is a tradition of substituting *adonai* for *Yahweh*. Sitting here in Bangladesh, I can't consult with my usual source if I am to make the deadline. It is unlikely that the missionaries translating the Bible into Bengali were aware of this. *Shoda* is a Sanskrit-origin prefix roughly meaning "always." I believe it is an attempt to catch the sense of "almighty." And now the word recedes into a marked enclave as Christianity becomes a largely ignored minority religion in Bengal. In some parts of India, there is murderous violence against Christians.

I believe West Bengal remains largely clear of this. I do not know what the equivalent of *shodaprobhu* would be in the other Indian languages. For my mother the word remained real and affectionately cumbersome, belonging to her childhood rather than to her 1937 MA in Bengali literature. And, as I entered the US ahead of the line without papers, she said to me: *Shodaprobhu amar palok amar obhab hoibey na*. My mother went the first few years to Christ Church School. The Indian Hindus were a tough nut to crack for the missionaries, especially the upper-caste Hindus, the collaborative Bengalis whom the East India Company encountered first when they became territorial.

My parents were smart planners in putting us sisters in St. John's Diocesan Girls High School. Diocesan made me, undoubtedly. It was not a convent school, where the teachers were mostly white nuns. We were not taught by upper-caste Hindus, upper-class Muslims. We were taught by Christian converts from the so-called low castes and aboriginals, who were supposedly in India from before the arrival of the Indo-European speakers between five and eight thousand years ago.

The Church dealt well with these people, whom we caste Hindus had treated like dogs. They were our teachers, and as such they were teaching upper-caste Hindus and upper-class Muslims. It was an altogether passionate kind of teaching. My role model was Miss Dass, a low-caste surname, our principal. As the years go by, she becomes, more and more, my role model.

I managed to forget all this in the first flush of PoCo in the 80s. I did write irresponsibly about the Christianization of the Indians, not recognizing how complicated the situation was. I have just given you an example of how the caste Hindus in my region have taken it in without really losing anything. I should also have thought of the pre-colonial "Syrian" Christians in the South. It is like an invagination, the part becoming bigger than the whole. The situation determines which is which.

Let me give you another example of the resources of my schooling. Because Miss Dass was much more interested in general ethics than in indoctrination (I think), she used "secular" prayers at morning assembly. One of them was "Be Thou, oh Lord, above us to draw us up, beneath us to sustain us, before us to lead us, behind us to restrain us, round about us to protect us." I was able last year to explain English conjunctions (in Bengali, of course) to one of the teachers in my rural schools through this prayer, surreptitiously adding a word for the Christians. This is not, strictly speaking, an example of gender and translation, the topic I had agreed to speak on. I include it to indicate a gendered exchange between what would now be called Dalit Christianity and a lapsed Brahmin girl, as also an act of subaltern translation.

The vanguard must, of course, do its work of institutionalizing translation studies. The discipline must do its work. We are in a double bind with this necessary work. After all, something will have happened whatever you plan institutionally. That that future will never be identical with what you're planning—and one hopes that it won't be identical with our limits—impels some of us to work seemingly against the grain. We're not against the grain. This is auto-critical from within. We are not to be seen in the binary-opposition model. There are a few of us persistently to remind the vanguard that we cannot simply plan the short haul with unassailable concepts. We have to look toward a future remembering that the one who wins loses. We must continue to invoke the Braudelian texture of translation events—events that not only escape the institutional performative in the nature of things, but must deliberately be excluded from the system, at best allowed in as politically correct anecdotal support.

From here I began to read from my prepared paper, ad-libbing freely. The paper title was "Gender and Translation in the Global Utopia." My sense of utopia comes from the root meaning of the word—that it is a "no place," a good place that we try to approximate, not achieve. The utopia proposed by globalization—and that's why I spoke critically about the borderless, nationless, stateless place where liberal humanists hang out—is a level playing field. I think it is generally understood that this is a false promise, especially since the impossibility inherent in all utopian thought is ignored by it; the world is run on the aim, however, to achieve it more or less disingenuously.

I spoke recently to British students who had taken a stand against budget cuts—"Think locally, act locally," said I to them, "that's all we can do. But you have to realize that the local is defined differently today. There is no difference between the local local and the glocal, and the global local and the local global, and so on. Just act locally, but ask yourself again and again, 'Is this generalizable?' Who are you confronting? Remember you're talking about the British state when you say budget cuts. Who are you confronting? The state is in hock to a world trade defined in terms of finance capital. So, see if your demands are generalizable following the vulgarized Spinozan model of singularity, always universalizable but never quite universal." The students were distressed. And now they follow the Occupy Wall Streeters who have made an inchoate attempt to generalize, unable to make the opposite kinds of connections, with labor power in Wisconsin, for example, when developments beckon. There I spoke as member of a vanguard that can only be placed within a binary opposition by those who do not have ears developed by slow teaching to hear. The idea of cultural exchange and translation is also an ideological support for the false promise of globalization: a level playing field across which equal exchange can take place. In order to make this false promise, the sponsors of globalization emphasize that access to capital brings in and creates social productivity. Hence fundraising. They do not emphasize the fact that such productivity must be humanly mediated by decision-makers who are deeply trained in unconditional ethics. With the decline and fall in education in the humanities, this group is extinct. I had written to the president of the University of Toronto when they were about to close the Comparative Literature Department: "Think of [education in the humanities] as epistemological and ethical health care for the society at large." In the absence of philosopher-kings directing the global utopia, what is also and necessarily ignored is that for capital to work in a capitalist way, there must be what used to be called proleterianization and what today has been revised to subalternization.

I am just back from rural southern China. The one-room, one-teacher schools I know, where there was an ethical connection between the teachers and students, are being closed down as partially-corporate-funded central schools are being established. Families are disrupted. The number of students is significantly down. The rural teachers with whom I work there were openly talking about the death of socialism to me this time. Of course, we were speaking in my halting Chinese so they couldn't speak very complicatedly. But the ethical impulse that can be nurtured with students who are in these primary schools with local teachers has been killed at the central schools, where all is speedy statisticalizable rational choice, value-adding that is globally recognized.

Please remember that what used to be called proletarianization and has been revised to subalternization must work for capital to work in a capitalist way. In order to establish the same system of exchange all over the world, the barriers between individual national economies and international capital have to be removed—the bottom line of globalization. This has an analogy with translation. We must look at what language we are translating into. I was recently at a European Cultural Congress in Wroclaw, Poland, where there were possibilities of translation into all kinds of languages, but of course not my mother tongue. It doesn't count. Only 270 million people speak it. That's not enough. It came into being from Sanskrit creoles in the eleventh century. That's not enough. There's a great deal of literature there. That's not enough. It's my mother tongue. That's not enough. So think about how you decide. You cannot have all the languages of the world. Your principle has to be practical and political. And, what we, the in-house auto-critical contrarians, say is impractical, in view of the future anterior.

In order, then, to establish the same system of exchange all over the world—the bottom line of globalization—the barriers between individual national economies and international capital have to be removed. When this happens, states lose their individual and idiosyncratic constitutional particularities in history and become recoded as agents for managing the interests of global capital. This is also why translation flourishes within these nation-states in different ways. In such a situation, when demand and supply begin to become the organizing principles of running a state we come to realize that items such as clean water or HIV/AIDS research do not necessarily come up in terms of the demands of the global economy. These kinds of needs then begin to be supervised by a global collection of agencies that are separate from nation-states. This group is often called the "international civil society," a more palliative description of what is also and still called nongovernmental organizations supported by the United Nations. Thus we can say that the structure of the utopianism of globalization brings forth restructured states aided by an international civil society and other instruments of world governance. In order to be realistic about this we should also speak of geopolitical interests and geomilitary interests, international criminal courts, where translation is necessary in rather a different protocol. But that would take us too far afield for the moment.

Let me now say something about today's bible of humanism, the Universal Declaration of Human Rights. The translation of that thing— it's been translated into many, many languages—is useless for those who do not know the imperial languages. The way in which it is translated is inaccessible to the people whom the international civil society teaches self-interest. They cannot understand a word of the document. What is actually happening is the creolization of English with which the top-down do-gooders are out of touch. Attending to creolization is a way of teaching on the ground translation which is different from what we teach at school where disciplinarization is obliged to follow the very tight rules of disciplinarization as such in systems that go back, in most "democratic" countries, to a post-Medieval European structure.

It is well known that the management of gender provides alibis for all kinds of activities—from military intervention to various kinds of platforms of action—where experience deeply embedded in cultural difference is translated into general equivalence. Often this happens because women are perceived to be a more malleable and fungible sector of society—especially women below a certain income line. If in a global utopia, it is also imagined that sexual preference would be translated into the language of general affective equivalence, this exists on a separate plane.

Already we can see that in order to establish the same system of exchange all over the globe, we are also obliged to establish the same system of gendering globally. How does translation enter here?

To gather singularities into a system of equivalence is also called "abstraction." I have often argued that gender, or what many of us have been calling gender for the last forty years or so, is humankind's, or perhaps the most intelligent primates', first instrument of abstraction, as follows.

Let us think of culture as a package of largely unacknowledged assumptions, loosely held by a loosely outlined group of people, mapping negotiations between the sacred and the profane, and the relationship between the sexes. To theorize in the abstract, as well as to translate, of course, we need a difference. However we philosophize sensible and intelligible, abstract and concrete, etc., the first difference we perceive materially is sexual difference. It becomes our tool for abstraction, in many forms and shapes. On the level of the loosely held assumptions and presuppositions which English-speaking peoples have been calling "culture" for 200 years, change is incessant. But, as they change, these unwitting presuppositions become belief systems, organized suppositions. Rituals coalesce to match, support, and advance beliefs and suppositions. But these presuppositions also give us the wherewithal to change our world, to innovate and create. Most people believe, even (or perhaps particularly) when they are being cultural relativists, that creation and innovation is their own cultural secret, whereas "others" are only determined by their cultures. This is the basis of translation theories in general. This habit is unavoidable and computed with the help of sexual difference sustained into "gender." But if we aspire to a global utopia, we must not only fight the habit of thinking creation and innovation are our own cultural secret, we must also shake the habit of thinking that our version of computing gender is the world's, and in fact, must even ignore our own sense of gender unless we are specifically speaking of women and queers.

Thought of as an instrument of abstraction, gender is in fact a position without identity (an insight coming to us via queer studies from David Halperin).[3] Because, however it is sexualized in cultural practice, we can never think the abstracting instrumentality of gender fully.

---

3 David Halperin, *Saint Foucault: Towards a Gay Hagiography* (New York: Oxford University Press, 1995), p. 62.

This broad discussion of gender in the general sense invites us to realize that gender is not just another word for women and that the (non-)place of the queer in the social division of labor is also contained within it. And yet, because gender, through the apparent immediacy to sexuality, is also thought to be the concrete as such (with commonly shared problems by women), the international civil society finds it easiest to enter the supplementing of globalization through gender. This is where translating becomes a word that loses its sense of transferring meanings or significations. A certain human-to-human unmediated affect-transfer is assumed as history is denied.

Yet it is possible that gender(ing)-in-the-concrete is inaccessible to agential probing, mediated or umediated.

I am assuming a distinction between agent (intention institutionally validated, most basically by the institution of reproductive hetero-normativity) and subject (the mental world shored up by the metapsy-chological, beyond the grasp of mere reason). I should add that I use "mere reason" in Kant's sense, which I cannot elaborate here in the interest of time.[4] (A rule of thumb: "mere reason" is the version of reason that substitutes "accountability" for responsibility; the connec-tion with globalization and certain dominant translation theories are obvious.)

Let me, then, repeat: it is possible that gender(ing)-in-the-concrete is inaccessible to agential probing, mediated or unmediated, as follows.

As I have argued elsewhere, the human infant grabs on to some one thing and then things.[5] This grabbing of an outside indistinguishable from an inside constitutes an inside, going back and forth and coding everything into a sign-system by the thing(s) grasped. One can certainly

---

4 Immanuel Kant, "Religion within the Boundaries of Mere Reason," in *Religion and Rational Theology* (Allen W. Wood and George di Giovanni eds and trans) (Cambridge: Cambridge University Press, 1996), pp. 39–215.

5 See "Translation as Culture" in this volume, pp. 69–88.

call this crude coding a "translation," but it is taking place (if there is a place for such virtuality) in infancy, between world and self (those two great Kantian "as if"-s), as part of the formation of a "self." In this never-ending weaving, violence translates into conscience and vice versa. From birth to death, this "natural" machine, programming the mind perhaps as genetic instructions program the body (where does body stop and mind begin?) is partly metapsychological and therefore outside the grasp of the mind. In other words, where parental sexual difference helps the infant constitute a world to self the self in, the work that we are calling "translating" is not even accessible to the infant's mind. So it is not much use for the kind of cultural interference that NGO gender work engages in. For all of us, "nature" passes and repasses into "culture," in this work or shuttling site of violence: the violent production of the precarious subject of reparation and responsibility. To plot this weave, the worker, translating the incessant translating shuttle into that which is read, must have the most intimate knowledge of the rules of representation and permissible narratives which make up the substance of a culture, and must also become responsible and accountable to the writing/translating presupposed original. That is the space of language-learning, not the space of speedy gender-training in the interest of achieving utopia in globalization. This is why books such as *Why Translation Studies Matters*, published through the European Institute for Translation Studies, are of interest to me, and I hope my words resonate with their sense of mission.[6]

I have given above an account of how the "self" is formed, through sexual difference. Let us move just a bit further in the infant's chronology and look at the infant acquiring language. There is a language we learn first, mixed with the pre-phenomenal, which stamps the

---

6 Daniel Gile, Gyde Hansen, and Nike K. Pokorn (eds), *Why Translation Studies Matters* (Amsterdam: Benjamin, 2010).

metapsychological circuits of "lingual memory."[7] The child invents a language, beginning by bestowing signification upon gendered parts of the parental bodies. The parents "learn" this language. Because they speak a named language, the child's language gets inserted into the named language with a history before the child's birth, which will continue after its death. As the child begins to navigate this language it is beginning to access the entire interior network of the language, all its possibility of articulations, for which the best metaphor that can be found is—especially in the age of computers—"memory." By comparison, "cultural memory" is a crude concept of narrative re-memorization that attempts to privatize the historical record.

Translation studies must imagine that each language may be activated in this special way and make an effort to produce a simulacrum through the reflexivity of language as habit. Walter Benjamin, like all male theorists, ignoring the play of gender in the constitution of language except through its use in the Adamic narrative, ignores therefore this aspect of the task of the translator.[8] Here we translate, not the content, but the very moves of languaging. We can provisionally locate this peculiar form of originary translation before translation on the way, finally, to institutionally recognizable translation, which often takes refuge in the reduction to equivalence of a quantifiable sort. Mere reason.

This is not to make an opposition between the natural spontaneity of the emergence of "my languaged place" and the artificial effortfulness of learning foreign languages. Rather is it to emphasize the metapsychological and telecommunicative nature of the subject's being encountered by the languaging of place. If we entertain the spontaneous/artificial

---

7 Alton Becker, *Beyond Translation: Essays Toward a Modern Philology* (Ann Arbor: University of Michigan Press, 1995), p. 12.

8 Walter Benjamin, "The Task of the Translator" (Harry Zohn trans.), in *Selected Writings, Volume 1: 1913–1926* (Marcus Bullock and Michael W. Jennings eds) (Cambridge: Harvard University Press, 1996), pp. 253–63.

opposition, we will possibly value our own place over all others and thus defeat the ethical impulse so often ignored in competitive translation studies. Embracing another place as my creolized space may be a legitimation by reversal. We know now that the hybrid is not an issue here. If, on the other hand, we recall the helplessness before history— our own and of the languaged place—in our acquisition of our first dwelling in language, we just may sense the challenge of producing a simulacrum, always recalling that this language too, depending on the subject's history, can inscribe lingual memory. In other words, a sense of metapsychological equivalence among languages, at the other end from quantification, rather than a comparison of historico-civilizational content alone. Étienne Balibar has suggested that equivalence blurs difference, whereas equality requires them.[9] Precisely because civil war may be the allegoric name for an extreme form of untranslatability, it is that "blurring" that we need.

There are two theories of literary translation: you add yourself to the original, or you efface yourself and let the text shine. I subscribe to the second. But I have said again and again that translation is also the most intimate act of reading. And to read is to pray to be haunted. A translator may be a ventriloquist, performing the contradiction, the counter-resistance, which is at the heart of love. Does this promote cultural exchange? This for me is the site of a double bind, contradictory instructions coming at the same time: love the original / share the original; culture cannot / must be exchanged.

How intimate is this "intimate act of reading"? Long ago in Taiwan, my dear friend Ackbar Abbas had said that my take on reading was a "critical intimacy" rather than a "critical distance." And now, another perceptive reader, Prof. Deborah Madsen, has found in my idea of "suture (as translation)" a way into Derrida's sense that translation is

---

9 Étienne Balibar, *La proposition de l'égaliberté. Essais politiques, 1989–2009* (Paris: Presses Universitaires de France, 2010), pp. 55–89.

an intimate embrace, an embrace that is also something like a physical combat.[10]

One prays to be haunted, Derrida asserts, because "I cannot be in the other's place, in the head of the other." In all reading, but more so in translation, we are dealing with ghosts, because "to translate is to lose the body. The most faithful translation is violent: one loses the body of the poem, which exists only in [the 'original' language and once only] [. . . T]ranslation is desired by the poet [. . .] but [. . .] ," and here we enter the place of violence in love, "love and violence." And the language of the "original" is itself "a bloody struggle with [that very] language, which [it] deforms, transforms, which [it] assaults, and which [it] incises." We have to inhabit the "original" language against its own grain in order to translate.[11]

Following these thinkers, then, I come to the conclusion that the double bind of translation can best be welcomed in the world by teaching translation as an activism rather than merely a convenience. In other words, while the translated work will of course make material somewhat imperfectly accessible to the general reading public, we, in the academy, should primarily produce translators rather than translations. We can expand this analogy to the necessarily imperfect translations of the images of utopia. The translations, in a classroom, at the Center, are lovely byproducts. We produce critically annotated and introduced translations, fighting the publishers some. In other words, we have to have the courage of our convictions as we enter and continue in the translation trade. Our international students' practical step of declaring a native language as "foreign" cannot dictate our teaching of translating from or into a learned language.

---

10 Deborah Madsen, "The Making of (Native) Americans: Suturing and Citizenship in the Scene of Education," *Parallax* 17(3) (2011): 32–45.

11 Jacques Derrida, *Sovereignties in Question: The Poetics of Paul Celan* (Thomas Dutoit and Outi Pasanen trans) (New York: Fordham University Press, 2005), pp. 164–69.

At the end of Benjamin's essay on "The Task of the Translator," there is the mention of a meaning-less speech, "pure speech," which makes translation possible. There is a famous scandal about the accepted English and French translation translating this as "makes translation impossible." In closing, I would like to invoke this intuition, which in Benjamin, to me unfortunately, takes on the guise of the sacred. But this idea—that the possibility of the production of meaning is a system without meaning but with values that can be filled with meaning—is in today's informatics, which is rather far from the language of the Scripture. We will recall that the distinction between meaning and value is already there in Saussure's *Course in General Linguistics*.[12]

In this understanding, signification means to turn something into a sign—rather than to produce meaning—and make it possible for there to be meaning within established conventions. This originary condition of possibility is what makes translation possible—that there can be meaning, not necessarily tied to singular systems. About sixty years ago, Jacques Lacan suggested that the unconscious is constituted like a conveyor belt, rolling out objects susceptible to meaningfulness—for use in building the history of a subject, with imperfect reference to whatever one could call the real world.[13] In these mysterious thickets, the possibility of translation emerges, but only if, institutionally, the so-called foreign languages are taught with such care that, when the student is producing in it, s/he has forgotten the language which was rooted in the soul—roots which, Saussure, Lacan, information theory, and in his

---

12 In this connection, Derrida also invokes the intuition of the transcendental but distances himself in the end: "every poem says, 'this is my body,' [. . .] and you know what comes next: passions, crucifixions, executions. Others would also say"—mark these words—"resurrections [. . .]" (Derrida, *Sovereignties in Question*, p. 169). For meaning and value, see Ferdinand de Saussure, *Course in General Linguistics* (Wade Baskin trans.) (New York: Philosophical Library, 1959), p. 111–22.

13 Jacques Lacan, "Subversion of the Subject and the Dialectics of Desire," in *Ecrits* (Bruce Fink trans.) (New York: W. W. Norton, 2007), pp. 671–702.

own way Benjamin, see as themselves produced, dare I say, as rhizomes without specific ground?[14] It gives me pleasure to recall that Saussure was a student of Sanskrit who may have arrived at this sort of intuition through his reading of the fifth-century BCE Indian grammarian Bhartrihari's notion of *sphota*.[15]

I have often said that globalization is like an island of signs in a sea of traces. A trace is not a sign. A sign-system promises meaning; a trace promises nothing—rather, it simply seems to suggest that there was something here. In this connection, one inevitably thinks of the established patriarchal convention, still honored by most legal systems, that I, especially if I am recognizable as a man, am my father's sign and my mother's trace. What is important for us within my argument is that, rather than theorize globalization as a general field of translation which in spite of all the empiricization of apparently impersonal mechanical translation, in fact privileges host or target, ceaselessly and indefinitely, we should learn to think that the human subject in globalization is an island of languaging—unevenly understanding some languages and idioms with the "first" language as monitor—within an entire field of traces, where "understanding" follows no guarantee, but where there is just a feeling that these words are meaningful, not just noise; an undoing of the *barbaros*. This may produce a new call for a different "non-expressional" art, a different simultaneous translation.

Global translating in the achievable utopia, on the other hand, ceaselessly transforms trace to sign, sign to data, undoing the placelessness of utopias. This arrogance is checked and situated, if we learn, with humility, to celebrate the possibility of meaning in a grounding medium that is meaningless.

---

14 Karl Marx, *Surveys from Exile: Political Writings*, VOL. 2 (David Fernbach ed.). New York: Penguin Books / New Left Review, 1973), p. 147; translation modified.

15 Bimal Krishna Matilal, *The Word and the World: India's Contribution to the Study of Language* (Delhi and New York: Oxford University Press, 1990).

In the interview from which I have already quoted, given a few months before his death, Derrida puts it in a lovely, empirical way: "there may be an allusion to a referent from [the author's] life that is hidden or encrypted through numerous layers of hidden literary references. [. . . I]n a word, there will always be an excess that is not of the order of meaning, that is not just another meaning."[16]

If we claim a successful translation, a successful recoding into a general system of equivalence, we forget the ghostliness of utopias, we betray gendering, our first instrument of translation. All attempts at fundraising are foiled by this, as Socrates knew. He could not "dumb himself down" for the city fathers, the social engineers.

The global contemporaneity that we now empirically supposedly have exists because the silicon chip allows us to travel on the web, and because other kinds of empirical travel are also possible. Actually this contemporaneity has always been a fact. Now that it is seemingly empirically available to many, we have to change ourselves into thinking that whatever is synchronic is modern. The different diachronies make it historically and politically uneven—this is the field within which translation must think itself. All of the different diachronies make this synchrony a relief map. Within this difference, translation begins to work. We cannot just talk about others. We must persistently change ourselves.

In 1982 in Essex I had said that the conference "Europe and Its Others" should have as its title, "Europe as an Other." It was deemed inappropriate then. Thirty years went by, and then it was possible to give me a twenty-minute slot on a panel called "Alien Europe: Europe as an Other" in Wroclaw, Poland. What was the history that happened? Translation is deeply involved in this history and you have to thank the world. But you must listen to us when we, the in-house auto-critical contrarians, haltingly make our instructive mistakes. The practical short

---

16 Derrida, *Sovereignties in Question*, p. 165.

haul can be evaluated. But if one wants this not to be identical with the other side, then one does not just put a plus in the place of the minus.

What we say—impractical as it may sound, impossible as the tasks are—should be attended to so that you, the disciplinarians, know that what you are doing has to be based on a grounding error: that translation studies as a discipline is possible. You should inhabit that grounding error because if you don't—since everything is a double bind—you cannot begin. If you're living, you have to make that into a single bind so that you can make decisions. But the difference between the real people (states people, the real activists, the real parents) and the unreal people is that the former know that the decision is going to have to be changed because it was too dependent on the circumstances given. Whereas the latter thinks that they were going to go forward but comes instead to a moment of racism, as in the Millennium Goals: "Hey we gave all these things to the African villagers and they don't know how to use them." That unacknowledged racism then begins to fester until there's a situation worse than the one being originally corrected and human rights come to depend on enforcement. This is all very deeply connected with the impulse to translate. It's a good impulse to create European institutions moving towards "Europe's Others," and to create US institutions moving towards "US's Others." It's a fantastic thing and I certainly talk to deans and vice presidents in favor of these things. At the same time, when you choose the others—we are talking now about the area studies disciplines that came in just after the Cold War because of national defense—there's also hierarchy. I am therefore not in translation studies, I teach reading, how to read in the most robust sense. And I repeat: translation is the most intimate act of reading. I remain a literalist, not because I think literalism is good, but because literalism is impossible. If you try to be literal, dynamic equivalence, which is a wonderful phrase, will come in anyway because no one is capable of being completely literal. Literalism between two languages is impossible and as I say, "Translation begins with the violent act of killing the sound." So we have to, and yet, I'm a translator and root for translation.

A postscript on proletarian and subaltern. The distinction was first made by Antonio Gramsci. As Frank Rosengarten, Gramsci's translator, pointed out in conversation, in the army, the definition of subaltern is "those who take orders." As soon as we look at this category, rather than those who are trashed within and by the logic of capital, we think gender, we think the paperless, we think of those outside the system of equivalences, we think of those with no social mobility who don't know that the welfare structures of the state are for the use of the citizen. I should tell you in closing that this final definition of the subaltern I wrote recently for a second cousin, deeply involved in global capitalism, who happened to see a video where women workers gently and with affection mocked me for my fixation on the subaltern. My cousin the capitalist didn't know what the word meant, as Lawrence Eagleburger, the sixty-second US secretary of state and chairman of the Board of Trustees for the Forum for International Policy, did not, in 1998, know what was meant by "New Social Movements," just as they were being co-opted into "the international civil society."[17]

Let us not permit our sanctioned ignorance, our unacknowledged ignorings, keep translation quarantined within the confines of an empiricized utopia.

---

17 The UN initiated the move in 1994, by opening an "NGO Forum" for the first time at the International Conference on Population and Development. Eagleburger, when questioned about new social movements at a conference on "Does America Have a Democratic Mission" at the University of Virginia on March 19–21, 1998, turned to the moderator (who happened to be Fareed Zakaria) and asked what was meant by the phrase.

Translating in a World of Languages

(2010)*

Let us point to Africa before we begin. Because historically it has been treated as a scandal, Africa makes theory visible. In our case, for example, it makes clear, in tranquility as well as in violence, that a nation is not identical with a language. Let us think also of the itinerary of the ethical in the Buddhist diasporas and the vicissitudes of imperial knowledge in the translation enterprises of the Arabo-Persian empires. These reminders stand as narratives that would annul many of the commonly held presuppositions that support varieties of dominant translation theory. Even attempting such rethinking, we should remember that, whereas much is published on the westward translating arm of the Arabs, little is published on the eastward arm. Let us begin, then, with an appeal for a person with knowledge not only of Arabic, Persian, and Sanskrit but also of Pahlavi.

The best gift of all enlightenments is reasonable doubt. The best guarantee of all worldliness is attention to space and time.

The title of the Presidential Forum invokes Walter Benjamin as well as Paul de Man's Messenger Lecture, a reading of Benjamin. It also invokes Benjamin's book *The Work of Art in the Age of Mechanical Reproduction*[1]—I deliberately choose the mistranslated title that has

---

* First published in *Profession* (2010): 35–43.

[1] See Walter Benjamin, *The Work of Art in the Age of Its Technical Reproducibility* (Michael Jannings trans.) (Cambridge, MA: Harvard University Press, 2008), pp. 251–83.

passed into common currency to show how much power an English wields. These are great texts caught in a historical moment. Our moment, speaking through us as reasoned spontaneity, produces a difference. Our collective title, unlike Benjamin's and de Man's, is abstract and plural: the tasks of translation. I can read this already as meeting certain demands of globalization, which deals with the abstract. If it is true that capital translates all objects into abstractions, the appropriate behavior of the organic intellectuals of globalization may be to situate translation as the abstract task of reducing all linguistic performance to equivalents, of establishing the emergence of the languages of the Security Council of the United Nations as general equivalents—in other words, of homogenizing them into a dominant. Yet a context is concrete. And since we are teacher-translators, the context presupposes readers, as we specify in every publisher's marketing proposal. These are Benjamin's well-known words:

> We may define [a bad translation] as the inexact transmission of an inessential content. This will be true whenever a translation undertakes to serve the reader. However, if it were intended for the reader so must the original be. If the original does not exist for the reader's sake, how could the translation be understood on the basis of this premise? Translation is a form.[2]

In his comments, de Man explains the dismissal of the reader by literally reading *Aufgabe* as "giving up"—the failure of the translator—and glosses Benjamin in a resolutely Euro-specific deconstructive context, where we can take the risk of saying, "[W]e have no knowledge of the vessel [the original], or no awareness, no access to it, so for all intents and purposes there never has been one."[3]

---

2 Walter Benjamin, "The Task of the Translator," in *Illuminations* (Harry Zohn trans.) (New York: Schocken, 1968), p. 70; translation modified.
3 Benjamin, *The Work of Art*, p. 44.

How, then, has the translator's right to determine this form been changed in what we have nonetheless called the global context? Let me quote my current formula: Globalization takes place only in capital and data; everything else is damage control. From my vantage point, to contextualize the global is to step into damage control, and it makes sense for me to unfurl my argument as a development of this gesture. Let me turn the decision we confront into a story. Hegel recoded Christianity as philosophy. Marx put capital in place of the Idea in Hegel. Capital asks for the destruction of the Tower of Babel. The context of this call is not global. It is in the agency of a tribal god. In the global context, the Tower of Babel is our refuge. How and why?

In this forum, we are speaking of translation in the broad purview of the humanities. I don't believe the humanities can be global. I think our task is to supplement the uniformization necessary for globality. We must therefore learn to think of ourselves as the custodians of the world's wealth of languages, not as impresarios of a multicultural circus in English. The task of translation is to translate before translation: languages into equivalence, a different kind of commensurability. This is a suggestion that I have made at greater length in "Rethinking Comparativism."

There is a language we learn first; mixed with the prephenomenal, it stamps the metapsychological circuits of "lingual memory."[4] Each language of study may be activated in this special way in order to make an effort to produce a simulacrum through the reflexivity of language as habit. Here we translate not the content but the very moves of languaging. This is a form of translation before translation. Naoki Sakai asks us to think of language not as one but as many. The thinking of languaging before language makes this possible. Reproductive heteronormativity, the emergence into birth as death from the uterine world (Melanie

---

4 Alton Becker, *Beyond Translation* (Ann Arbor: University of Michigan Press, 1996), p. 12

Klein) as the theater of the staging of each language, makes Sakai's Kant possible as well.[5]

This is not to make an opposition between the natural spontaneity of the emergence of "my languaged place" and the artificial effort of learning foreign languages. Rather it is to emphasize the metapsychological and telecommunicative nature of the subject's being encountered by the languaging of place.[6] If we entertain the spontaneous-artificial opposition, we will end up valuing our own place over all others and thus defeat the ethical comparativist impulse. Embracing another place as my creolized space, as in migration, may be a legitimation by reversal. If the making and unmaking of an ethical subject—a knowing, feeling, judging subject—are to begin, it does not matter whether the language instrumental in this is recognizably hybrid or not. If, on the other hand, we recall the helplessness of subjects before history—our own history and that of the languaged place—in their acquisition of their first dwelling in language, we just may sense the challenge of producing a simulacrum, always recalling that this language too, depending on the subject's history, can inscribe lingual memory. In other words, I am calling for a sense of equivalence among languages rather than a comparison of historico-civilizational content. Étienne Balibar has suggested that equivalence blurs differences, whereas equality requires them ("Entretien"). Precisely because civil war may be the allegoric name for an extreme form of untranslatability, we need such blurring. The Tower of Babel, the condition of impossibility of translation, is thus a refuge in thinking the apparent global contemporaneity of languages before their historical inequality.

Listening to a version of this argument, my colleague Suva Chakravarty Dasgupta, of Jadavpur University, made me think of the value

---

5 See the opening of "Translation as Culture" in this volume, pp. 69–88.
6 "It would be bad natural history to expect the mental processes and communicative habits of mammals to conform to the logician's ideal" (Gregory Bateson, *Steps to an Ecology of Mind* [Chicago: University of Chicago Press, 2000], p. 180).

form in its expanded format. Indeed, Marx was productively counter-intuitive in suggesting that value is already implicit in use and in deepening the value form unconfined to the economic. If in languaging we are equivalent, as it were, and we want to disciplinarize this equivalency and keep it upstream from verbal translation, we understand Marx's insistence that the value form is contentless and his choice of foreign language learning as an example of revolutionary practice.

The task of translation in the global context should be thought in this frame, where the learning of languages is the first imperative—the production of translation an activism—and not simply a giving in to the demand for convenience in a country where multiculturalism goes hand in hand with monolingualism. Our obligation to translate should be recognized as, at the deepest level, determined by "the idea of the *untranslatable* as not something that one cannot translate but something one never stops (not) translating," a persistent epistemological preparation rather than merely a response to a global market understood as a call to equitable pluralism.[7]

Globalization demands from us an epistemological change. Claims for an epistemic change are often quickly made on the grounds of immediate information command. An epistemic change is in fact diagnosed only belatedly, *nachträglich*. We cannot look around that corner; it is in the future anterior, something that will have happened. We can, however, be responsible for epistemological change as tertiary and post-tertiary teachers. As such, we might tell heritage students; multicultural students; military, diplomatic, human rights, and business students that you do not learn culture as content, you learn language as practice. We learn to think a tremendously diverse shared history, literally an inventory without traces, where a trained imagination may be our only practical refuge. Some years ago, Jack D. Forbes described something like

7 This definition of the untranslatable, in Barbara Cassin's dictionary, was provided to me by Alessandra Russo (Barbara Cassin [ed.], *Vocabulaire européen des philosophies: Dictionnaire des intraduisibles* [Paris: Seuil, 2004]).

such an imagination in his account of the racial heterogeneity of the greater Caribbean:

> [T]hree hundred to four hundred years of intermixture of a very complex sort, [and] varying amounts of African and American ancestry derived at different intervals and from extremely diverse sources—as from American nations as different as Narragansett or Pequot and the Carib or Arawak, or from African nations as diverse as the Mandinka, Yoruba, and Malagasy.[8]

"For the perceptive reader," I then commented, "Forbes's book at once opens the horizons of Foucault's work, shows the immense, indeed perhaps insuperable complexity of the task once we let go of 'pure' European outlines, and encourages a new generation of scholars to acquire the daunting skills for robust cultural history."[9] Today, ideologically held by a simulacrum of contemporaneity in the global, the call is to rethink the historical as such as always contemporary and to train for a mindset that will be equal to the task. It is precisely in this contemporaneity that we have to train ourselves to imagine the equivalence of all languages. Jacques Derrida has a lovely passage, which I often quote, on the need for learning to translate today: "It remains to be known, so as to save the honor of reason, how to *translate*. For example, the word *reasonable*. And how to pay one's respects to, how to [. . .] greet [. . .] beyond its latinity, and in more than one language, the fragile difference between the *rational* and the *reasonable*."[10]

---

8 Jack D. Forbes, *Black Africans and Native Americans: Color, Race, and Caste in the Evolution of Red-Black Peoples* (Oxford: Blackwell, 1988), pp. 270–71.

9 Gayatri Chakravorty Spivak, "Race before Racism: The Disappearance of the American," in Paul A. Bové (ed.), *Edward Said and the Work of the Critic: Speaking Truth to Power* (Durham, NC: Duke University Press, 2000), p. 53.

10 Jacques Derrida, *Rogues: Two Essays on Reason* (Pascale-Anne Brault and Michael Naas trans.) (Stanford, CA: Stanford University Press, 2005), p. 159.

You see here not an abdication of translation but, once again, a recognition of it as an active practice: the idea of the untranslatable as not something that one cannot translate but something one never stops (not) translating.

The unending negotiation with the untranslatable will today be judged an impractical project. But in our professional organization, we should at least talk about the philosophy of our task instead of simply accepting that, caught up in the current corporatization of the university and in the financial crisis, we will never be able to perform the task that translation must carry on in the mode of pursuing what is persistently around the corner, in order to supplement the uniformization of the global.[11] Immense structural changes will of course be needed in order to think the equivalence of languages. The lack of parity that currently exists between established and less-taught languages goes against the very spirit of an enlightened globalization of the curriculum. This lack of parity is matched by that between teachers of language and teachers of literature at all United States universities and probably at universities everywhere. I continue to think of the MLA as a force of change rather than compromise. I have been a member since 1964, and in those early times we believed that the MLA could make some changes—and indeed it did. In this hope, I make these untimely suggestions.

I am myself a translator. I recently finished a translation of Aimé Césaire's *Une saison au Congo*.[12] And, because there is no market

---

11 I am revising this piece at Mahatma Gandhi University in India, and it fills me with despair that, as India rises, not only are the humanities dispensed with as excess baggage but the idea of teaching more than English and the local language is not even remotely entertained outside the megacities.

12 Available as Aimé Césaire, *A Season in the Congo* (Gayatri Chakravorty Spivak trans.) (London: Seagull Books, 2005). The haunting footprint of that experience of translating is to be found in Spivak, "Who Killed Patrice Lumumba?" Keynote address at the Conference on Translating Postcolonial into French, Columbia University, New York, March 26, 2010.

demand for it, I have put aside in a long-term way the project of translating Assia Djebar's *Loin de Médine* into Bengali for the Bangladeshi women's movement. I translate as an act of transgression, because I cannot not do it, always aware that it levels the text. Walter Benjamin was not allowed to become a university teacher. If things had fallen otherwise, one wonders if he would have dismissed the reader so easily. I also engage in the plurality indicated in the title of our forum. With Palgrave and with Hosam Aboul-Ela's able co-editorship, I am running a translation series, Theory in the World, which brings non-Euro-US texts into English. We will soon celebrate the appearance of our first translation, the Brazilian theorist Mariolena Chaui's *Resistance and the World*. I am at the moment engaged in organizing the translation of Arindam Chakrabarti's *Deho, Geho, Bondhutto*, a text in my native language. We focus on transgressions and impossibilities—rather than acknowledge the normative.

There are therefore no statistics in my presentation. My dear friend and ally Kenneth Prewitt, a distinguished social scientist at Columbia University, talks about the way in which a set of statistics is calculated in order to come to what is basically an English word—a species of translation. Once the statistics are established, Prewitt pointed out, it is easy to endow them with all the aura of the word in the history of the language. The word of the moment, he told me, is *progress*. Once you know the statistics, you know if there has been progress. My friends in rural India show the power of this logic in accepting the absence of development.

We need a deep change of mind in order to thrust the contextualization of the global into its own repeated displacement, into its supplement. Otherwise the equation of globalization and Americanization continues as the task or burden of translation. We forget then that the phonetic elements of languages do not translate—that is also an abstraction. I am often told that when I speak in my mother tongue, it sounds beautiful—it is a legitimation by reversal of the argument behind the word *barbaros*. Meaningless sounds, whether ugly or beautiful. In place of such culturalist exoticization of the MLA, the task of the translator as member might be to rethink the current workaday definition of translation and try to make translation the beginning, on the way to language learning, rather than the end.

I close with Abderrahman Sessako's 2006 film *Bamako*. In one scene, a Malian Muslim woman swears by Allah in a secular African symbolic court judging the World Bank. A global context. Unlike all the other witnesses, she will not be shown any further in the film. In other words, this particular limit-case will not translate into a Euro-specific practice, although the practitioners are African and the country calls itself secular. In another scene, a traditional healer is dismissed by court protocol but later reappears to sing most movingly. My colleague Mamadou Diouf tells me that the song is incomprehensible even to the Malians who crowd the compound. Here is an entry into the abstract task of translation: the court of law, engaged with world governance even if inhabited by fellow Africans in a good cause, is faced by an incomprehensible traditional desire to supplement, literally beside the task. Tradition here remains undecidable, incomprehensible, not immediately usable unless, through social translation, as in W. E. B. Du Bois's long-ago practice in *Souls of Black Folk*, it is actively translated—as Du Bois did the Negro spiritual—into European notation. He managed the text so that by its end, the performative had been translated into performance, and the entire text was managed by that move.[13] If you were born in a world of so-called less-taught languages, pick up the challenge, make a decision. It will not happen if you merely crave power. And it will not emerge from the appropriative benevolence of the languages that are perennially taught. Raymond Williams, who certainly could not imagine a globalized world, nor did he take note of gender,

---

13 I have developed this in my DuBois lectures of November 2009, forthcoming from Harvard University Press.

gave us this invaluable clue: the dominant ceaselessly appropriates the emergent and rewards it as part of the thwarting of its oppositional energy, channeled into a mere alternative.[14] Losing that which is to come in the future anterior for mere institutional rewards will break our promise to the philosophers of the future.

Postscript

The Tower of Babel is our refuge. In Derrida's reading, it is a God who asks men, his children, to translate and not to translate at once.[15] Babel/Bavel is His name. Long ago I argued that when God becomes history and the sacrifice is gendered, the Mother's hand is not arrested into the making of a covenant, comparing Toni Morrison's *Beloved* with the story of Abraham and Isaac.[16] Here I substitute "other people's children" for the messianic singular—by way of the thesis that every language can be an instrument for moving into the phenomenal. This thought for me is grasped before one's desire to undo historical damage to one's own mother tongue (the objection invariably brought to the plea for imagining equivalence).

If the effort to imagine the equivalence is rethought as "other people's children" as equivalent to my own, we have X-rayed comparative literature—translating before translation—into the semiotics of reproductive heteronormativity at its most impersonal.[17] Derrida chose

---

14 Raymond Williams, *Marxism and Literature* (New York: Oxford University Press, 1977), p. 121–27.

15 Jacques Derrida, "De Tours de Babel" (Joseph Graham trans.), in *Acts of Religion* (Gil Anidjar ed.) (New York: Routledge, 2002), p. 118.

16 Gayatri Chakravorty Spivak, *A Critique of Postcolonial Reason: Toward the History of a Vanishing Present* (Cambridge, MA: Harvard University Press, 1999), p. 305.

17 For an analysis of rationalizing social formation by reproductive heteronormativity, see B. R. Ambedkar, "Castes in India," in *The Essential Writings of Ambedkar* (Valerian Rodrigues ed.) (New Delhi: Oxford University Press, 2002), pp. 241–62.

hymen and marriage as his concept-metaphors for translation. I speak of reproductive heteronormativity upstream from sexual contract or preference, as the irreducible. It is the baseline coding assemblage at our disposal. Reproduction from difference as the norm is the irreducible; upstream from straight/queer/trans as phenomenally understood. *Hetero-* here is the antonym of *auto-*. The queer use of childbearing, for example, is an important extramoral use of difference. Language is always already (reproduced in difference; so are capital and translation. Examining the specificities of each reproduction, we see the predicament of phenomenal reproduction (sex-gender systems) in each.

Translation in these understandings marks being/becoming-human. Do animals translate? Elsewhere I have quoted Oedipus's lament: "O marriages, marriages, you put us in nature, and putting us back again, reversed the seed, and indexed fathers, brothers, children, kin-blood mingled, brides, women, mothers, a shameful thing to know among the works of man [. . .]"[18] Derrida cites Porphyry on the Roman Crassus: "A lamprey [toothed eel] which belonged to the Roman Crassus would come to him when called by name [*onomasis kaloumene*] and had such an effect on him that he mourned when it died, though he had earlier borne with moderation the loss of three children."[19]

Even if we recognize that the Law of the Father (the very mark of being/becoming human) staged in *Oedipus* is also a longing to follow our animality, we who belong historically to a sector of the human that accessed the Law through a language less taught in the United States

---

Although he is ostensibly speaking of caste formation, the argument applies to group formation in general.

18 Sophocles, *Oedipus the King*, ll. 1403–07. My translation is as literal as possible, to show that Oedipus reproaches marriage for the reversed inscription of human kinship, which makes incest possible (Spivak, "Tracing the Skin of Day," in *Undated: Nightskin* [Dubai: 1x1 Art Gallery, 2009]).

19 Jacques Derrida, *The Animal That I Am* (David Wills trans.) (New York: Fordham University Press, 2008), p. 85.

will not want to humanize that longing into Crassus's eel's ability to translate human speech, will not want to follow a cited animal incorrectly, by translating capital/English's call for translation as if it were our proper task/name, even if our master mourns for us.[20]

---

20 Derrida's taking up the untranslatable French pun in *suis*, first-person singular for both "to be" and "to follow," as a stable essential description of being human, and a "mad pursuit" of the animal in search of questions too complex to summarize here, is relevant to my use of this final example (*The Animal That I Am*, p. 78).

Global?

(2015)*

The real title of the book that I published in 2013 is *An Aesthetic Education in the Era of Globalizability.* In the end of the book this secret is revealed. That to me is more important than globalization: that nearly everything is globalizable, medicine and poison. Yet it is also true that "globalization takes place only in capital and data. Everything else is damage control."[1] If we catch up epistemically with this situation we will have just a couple of global languages, and a world governance, undoubtedly pernicious and feudal in its workings, which will operate not in a nation, not in a political way, but in a cosmopolitical way. When we emphasize ideal global communities we begin to sense that there is a mismatch between nation-state and world governance. The answer to that is not notions of community, however. They take us back to somewhat primitive social contracts subsumed under a financialized global economy.

The global histories that we project today are usually international histories. A group of us have started a project involving Africa and Asia, variously called "Radiating Globality" or "Old Histories, New Geographies," which tries to undo this tendency. I hope you will be able to read

* First published in Henrik Enroth and Douglas Brommesson (eds), *Global Community? Transnational and Transdisciplinary Exchanges* (London: Rowan and Littlefield, 2015), pp. 9–18.

1 Gayatri Chakravorty Spivak, *An Aesthetic Education in the Era of Globalization* (Cambridge, MA: Harvard University Press, 2013), p. 1.

some of these efforts in the coming years. Today I ask you to look back in another direction as well.

The tacit globalizer before the globe was ever thought of is reproductive heteronormativity. The word hetero here is not the opposite of homo but the opposite of auto. Everything, including capital, rises in this difference between the auto and the hetero. This is a much larger globalizer. If one could in fact begin to think of plotting such a history, which cannot be fully done because it goes beyond the idea of agency, it would be different from international histories of people traveling, or world system theories which think that economic systems automatically mean cultural systems.

Part of the work of the "Radiating Globality" group is to understand the relationship between my hometown Kolkata and the Chinese city of Kunming. They have traded since the eighth century. We are trying to reestablish what this might mean in the making of global histories. As for "world literature," it aims for a kind of cosmopolitan fusion cuisine.[2]

What is at stake in seeking to restore the word "community," here in the heart of successful European socialism, crumbling since the late 1980s under the weight of ethnic immigration, free of the bad austerity news of the euro zone making international headlines every day, thanks to a unification proposed on grounds of economic expediency without the sharing of power. And now as the Arab spring is being managed, as Chinese internet is censoring reporting of the prime minister's wide and deep involvement in capital accumulation, as IMF hands become heads of state in Spain, Italy, and India—is it a return of the golden repressed, in a loose analogy with Freud fabulated, a digitally idealized utopian socialism? "Community" is a topos in existence since at least McLuhan and Lyotard, as I remarked to an audience in Sweden in

---

2 Wole Soyinka gives us a hilarious early example of this in Soyinka, "Othello's Dominion, Immigrant Domain," *Savannah Review* 3 (May 2014): 1–20.

1992.[3] Is the invocation of community especially a task for the organic intellectual of globalization? We could spin a tale here of how to describe the contemporary mode of production as it relates to the changes in the epistemological projects of intellectuals, as the conjunctures change. Perhaps there is a story of intellectual community formation here. Story. I prefer the abstract fictionality of class formation rather than communities, expanding it beyond capital logic as did Gramsci and beyond sexual logic as did Zillah Eisenstein and Gayle Rubin. The mobility and contingency of class carried an implicit acknowledgment that the hunkering together was an epiphenomenon, that it was not the main point.

A splendid example of this comes long before our time when the mobility was much slower. It is the great novel of Chartism, Mrs. Gaskell's *North and South*. This epiphenomenality was proved in that novel, if proof is needed. Communities are always metonymic, although they are constituted by the effort to think of themselves as holistic, often by way of gender control.

Let me pause a moment on another literary example, Tillie Olsen's novella *Tell Me a Riddle*. Olsen's parents were in the 1905 Russian Revolution. In this novel Olsen presents a fictional representation of her mother, who wonders about this riddle. It relates obliquely to a riddle that W. E. B. Du Bois mentions in an early lecture to what he calls "Smughampton," a small community of upper-class Black people at a small university:

> You are the type and representative of that fateful class through whom the great army of tomorrow's men are learning the riddle of the world, the meaning of life and the life worth living. And so when I speak to you, I feel that in a peculiar way I am speaking to the future world and if I way well what I am moved

---

3 Gayatri Chakravorty Spivak, "Love, Cruelty, and Cultural Talks in the Hot Peace," *Parallax* 1 (November 1995): 1–31.

to say and force my words into your souls then somehow and sometime those words will fire the hearts of men.[4]

Du Bois is thirty-eight at the time and speaks prospectively to an unlikely group. Olsen gives an old woman's version, looking at a failed revolution: why do people lose interest in social justice once they taste prosperity? Why do socially articulated communities disappear?

This riddle is generalized by Derrida in the notion that the event escapes the conventions of the performative. The performative operates because of the existence of conventions, otherwise it wouldn't operate at all. I am suggesting that we continue to think of community as something happening as a result of global formations coming together but then dissolving rather than something that we recognize and establish and possess. Think of ourselves at this conference for example as a "community" metonymically held together by our shared concern for what you have called alterity in a post-national condition. So our task would be to ask what a global community might be in the fullest sense, things held in common. Networking through the silicon chip, the other side of which is finance capital and derivatives. An electronic network is a new thing and to call it by that old dream is to bring in certain kinds of unacknowledged behavior that might not be appropriate. I am not a technophobe, but I think, as I was saying to you yesterday, that this incredible genie out of a bottle is medicine as well as poison. In order to be able to use it as medicine you need agents who are produced outside of the speed of the thing itself.

This would imply a fully socially articulate community rather than a networked collectivity named a community. The real question is not can the word community be salvaged, but that it is repeatedly salvaged and used mostly to describe a group of people metonymically marked

---

4 W. E. B. Du Bois, "The Hampton Idea," in Herbert Aptheker (ed.), *The Education of Black People: Ten Critiques, 1906–1960* (Amherst: University of Massachusetts Press, 1973), p. 6.

. . . toward whom we feel as non-sufferers—a term coined by Marilena Chaui of Brazil—a certain obligation, survivor's guilt. You mention *A Critique of Postcolonial Reason* in your invitation. My argument there would take on board this sort of behavior toward minority groups whose upper reaches collaborate by self-ethnicization. Given the pervasive low-grade racism and sexism that make the world go around, the self-ethnicized leaders create voting blocs that in principle contravene the austere outlines of democracy.

Post-national alterities: even in referring to paperless immigrants in the metropole, that description is not accurate. In fact even the waves of underclass immigrants are not *post*-national. They are the result of the full displacement of national responsibility from citizen to global capital. How under those circumstances can we call the world post-national, but you pointed out in your opening remarks that you were well aware that everything was in fact not pre-post national, as it were, but at the same time. How can we call the world post-national, except as organic intellectuals of globalization? The globe is borderless only in the movement of finance capital and derivatives, moving twenty-four seven all over the grid in heliocentric time. Yet it must seek to preserve the difference between nation-state-based currencies further divided by the global north, the G20 and the global south. Without this the currency speculations, which is one important basis of finance capital, and financialized world trade, could not flourish. These virtual and electronic divisions are added to more conventional borders, so that capital can travel across borders in a digitally borderless fashion. Borderlessness in other words needs borders of a certain sort in order to be borderless. It is within this performative contradiction that the problematic of immigration is lodged. You are describing this as post-national alterity. Capital cannot let go of massively underpaid labor, with no workplace safety or benefits requirements, and yet it must racialize, sexualize, oppose.

This post- is too easily said: We are in a world which is not only far from post-national but where borders have to be kept up, because of the double bind of capital, which cannot survive without the captive workforce. These are the new subalterns, undocumented immigrant labor, post-national alterities. And, if the visible minorities are alterity, does the invisible majority retain ipseity as well? If there is a global community, it is bound by capital logic. Labor must therefore cross frontiers, not borders, under cover, where hard currency beckons.

If we are obliged to become what Gramsci would call the organic intellectuals of capitalist globalization, let us do so in a supplementing spirit. In the best of all possible worlds, the performative contradictions of literary borderlessness supplement the cruelties, in our case English, in the case of North Africa French, in the case of Mozambique Portuguese, and so on. This borderlessness of the imperial literatures supplements the cruelties as well as the social productivity of seemingly borderless capital, and you know well what the outline of supplementation is. The person or the group or whoever wants to supplement has to know what it is that one is adding to, has to know the other object very well to know the shape of the hole that must be filled, sometimes called a textual blank. It is threatening for the borderlessness of those literatures, dangerous. This is how one supplements. Not just from the outside; achieving a sort of critical intimacy rather than a critical distance. So think again of our benevolence towards so called post-colonial alterity, an abstract phrase to which it is difficult to give supplementational gravity, without giving time and labor. Not to mention deep language learning. This is not practical and fast, and it cannot be planned in conferences. I have been for thirty years trying to do this in a very small focus. A small group of landless illiterates, six schools. The idea of doing this, producing intuitions of democracy, rather than simple employability, in this largest sector of the electorate in the so called world's largest democracy. There is no "culturalism" there, no "community." It is not something that can be just proposed. This kind of relationship to the experiential textuality of post-national alterity will undo the universalizing abstractions coming out of a Euro-US as well as North-in-the-South perspective. The subaltern is not generalizable. As you can see, what you call post-national alterity is very close to my concerns today. The nation-state needs to be noticed today rather than dismissed as "post." Like Socrates in the *Apology*, we must be a gadfly on the horse's ass, on the backside of the hippo megalo that is the state.[5]

Imaginative training of epistemological performance for the intellectual is the insertion of the subaltern into the circuit of hegemony on the Gramsci–Du Bois model. And for that we need the nation-state and we need to fight for constitutionality rather than the unconstituted "rule of law" imposed by neoliberal economic re-structuring. The liberated subaltern can access the state as an agent but not the global capitalist cosmopolis. Enlightened capitalism, corporate philanthropy, international civil society. Their talk of giving back, of repaying the global community, has its limits. It is obliged to ignore the continued need for subalternization in order for social productivity to be so visible. As a Humanities teacher, I add unconditional ethics.

For some years now I have been focused on the fact that in life as in thought, we almost always receive contradictory instructions at the same time. The greatest example is that even as we are living we are dying and the exigencies of the two positions are contradictory. Nestled in this contradiction we still go forward, hoping for the continuity of our world beyond the limits of our lives. The general name for this situation is double bind, and it is, paradoxically, a productive structure. The idea of a global community is in a double bind with the fact that feelings of community are necessarily connected with the first language(s), most often also connected through the group of human beings claiming it as

---

5 Plato, *Euthyphro, Apology, Crito, Phaedo, Phaedrus* (Harold North Fowler trans.), Loeb Classical Library 36 (Cambridge, MA: Harvard University Press, 1914), pp. 111–13.

such, not necessarily identical with nation or class but somehow tied with these ideas as they harbor something like imagined neighborhoods, even blood, which brings in gendering and the family romance. This is a problem, and these are part of the philosophical representation of the double bind between the global and the local. We have to take this into consideration, if we are going to look at the productive double bind within translation as such.

The double bind operates unevenly between deep language learning in order to access lingual memory, memory of the language in the language, and the imperative to translate, which also requires such deep language learning. Such considerations drive me to think of translation as an activity rather than a convenience. There is no cultural exchange through translation. I do not think cultures can be exchanged, I do not think cultures can be named. I think culture is a word that one should take a moratorium on. Translations of convenience are a way of coping with the fact that there can be no global community except at the very top. And even then, even with just a handful of well-known languages, the convenience of translation must constantly be used and the double bind between the necessity and impossibility of translation denied. There would be much to say about this but I will for the moment turn aside from it, except to repeat here, in the bosom of a university, that we focus on translation as an activity. That most intimate act of reading is different from the benevolence of communitarianism. It requires the ability to suspend the interest of the self in the interest of the other. The goal of translation as an activity rather than a convenience is to generate a dissatisfaction rather than a satisfaction in the product.

In an ethical situation that is unconditional rather than focused on a single kind of problem, we know that the extent of the suffering is altogether larger than whatever it is that we are able to address. Such reading has to be used by minds that have been made ready for the use of digitality as medicine rather than poison.

A word in closing about my specific discipline. Disciplinarily I do of course always insist on comparative literature. Comparative literature perceived from the perspective of globalization thinks that the experience of first language learning shared by the overwhelming majority of infants in the world—before acquired rationality—puts in place the instrumentation for unconditional ethics. That stuff is learned before you begin to reason. Any language, big or small, rich or poor, endangered or triumphant, can activate the metapsychological circuits of the infant subject and launch it on the contingent track of the ethical. When we translate the mother tongue this relationship between subject and language is displaced. Comparative literature at its best tries to learn language the child's way, the impossible way, entering the lingual memory, the memory of the language in the language. A private and singular hold on its history also requires such deep language learning, suspending itself in it. By so doing it enlarges the scope and range of ethical practice.

Then we can at least think of the other side, where the wounds bleed, where people feel these departures rather than just wanting to find justice under capitalism in the place to which they have come. I was recently at a conference of ethnicity, identity, literature in upper Assam in North-East India. Along the border between the state of Assam and upper Bangladesh, there is a great deal of ethnic conflict, resembling such conflicts as the US–Mexico border, Israel–Palestine border, and other well known international boundaries. Studying some literature from the area, I read a novel based on this problem. Assamese is not my language. We the Bengalis are the cultural imperialists in that area. "Kick the Bengalis out" is a slogan that has been around, to the extent that one of my class friends, Assamese himself, having taken a stand against it, was beaten up so badly—a brave intellectual taking a political stand—that he was hospitalized for a long time and has suffered nervous damage. I learned how to read Assamese for the sake of the conference, so that I could read Assamese literature to an Assamese audience in Assamese. It was not so easy, especially since the two languages are close enough that you can slip into Bengali easily and then the attempt is undone.

Studying some literature from the area, I read the novel *Rupabalir Palash* by Syed Abdul Malik, a member of the migrant Bengali community from Eastern Bengal (now Bangladesh) who have been mowed down by the indigenous Ahom. Malik describes the way in which the migrant, especially the underclass migrant, makes the language of the ironically named host state his or her own, and how, for the second generation it becomes a first language. Coupled with this, in the last section of Malik's novel, there is a lament that in spite of such an effort voting rights, idealized throughout the novel, are denied, that the model of deep language learning is not just the institutional humanities model of comparative literature, but the practical humanities model of these so called illegal immigrants, a global phenomenon, a group that I have described as the new subaltern. I believe that the sensibility trained in the humanities, as I have continuously been describing for the last few years, can also begin to see that the border between the new subaltern and disciplinarized humanities teachers in a globalized world that trivializes the humanities is unstable. Subaltern classes cannot use the state in a democracy where people supposedly control the state. In Abdul Malik's novel we find the words "those who, thinking to stay alive, have given up the enchantment of the motherland, come to Assam and, taken her for mother, forgetting their own language, have made Assamese their own language." In a passage that I often quote, Karl Marx provides a less affective description of this as revolutionary practice. "In like manner the beginner who has learned a new language always translates it back into his mother tongue, but he appropriates the spirit of the new language, and can produce in it freely only when he moves in it without remembering back, when he forgets the language rooted in him."[6] Within the

---

6 Karl Marx, "The Eighteenth Brumaire of Louis Bonaparte," in *Surveys from Exile* (David Fernbach ed.) (New York: Vintage, 1973), p. 147.

actively translating teacher and student in our classrooms, this practice brings the awareness that the first step in translation is violent, the destruction of the body of the language, the sound that is so deeply tied to the structural feeling, especially but not only if one is translating from the first language. Perhaps it is a reminder of the setting aside of the interest in the self that must accompany translation as an encompassing model of ethical practice as such. We must imagine that this violence is called for in all efforts of communication. In other words, I am trying to explain the difficult set of ideas that crowd my mind, because I am a comparativist, when I try to open up the unexamined conviction that translation can naturally create cultural exchange and global community. In the wholesale acquisition of texts in other languages, the idea of translation as convenience begins to win over the idea of translation as activity. Can translating rather than translation be the future of the humanities? We will then be a global "community," each one of us globalizable, upstream from politics, an island of languaging in a field of traces. The trace of an unknown language is where we know meaningfulness is operating, but we do not know how. Our task as teachers and translators calls us into this challenge, the recognition that a fully translated globe is nothing that we should desire.

In conclusion: first I asked what is at stake in talking community in this corner of Europe today. Next I stopped on the words "post-national alterity" and tried first to say that "post-national" is too superficial. Under the encompassing word "alterity," used as the consolidating opposite of ipseity, I tried to think about the heterogeneity of alterity, especially if agency is restored to the other side as extant, not only here, but also there. A few words on translation, on comparative literature. Two words left out: cosmopolitanism and planetarity. Think upon them and let these words be complete.

Teaching *Black Skin*

(2022)*

I dedicate these words to Ella Turenne, a Haitian-US poet, who came into my life at the beginning of the century; because I believe Haiti is a cryptonym in Fanon, Du Bois, and others. Cryptonym: a name in the crypt of the soul. Look for the discussion in my forthcoming book *My Brother Burghardt* with Harvard University Press. For here, Derrida commenting on Nicolas Abraham and Maria Torok: "Everything happens as if the cryptonymic transcription, playing with the allosemes ["It" and "which" are allosemes—from OED] and their synonyms (always more numerous in their open series than is indicated by a dictionary), acts like an angled hook to put the reader on a detour and to make the itinerary illegible."[1]

How does someone not of African or Antilles origin, except in the broad sense in which the origin of the human is in Africa, and not a specialist of those areas, teach *Black Skin, White Masks*—seventy years

* Paper presented at "Seventy Years of *Black Skin, White Masks*," Modern Language Association Convention, Washington, DC, January 7, 2022. [My deepest gratitude to Surya Parekh for working with me in preparing this essay for publication.— GCS]

1 Jacques Derrida, "Fors: Les mots de Abraham et Torok," preface to Nicolas Abraham and Maria Torok, *Cryptonymie: Le verbier de l'Homme aux Loups* (Paris: Aubier Flammarion, 1976), p. 62; "Fors: The Anglish Words of Nicolas Abraham and Maria" (Barbara Johnson trans.), foreword to Nicolas Abraham and Maria Torok, *The Wolfman's Magic Word: A Cryptonymy* (Nicholas Rand trans.) (Minneapolis: University of Minnesota Press, 1986), p. xlii; translation modified. The translation translates *transcription* as "translation." Much to think about here.

old this year?[2] First, as Jean Khalfa suggests, we must teach it with sustained reference to Fanon's actual dissertation for a medical degree (*Black Skin* was apparently submitted as such and rejected.), "Mental Alterations, Character Modifications, Psychic Disorders and Intellectual Deficit in Spinocerebellar Heredodegeneration: A Case of Friedrich's Ataxia with Delusions of Possession," which he dedicated to his family, and to his brother Joby, and he included this epigraph from Nietzsche's *Thus Spoke Zarathustra:* "I speak only of lived things and do not simply present cerebral processes."[3] The dissertation seeks to undo the barrier between the neurological and the psychological, and attempts to connect the individual and the collective; for colonizing white societies, the genetic family. In *Black Skin* the genetic, racializing Eros writes it into colonialism. Much has been made of Fanon's appreciation of Lacan. To my mind, the greatest affinity is with the Lacan who suggests that in rememoration, the analyst helps the patient to occupy with desire a psychic network on different levels, including traces deposited on mnemic material, the Fliess–Freud–Lacan rewriting of the neurological.[4] To

---

2 Frantz Fanon, *Peau noire, masques blancs* (Paris: Éditions du Seuil, 1952); *Black Skin, White Masks* (Charles Lam Markmann trans.) (New York: Grove Press, 1967); *Black Skin, White* Masks (Richard Philcox trans.) (New York: Grove Press, 2008). Page numbers hereafter given in the text, with F for French, EP for the Philcox translation, and EM for Markmann. I cite both translations because, following the track laid by my essay, I check both when I feel the activism of Fanon's language is lost in the English.

3 Frantz Fanon, *Alienation and Freedom* (Jean Khalfa and Robert J. C. Young eds; Steven Corcoran trans.) (New York: Bloomsbury, 2019), p. 204.

4 Jacques Lacan, "Du réseau des signifiants," in *Le Séminaire de Jacques Lacan Livre XI: Les Quatre Concepts Fondamentaux De La Psychanalyse* (Jacques-Alain Miller ed.) (Paris: Éditions du Seuil, 1964), pp. 43–52; "The Network of Signifiers," in *The Seminar of Jacques Lacan Book IV: Four Fundamental Concepts of Psychoanalysis* (Alan Sheridan trans.) (New York: W. W. Norton, 1981), p. 42–52. Though the actual seminar happened after Fanon's death, I am pointing at what Taraknath Sen called "the community of spirit" between Tagore, Goethe, and Shakespeare (in Taraknath Sen, *A Literary Miscellany* [Kolkata: Avant-Garde, forthcoming]).

achieve that affinity, Fanon has to pass through many steps on the task of finding agency of semiosis for the pluralized colonized. He can call Lacan a metonym for his undertaking as Lacan calls Hegel a metonym for psychoanalysis.

Secondly, we who cannot make identity-connections, must go over contextual research carefully.

But then, and thirdly, we must see how Fanon sublates his context.

Martinique (circled in the extreme right of the map below) is tiny, about 50 miles long and reaching a maximum width of 22 miles.

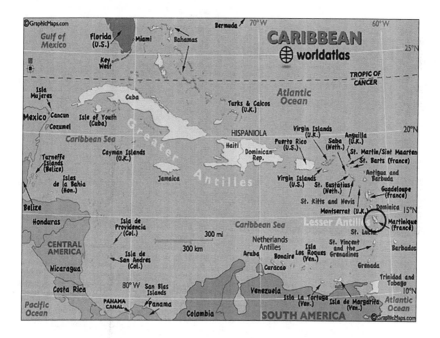

Russia is 6,612,073 square miles, and encompasses more than one-eighth of Earth's inhabitable land area. China is 3,250 miles from east to west and 3,400 miles from north to south. The continent of Africa is 11.73 million square miles.

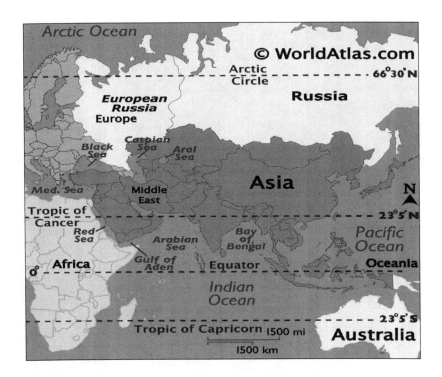

And yet we think Fanon can speak to the educated world beyond these limits. He lived only thirty-six years. He is therefore constrained in both time and space; yet he is a big voice.

How, then, does he sublate his context? First off, by asking the reader to pay attention to it, posit it. Learn to distinguish between the Antilles and Africa says he. And then, in the Antilles, he categorizes three groups: never been to the metropole, been and returned, and the diasporic. In terms of the diasporic, he finds room to generalize, with all colonized peoples.

His attitude towards the diasporic is deeply distrustful. And yet, he clearly speaks as a diasporic claiming metropolitan validation. This is indeed his undertaking, access to the ingredients for a Black semiosis and the possibility to write a psychiatric dissertation as a self-diagnosed subject. "L'artiste est quelqu'un qui ne devient artiste que là où sa main tremble, c'est-à-dire où il ne sait pas, au fond, ce qui va arriver ou ce qui va arriver lui est dicté par l'autre."[5] I differ from my brilliant and dear friend Françoise Vergès perhaps precisely because I cannot be within identity politics here.[6]

(Fanon speaks as self-translated into "French" diasporic—even as a Jean Veneuse, René Maran's hero—but, unlike Veneuse, Frantz does not go back. Let us consider a telling example:

When he comments on "mastery"—shades of Hegel here—"of language afford[ing] remarkable power," he cites a line from Paul Valéry's "La Pythie," from the same stanza chosen by Jean Hyppolite's—Fanon read his translation of Hegel, and no doubt encountered him as he attended Kojève's and Merleau-Ponty's seminars—commentary on Hegel's locating of language in his essay entitled "Sense and Sensible,"[7] the only difference in the "French"-translated diasporic is that he chooses a different line, mentioning flesh. Here is the stanza, Hyppolite chooses the first line and Fanon the fourth:

Honor of Men, Saint LANGUAGE,
Prophetic and adorned discourse,
Beautiful chains in which enwinds
The god strayed into the flesh[8]

---

5 Jacques Derrida, "Comment ne pas trembler?", *Annali, Fondazione Europea del Disegno* (*Fondation Adami*) 2 (2006): 97.

6 In "Creole Skin, Black Mask: Fanon and Disavowal" (*Critical Inquiry* 23[3] [Spring 1997]: 578–95), Françoise Vergès sees him as disavowing the Antilles and finding his fathers in Algeria.

7 Jean Hyppolite, *Logique et existence* (Paris: Presses Universitaires de France, 1953); *Logic and Existence* (Leonard Lawlor and Amit Sen trans) (Albany: SUNY Press, 1997).

8 Paul Valéry, *Charms and Other Pieces* (*A Bilingual Edition*) (Peter Dale trans.) (London: Anvil Press Poetry, 2007), pp. 176–77; translation modified.

Hyppolite and Fanon share their French-ness in not acknowledging Valery's epigraph which asks us to read Virgil's *Aeneid,* Book IV. The epigraph indicates that Dido has just said something, thus provoking the reader to go back to the *Aeneid* and discover what it was that Dido did say. In Dido's account we encounter the Ethiopian Sybil who can teach Dido how to die. This is a contrast to the Cumean Sybil, the good Sybil who will appear later, to lead Aeneas into Lethe. The Romans knew that part of Africa pretty well and Virgil mentions the ethnic origin of the Black Sybil. Of course Valery does not go that far but, in the poem, he describes this Black Sybil in her immense suffering and turbulence at last giving birth to a language that comes from no human agency. Shelley Haley, an eminent Black feminist classicist, locates the Black Sybil as Maasai and she also suggests that details of the sacrifice of blood and the presence of serpents resemble vodou.[9] Tracking the cryptonym here is a massive historico-geographic exploration where Fanon is absent.)

If this is the positing of the diasporic subject as an inadequate enunciator of the semiotic system he is obliged to inhabit, its negation comes in the most powerful chapter of the book: "L'expérience vécue du Noir"—the lived experience of the Black—and Richard Philcox adds the "Man" that English requires.[10]

In my office hangs a photo of Lyle Ashton Harris's "Mama see the Negro, I am Frightened."

---

9 Shelley Haley, "Be Not Afraid of the Dark: Critical Race Theory and Classical Studies," in Laura Nasrallah and Elisabeth Schüssler Fiorenza (eds), *Prejudice and Christian Beginnings: Investigating Race, Gender, and Ethnicity in Early Christian Studies* (Minneapolis, MN: Fortress Press, 2009) pp. 27–49.

10 Lydie Moudelino's distinction—*Nègre* as African and *Noir* as Caribbean—is particularly important as the shunning of the encrypted Haiti ("Contextualizing Fanon, Again: On the Black Man and His 'Fellows' in 1950s France," paper presented at "Seventy Years of *Black Skin, White Masks*," Modern Language Association Convention [MLA], Washington, DC, January 7, 2022).

FIGURE 4. "Mama See the Negro, I'm Frightened" (1993) © Lyle Ashton Harris.

As the visitor exits Spivak's office:

FIGURE 5. Office door. *Courtesy: Gayatri Chakravorty Spivak.*

In 1963 I went to Franco's Spain, to see what was happening in Catalonia because in India I had read George Orwell's *Homage to Catalonia*.[11] I wore nylon saris as the most packable clothing. I hitch-hiked to Pamplona to see bullfights. I cannot count how often fathers and mothers of families with children would point at me and utter "mira mira mira gitana Indiana caballeros oklahoma" and so on. I identified with "Mama, see the Negro." I squatted in the dust and drew maps of the world with a twig to show where I came from, trying to grasp the agency—*l'instance*—of semiosis, only to arouse fear, Was I a witch? In Britain I was hit four times—once concussed badly—always while jogging—how dare a mature woman of color run for fun? I went to the *Guardian* with the story, trying to grasp the agency of semiosis, but they didn't think the story was of interest. This is Fanon's lesson, grasp the agency of semiosis. Otherwise there is no thematization, no reflexive démarche. (The translations miss the activism of the sentence.)

What does *Black Skin* suggest that I was not doing? Now I push the students to find the answer. I ask them to look for a hard word: lysis, analysis without the "ana."

Corey McEleny considers Fanon's use of lysis in *Black Skin* within the Euro-US film-theoretical field and, since he clearly does not want to be politically incorrect, he cannot say too much:

> In the domain of biochemistry, for instance, *lysis* refers to the "disintegration or dissolution of cells" through a breakdown of the cellular membrane (*OED*). This is the sense of the word on which Frantz Fanon riffs when, in the introduction to *Black Skin, White Masks*, he calls for "a complete lysis of this morbid universe." [. . .] Fanon states his intentions for that complex in a way that prefigures Mulvey's formulation. "By analyzing it," he writes, "we aim to destroy it."[12]

---

11 George Orwell, *Homage to Catalonia* (Orlando, FL: Harcourt Brace Jovanovich, 1952).

12 Corey McEleney, "The Resistance to Overanalysis," *Differences* 52(2) (2021): 19.

Of course McEleny cannot see that analysis is psychoanalysis here (although Fanon is not, of course, a psychoanalyst) if she thinks Fanon is prefiguring Laura Mulvey! And, he cannot see that the destruction—I must think Ambedkar's annihilation of caste—is a move that precedes a new challenge to analytic practice, where the analyst occupies an "interested" position within a racialized field in order to discover pluralized problematics of new psycho-semiotics. I will warn the students to take the humanities beyond the discipline and allow them to appreciate how hard McEleney tries within the discipline. In a footnote he writes: "In the end, however, such categorical differentiations are of limited value;" whereas Fanon says that he "grasp[s] his narcissism with both hands and [. . .] pushes back on [*repousser*] on those who want to make of the human a mechanically unified field [*faire de l'homme une mécanique;* the translations miss the implications of *la mécanique* as a method]. If the debate cannot be opened up on a philosophical level—i.e. the fundamental demands of human reality—I agree to place it on a psychoanalytical level: other words the 'failures' [*ratés*]," just as we talk about engine failures.

His examples are therefore not representative, but "failures," whose access to the appropriate semiotic agency must be preceded by a lysis of their interpretation by way of a normative mechanical discourse of evaluation.

It is thus that he proceeds to Adler (the behaviorist) and Hegel (the philosopher/phenomenologist). In the mean time, all his examples are literary, "unverifiable." Freud says in "The Uncanny" (1919) that he can find in literature evidence of the sort that he cannot find in real life. Literature is "an experience of the impossible." Literature is giving Fanon those "failures" that he will treat in his office.

For him therefore, it is a *devoir d'analyse* to assess the significance of the reception of Mayotte Capécia's *Je suis Martiniquaise* in certain milieus, in other words of the "failure" of the collective as well and therefore he calls the book as "pushing [*prônant*] unhealthy [*malsain*] behavior" (F 34). The translations miss this self-proclaimed professional duty—making it into a "forcing" (EM 42), and an obligation (EP 25) where Fanon the analyst claims "no equivocation is possible," Markmann goes for "circumlocution," and Philcox "no doubt whatsoever." What is most alarming is Markmann's translation of *prôn[er] un comportement malsain* as "a sermon in praise of corruption." What is missed is Fanon's staging of himself as an analyst and also as marked by gendering, since that is the task of the text (to seek validation from an institution lyse-d from under his feet). It remains to add that the task of Fanon the analyst is to correct the "failure"—or, as he puts it, "Ce que nous affirmons, c'est que la tare doit etre expulse une fois pour toutes" (F 50). The more professional phraseology "what we affirm" is "what we can say" in Philcox (EP 44) and "what I insist on" (EM 62) in Markmann. *Tare*—a "defect," again less personal—becomes either a "flaw" (EP 44) or, what is much worse "the poison" (EM 62). My point is that the entire analytical play with the institution rhetorically staged in Fanon is missed by the translators.

It is in that mood that he writes "in other words, the question is whether the basic personality is a constant or a variable." "Basic personality" is, as the translators tell us, in English in the original. Notice below, in a poem by a major Bengali poet who was also schizophrenic, the underlined sentence that is written in English in Bengali script.[13] There will be a "reading" of this poem with my students, which is beyond the scope of this essay. Let us simply say that this is a statement uttered about the allosemic position of gendering in the embryo.[14]

---

13 The translator, Arindam Chakrabarti, who sent me the material by email, did not mark the line that is in English in both versions, in Bengali script in the original. A transcription? Claiming to be a translation? A lot to think of here (see footnote 2 above).

14 Malay Ray Chowdhury, "Binoy Majumdar: Kabitar Bodhi Briksha," available at www.binoy898180804.wordpress.com (last accessed on January 8, 2022). He makes an attempt to situate Majumdar's poetry within his schizophrenia. (I should warn

X, Y ও Z

দুটো ভ্যারিয়বল X ও Y
X ও Y থেকে তৃতীয় একটি ভ্যারিয়বল বানাতে চাই
আমরা। তৃতীয় ভ্যারিয়বল 'Z' সহজেই বানানো যায়
ক্যালকুলাসের দ্বারা।
একমাত্র ঐ ক্যালকুলাসের জন্যই ময়ূরীর সন্তান আরেকটি
ময়ূরীই হয়—ডিম থেকে ময়ূর হয়, তারপরে
'Z' হয়। Y আর X
Y ইজ আ ফাংশন অফ X
ঠিক ডিমটাও হয় সেইরকম। ডিমের ভিতরে
'Y'-ও আছে 'X'-ও আছে। সুতরাং 'Z' সহজেই
হয় Y নতুবা X-এর মতন হবে। ময়ূরীর ডিম
তার ভিতরে ময়ূরী'ও আছে ময়ূর'ও আছে।
সুতরাং ডেরিভেটিভ হয় ময়ূর হবে নয়তো ময়ূরী হবে।

X, Y, and Z

Two variables, X and Y:
We wish to construct a third variable
From X and Y and it is easy to make
Z, a third variable
By means of Calculus
It's thanks only to this Calculus
That the progeny of a peahen
Can only be a peahen—from the egg a peacock is
  born
And then there is Z; at first of course there have to
  be X and Y
Y is a function of X
Just like that is the egg, and inside the egg
There is 'Y' as well as 'X'
It follows easily from this that Z would be similar
To either Y or X and the egg of a peahen
Would contain, inside, both a peahen and peacock
Hence the derivative will be
Either a peacock or peahen.

A poem by Binoy Majumdar (1934–2006)
from his collection Short Pieces of Poetry
and Prose.

We are reading *Black Skin*. Its scenario will be transformed in the experience of Algeria: anti-colonial struggle, psychiatric practice, political violence, living with terminal disease. Again, you will notice my divergence from Vergès. My point is that as Fanon goes from Martinique to Algeria via Brittany, and the diaspora is not metropolitan. Indeed, it is the metropole that denies citizenship to him. We are not talking national identity here. We are talking of the usefulness of a non-metropolitan diasporic difference.

---

the reader that anything said about me in Ray Chowdhury's piece is factually incorrect.)

The last word in the title of Fanon's dissertation is "possession." And here, before the emergence of Algeria, we can look at what might be the cryptonym of Haiti as a good diaspora. The apparent argument is out of place and suffers from internal racism. "We have known and unfortunately still know comrades originary [originaires] from Daho-mey or the Congo who say they are Antillean; we have known and still know Antilleans who get annoyed at being taken for Senegalese" (F 20, EP 9, EM 25–26; translation modified). Markmann is less satisfactory here than Philcox. I have emphasized the word "originary" though I am not sure if Fanon intends the strict meaning which insists that each time something is done the same steps must be repeated. The way in which the "African" Haitians make Dahomey or their African places of origin come alive in the acts of possession might make the word important. We must remember, however, that vodou is mostly practiced by peas-ants and the urban poor, and Fanon himself in *The Wretched of the Earth*, in a sympathetic analysis, insists that the peasants as such, because they have mysterious beliefs, probably cannot be the agents of an anti-colonial revolution as such.[15] But cryptonymy knows no such rules. It is enough that Dahomey and Congo supplied African slaves to Haiti (and in small numbers to Martinique) to replace the Carib. And in this diaspora, they brought their gods from Africa and returned them so they could be haunted by them, possessed by them in vodou. This is reminiscent of the original diaspora in Alexandria.

Broadly understood, "possession" can travel beyond popular prac-tice and give a model for our own "modern" reading strategy. The "lit-erary" can then give you experience of this "possession." I can offer an example from my professor in Presidency College, Kolkata.

His way of teaching/reading was to efface oneself as far as possible and attempt to enter the space of the poem, to wish as it wishes, to

---

15 Frantz Fanon, *Les Damnés de la terre Les de la terre* (Paris: François Maspero, 1961); *The Wretched of the Earth* (Richard Philcox trans.) (New York: Grove Press, 2004).

experience it as a field of desire, from within. To be possessed by it, as it were. When he wrote, in "The Essential Wordsworth," "Mark the emotional intensity of such phrases as 'disturbs me with the joy of elevated thoughts,'"[16] he was practicing this kind of teaching/reading. Wordsworth himself describes the process in his "Preface to Lyrical Ballads:" "[. . .] it will be the wish of the Poet to bring his feelings near to those of the persons whose feelings he describes, nay, for short spaces of time, perhaps, to let himself slip into an entire delusion, and even confound and identify his own feelings with theirs."[17]

Joan Dayan sympathetically understands the Dahomey-Haitian notion of "possession" in vodou as something like this way of reading. It has been interesting for me to see this reflected in W. E. B. Du Bois's idea of reading the world's history, and to ask myself how much came through his half-Haitian parentage. No one can miss his obsession with Dahomey, and the ubiquity of the Black Messiah say, in *Darkwater*. (There are connections to be made here that are beyond the scope of this essay.)[18]

---

16 Gayatri Chakravorty Spivak, "Homage to Tarakneth Sen" (forthcoming). The politics of being possessed by English literature while being deeply loyal to the Bengali/Indian tradition and skeptical about the British state cannot be adequately discussed here.

17 William Wordsworth, "Preface [with additions of 1802]," in *Wordsworth's Poetry and Prose: Authoritative Texts, Criticism* (Nicholas Halmi ed.) (New York: W. W. Norton, 2014), p. 86.

18 Joan Dayan, *Haiti, History, and the Gods* (Berkeley: University of California Press, 1995). Here is Du Bois in 1903. When in 1961 he goes to Ghana to stay there until his death, his obsession with Dahomey is all too clear:

> Let us now trace this development historically. The slaves arrived with a strong tendency to Nature worship and a belief in witchcraft common to all. Beside this some had more or less vague ideas of a supreme being and higher religious ideas, while a few were Mohammedans, and fewer Christians. Some actual priests were transported and others assumed the functions of priests, and soon a degraded form of African religion and witchcraft appeared in the West Indies, which was known as Obi,* [Du

Bois's note: *Obi (Obeah, Obiah or Obia) is the adjective; Obe or Obi, the noun. It is of African origin, probably connected with Egyptian Ob, Aub, or Obron, meaning serpent. Moses forbids Israelites ever to consult the demon Ob, i.e., "Charmer, Wizard." The Witch of Endor is called Oub or Ob. Onbaous is the name of the Baselisk or Royal Serpent, emblem of the Sun, and, according to Horus Appollo, "ancient oracular Deity of Africa."—(Bryan) Edwards, (*The History, Civil and Commercial, of the British Colonies in the*) *West Indies*, VOL. II (London, 1807), pp. 106–19.] or sorcery. The French Creoles called it "Waldensian" (Vaudois), because of the witchcraft charged against the wretched followers of Peter Waldo, whence comes the dialect name of Voodoo or Hoodoo, used in the United States. Edwards gives as sensible an account of this often exaggerated form of witchcraft and medicine as one can get:

> "As far as we are able to decide from our own experience and information when we lived in the island, and from the current testimony of all the Negroes we have ever conversed with on the subject, the professors of Obi are, and always were, natives of Africa, and none other; and they have brought the science with them from thence to Jamaica, where it is so universally practiced, that we believe there are few of the large estates possessing native Africans, which have not one or more of them. The oldest and most crafty are those who usually attract the greatest devotion and confidence; those whose hoary heads, and a somewhat peculiarly harsh and forbidding aspect, together with some skill in plants of the medical and poisonous species, have qualified them for successful imposition upon the weak and credulous. The Negroes in general, whether Africans or Creoles, revere, consult, and fear them. To these oracles they resort, and with the most implicit faith, upon all occasions, whether for the cure of disorders, the obtaining revenge for injuries or insults, the conciliating of favor, the discovery and punishment of the thief or adulterer, and the prediction of future events. The trade which these imposters carry on is extremely lucrative; they manufacture and sell their Obeis adapted to the different cases and at different prices. A veil of mystery is studiously thrown over their incantations, to which the midnight hours are allotted, and every precaution is taken to conceal them from the knowledge and discovery of the

When such reading is carefully practiced, the reader attempts, however unverifiably, to inhabit the desires inscribed in the text in question. There is room here to think upon Fanon's insistence upon "desire" at this stage, especially in search of the reflexive *démarche*. The two— to be in desire and to lyse > analyse conflict at the end of the chapter and the analyst weeps.

After this, the book changes course; the subject cannot remain ironized. This part must show the method working. In any extended discussion of how one might teach this book, this section will call for an alternative approach. Fanon is twenty-six, he has no real model, and he is trying for validation within the institution that he wishes to transform. We read these chapters (a) to warn against "practicing" Fanon's staged analytico-philosophical mode diagnostically, and (b) take up this young man's relay by saying that this practice plays the certainty of "failure." "'C'est comme si l'image faisait un voyage' et la main en suivait le parcours privé avec la gomme autant qu'avec le crayon."[19]

In these "objective" chapters, with the Negro generalized,[20] solutions are offered but the necessary model of failure and persistence is located in the return of passion in what is "in place of"—even appears in the guise of (*en guise de*)—a conclusion. Here also the translators miss the theater of the text. There is an incredible amount of material

---

White people."* [Du Bois's note: *Edwards, *West Indies*, VOL. II, pp. 108–09.]

As Kate Ramsey indicates, the derivation of the word here is wrong (*The Spirits and the Law: Vodou and Power in Haiti* [Chicago: University of Chicago Press, 2021], p. 5). The Du Bois passage is from *The Negro Church* (Atlanta, GA: Atlanta University Press, 1903), pp. 5–6.

19 Valerio Adami, *Dessiner. La gomme et les crayons* (Jean-Paul Manganaro and Philippe Bonnefis trans) (Paris: Galilée, 2002), p. 17.

20 The generalization in the original of the Black as *Nègre* surely questions the earlier differentiation suggested by Lydie Moudileno of *Nègre* as "the Senegalese rifleman" and the *Noir* as the Antillean, as she proposed on her MLA panel.

in the conclusion, focused on persistence. I will just refer to the epi-graph and two sentences.

It is often pointed out that Fanon was critical of Marxism and indeed his criticism came from the Eurocentrism of the Marxism he knew. I grew up in a Left Front state which is now ruled by a fierce state/cultural identitarianism. When I address the leftover Left—mechanical Marxists—in that home state of West Bengal, I meditate upon Marx's description of the content of a revolution, the only rev-olution (failed) that he had witnessed. There his suggestion is what Fanon chooses as epigraph for his conclusion that is also an overture—"the social revolution [of the nineteenth century] cannot draw its poetry from the past, but only from the future": work toward a time still to come, and your method is poetry.[21]

The first sentence I quote is "I am not only responsible for the revolt in Saint Domingue [Haiti]" (F 183, EP 201). Here the class reads with me *The Black Jacobins*, in a new way, in terms of Dessalines the Black Messiah, in terms of C. L. R. James's account of how Jacobinism revealed its fault lines for French and Afro-Haitian in Haiti. This would throw light on what he wrote years later; that reading Du Bois he had understood that revolutions are carried out by the many little people rather than the named leaders but that understanding did not produce finished work. Garry Bertholf puts it well:

> In his third and final lecture (titled "How I Would Rewrite the Black Jacobins"), James exercises his hindsight in thinking more closely about what a "thicker" (more Du Boisian?)

---

21 F 181, EP 198; translation modified. My discussion of the passage is to be found in Spivak, "Global Marx?," in Theodore A. Burczak, Robert F. Garnett Jr., and Richard McIntyre (eds), *Marxism without Guarantees: Economics, Knowledge, and Class* (London: Routledge, 2017), pp. 265–87; reprinted in Spanish as "Una ética incondicional" in *Le Monde diplomatique*. To sense the difference when discussing the passage with a largely communist audience in West Bengal, see Spivak, *Jukti o Kalpanashakti* (Kolkata: Anustup, 2018).

description might have opened out for his history of the Haitian Revolution: "I would write descriptions in which the black slaves themselves, or people very close to them, describe what they are doing and how they felt about the work that they were forced to carry on. [. . .] I would write the actual statements of the slaves telling what they were doing [emphasis in original]" (99–100). And, of course, Du Bois's own historical descriptions of actors in the past often attend closely to their cultural (and especially musical) practices.[22]

It is in the context of "cultural . . .[/]musical[/dance] practices" that Kate Ramsey writes, in the Haitian case, a "social history of African diasporic religions under colonial, ecclesiastical, and postcolonial regions of the Atlantic world." We can then read C. L. R. James as practicing a "transformation of the traditional understanding of the Enlightenment."[23]

The second sentence from the semi-conclusion that I will quote is: "Dans le monde où je m'achemine, je me crée interminablement" (F 186). "In the world where I will go forward, I will create myself interminably" (EP 204). Philcox misses the *interminablement* and translates it "endlessly." But Fanon knew his Freud. He is undoubtedly referring to Freud's "interminable analysis."[24] That is the accepted French translation

---

22 Garry Bertholf, "Listening To Du Bois's 'Black Reconstruction': After James," *South: A Scholarly Journal* 48(1) (Fall 2015): 82.

23 Ramsey, *The Spirits and the Law*, p. 19. Her reading and Susan Buck-Morss's passionate book *Hegel, Haiti, and Universal History* (Pittsburgh, PA: University of Pittsburgh Press, 2009) can be supplemented by the humanities' imaginative activism—the invitation to practice being-possessed.

24 Sigmund Freud, "Die Endliche und Die Unendliche Analyse," *Gesammelte Werke*, Band XVI, pp. 59–99; "Analysis Terminable and Interminable," in *The Standard Edition of the Complete Psychological Works of Sigmund Freud* (James Strachey ed. and trans., with Anna Freud) (London: Hogarth, 1953–74), VOL. 23, pp. 209–53. Only half in jest, one can say that if Fanon were reading Freud in German, Philcox's "endlessly" would be "authentic."

of Freud's word *unendliche* as it is found in the essay "Die Endliche und Die Unendliche Analyse." In the classroom I will emphasize a reading of the conclusion and its insistence on the horizon-structure of this kind of engaged analysis.

The last page of *Black Skin* rewrites Adler even as his broad outlines are followed. The search for access to the ingredients of another semiosis is consistent, directed "to the open dimension of every consciousness" (F 188, EP 206). His main instrument is self-consciousness. (I can think of an extended discussion of Hegel's framing of the Subject in the Foreword to *The Phenomenology of Mind* and Fanon's bold sabotage of it as "fiction" through his use of Adler.)[25]

We have been watching a practice that must play to lose to win, writing for the open future, right now, ourselves in the vanishing present. To conclude my essay, this reading, perhaps on my eightieth birthday, I will quote the end of the abstract I presented to the Modern Language Association on the first occasion of the presentation of a shorter version of it:[26] Can raced and classed gender expand Fanon's urgency toward claiming the agency of semiosis convincingly, keeping in mind the world's wealth of languages, within which the legal entity understands itself variously—and the Abrahamic, polytheist, henotheist, animist, and non-theist varieties of religious intuitions? Only the failures in teaching can tell you and you will be instructed if you have opened up like a shell, so that sea water and sand can perhaps make a pearl, perhaps not.

---

25 Georg Wilhelm Friedrich Hegel, *Gesammelte Werke*, VOL. 9 (Hamburg: Felix Meiner, 1980), p. 17–20; *The Phenomenology of Spirit* (Terry Pinkard trans.) (Cambridge: Cambridge University Press, 2018), pp. 11–14.

26 Gayatri Chakravorty Spivak, "From Lived Experience to a Step Beyond Hegel," paper presented at "Seventy Years of *Black Skin, White Masks*," Modern Language Association Convention, Washington, DC, January 7, 2022.

Afterword

Translating the Planet?

AVISHEK GANGULY

To invoke the moment of a short "Afterword" that Gayatri Chakravorty Spivak had once written on the occasion of the publication of a volume of her translation of Mahasweta Devi's work, this time too there is an air of hectic celebration around the production of this book.[1] That was the imminent end of the year of the Indigenous; this is the imminence of the author's eightieth birthday. Hence, this afterword will also be necessarily brief.

How might the ethics and politics of translation in Spivak resonate with her imperatives for the necessary impossibility of imagining the subject as planetary, put forward in another set of equally compelling speculations? One place to look for an answer to this question would be the notion of "the untranslatable," which I would argue functions for Spivak as not only a limit of translation but also as a point of departure for thinking planetarity.[2]

In what follows I attempt to track the movement, never linear, between a necessarily inadequate onto-theological question of what

---

1 See "Translator's Afterword to *Chotti Munda and His Arrow*" in this volume, pp. 134–37.

2 For more on this see Avishek Ganguly, "Border Ethics: Translation and Planetarity in Spivak," *Intermédialités / Intermediality* 34 (Autumn 2019). Available at: https://doi.org/10.7202/1070871ar (last accessed on January 13, 2022).

planetarity is (other than intuition, better called untranslatable) and what planetarity does (works at its own heterogeneous behests under-ived from "us"). But first, a reverse genealogy: we could begin with what is probably one of the more recent instances of Spivak's thinking on the topic: the entry on "Planetarity" in the English version of *Dictionary of Untranslatables: A Philosophical Lexicon* (2014) first put together in French by Barbara Cassin.[3] That entry does invoke "translation" at the end and so I include that passage here:

If we imagine ourselves as planetary subjects rather than global agents, planetary creatures rather than global entities, alterity remains underived from us, it is not our dialectical negation, it contains us as much as it flings us away—and thus to think of it is already to trans-gress, for, in spite of our forays into what we metaphorize, differently, as outer and inner space, what is above and beyond our own reach is not continuous with us as it is not, indeed, specifically discontinuous. We must persistently educate ourselves into this peculiar mindset, of accepting the untranslatable even as we are programed to transgress it by "translating" into the mode of "acceptance."[4]

I should like to think that here Spivak submits planetarity as an "untranslatable" in the spirit of the philosophical dictionary in which it appears and proceeds to lay out her argument in brief befitting the form of such keyword entries. For what seems to me to be planetarity in a different discursive mode, let us look at Chapter 3 of *Death of a Discipline* published more than a decade earlier.[5] There Spivak presents

---

3 Gayatri Chakravorty Spivak, "Planetarity," in Barbara Cassin (ed.), *Dictionary of Untranslatables: A Philosophical Lexicon* (Steven Rendall, Christian Hubert, Jeffrey Mehlman, Nathanael Stein, and Michael Syrotinski trans.; Emily Apter, Jacques Lezra, and Michael Wood trans. eds) (Princeton, NJ: Princeton University Press, 2014). The version I cite here was reprinted as Spivak, "Planetarity (Box 4, WELT)," *Paragraph* 38(2) (June 2015): 290–92.

4 Spivak, "Translator's Afterword," p. 135.

5 Gayatri Chakravorty Spivak, *Death of a Discipline* (New York: Columbia University Press, 2003), pp. 71–102.

a reading (further developed as a representation of the task of planetarity in a forthcoming collection)[6] of how the figure of the prehistoric pterodactyl in Mahasweta Devi's eponymous novella, among other textual examples, could "claim the entire planet as its other"; how it could be read as "a figure of the mindset" that could make the "new Comparative Literature work"; the uncanny was planetary—the pterodactyl, after all, did not translate. But the tracks of the planetary as an experience of "the impossibility of translation in the general sense" were explicitly laid out in an even earlier text: "Imperative to Re-imagine the Planet / Imperative zur Neuerfindung des Planeten"—delivered as the inaugural Mary Levin Goldschmidt-Bollag Memorial Lecture "on refugee policy and the politics of migration" at the Stiftung Dialogik in Zurich, Switzerland in 1997 and published as an English–German parallel text edition two years later.[7] Spivak's lecture had inaugurated a shift in the foundation's priorities "from Holocaust asylum to migrant multiculturalism" with a new series of conversations on "refugees and immigrants" that wanted to respond to the crises not just with "advocacy or moral appeal," but with "critical imagination."[8] This text would later appear with minor modifications in *An Aesthetic Education in the Era of Globalization*.[9] In a troubling politics of citation contemporary discussions of the planetary often forget to revisit this earlier, prescient discussion of the planet in a more-than-ecological sense that perhaps came before its time. To close off this genealogical exercise, however, I would suggest that it was in Spivak's reading of Mahasweta Devi and Toni Morrison's work, way back in "The Politics of Translation" in 1992,

---

6 Gayatri Chakravorty Spivak, "Reading 'Pterodactyl,'" in Radha Chakravarty (ed.), *Mahasweta Devi: Writer, Activist, Visionary* (London: Routledge, forthcoming).

7 Gayatri Chakravorty Spivak, *Imperative to Re-imagine the Planet / Imperative zur Neuerfindung des Planeten* (Vienna: Passagen Verlag, 1999).

8 Spivak, *Imperatives to Re-imagine the Planet*, p. 30.

9 Gayatri Chakravorty Spivak, *An Aesthetic Education in the Era of Globalization* (Cambridge, MA: Harvard University Press, 2012), pp. 335–50.

perhaps her first (and still most cited) essay concerned exclusively with the discussion of translation, that we witness the initial lineaments of what was to coalesce as intimations of "planetarity" in later iterations.[10]

The untranslatability of planetarity, Spivak argues, lodges in the planetary system being unavailable to the lodgers on planet Earth "contained under another, prior concept of the object." This also brings to mind Emily Apter's recent call to imagine "just translation," which she argues could only come into being through "efforts to decolonize the language of 'damages,' by engagement with a politics of recognition that acknowledges where translation cannot tread or deliver."[11] Thinking of planetarity in this way resists any "smooth translation" into "contemporary planet-talk by way of environmentalism" and by extension, into "good"—now "green"—capitalist globalization. (When Spivak proposed "good" capitalism the idea of "green" capitalism was not yet there; always ahead of her time. She talked about globalization as electronification of the stock exchanges in the 1980s. Translate!) It is in a further refusal of Spivak's notion of planetarity to be identified with an "applicable methodology," in its reluctance to take the shape of a "solution" to an uncomplicated "problem" that the untranslatable, in my view, becomes a point of departure for thinking planetarity across disciplines. From discussions about reparations for historical wrongs to tackling climate change and interrogating the vagaries of biased algorithms used for interpreting big data—to use a dramatic set of shorthand—if the humanities want to address evolving contemporary realities then I

---

10 "The Politics of Translation" was published in two different volumes close to each other: Michele Barrett and Anne Phillips (eds), *Destabilizing Theory: Contemporary Feminist Debates* (Stanford, CA: Stanford University Press, 1992), pp. 177–200; Gayatri Chakravorty Spivak, *Outside in the Teaching Machine* (New York: Routledge, 1993[2009]), pp. 179–200. I am referring to the 1993 version of the essay here, which is included in the present volume, pp. 36–66.
11 Emily Apter, "What Is Just Translation?" *Public Culture* 33(1) (January 2021): 108.

believe they need to confront these newly ascendant designs and meet other disciplines halfway. The imprint of the Covid-19 pandemic is all over the production of this book; it would be delusional to think that our pre-pandemic systems will just click back into place when it is over because the status quo was already pathologized. The planet is not a problem to be solved; neither can it be reduced to an order of existence that first needs to be possessed in order to be saved. By resisting the smooth translation of a seemingly familiar concept into recognizable practices of making, the humanities as "imaginative activism" could not only contribute to the undoing of a reductive solutionism in the discourses of design and technology but also enable the uncoupling of planetarity from isolated, depoliticized environment talk. And here the most powerful lesson could well be "to continue to educate ourselves into the peculiar mindset of accepting the untranslatable, even as we are programmed to transgress that mindset by 'translating' it into the mode of 'acceptance,'" as mentioned above. I can only imagine the vast lives of Spivak's thinking on translation and planetarity beyond the humanities because that work is just beginning.

Gramsci and Spivak: Politics of Translation

MAURO PALA

With the recent publication of the critical edition in English of Notebook 25,[1] it has now clearly emerged how, with the subalterns, Antonio Gramsci reproposed a problematic that up to then had never been made explicit in the Anglophone world. This was, however, a theme that recurred throughout his entire work, with outcomes that remained unresolved to the same extent that they open out an extraordinary potential for the understanding of hegemonic mechanisms. In this essay I submit that in the light of Gramsci's full set of assumptions about subalternity, the praxis of translation in Gayatri Chakravorty Spivak presents significant points of contact, both at the epistemological and at the thematic levels, with the notions of "translation" and "translatability" in Gramsci's philosophy of praxis. While bearing in mind the differences bound to the historical period in which they work, for both of them translation constitutes the action of the intellectual in the role of "language operator [for whom] language is an ideology or a conception of the world":[2] language is here consubstantial to contents,[3] and for the

---

1 Antonio Gramsci, *Subaltern Social Groups: A Critical Edition of Prison Notebook 25* (Joseph A. Buttigieg and Marcus Green eds and trans) (New York: Columbia University Press, 2021).

2 Fabio Frosini, *Gramsci e la filosofia. Saggio sui Quaderni del carcere* (Rome: Carocci, 2003), p. 34.

3 See Peter Ives, *Gramsci's Politics of Language: Engaging the Bakhtin Circle and the Frankfurt School* (Toronto: University of Toronto Press, 2004); Peter Ives and Rocco Lacorte (eds), *Gramsci, Language and Translation* (Lanham, MD: Lexington Books,

speaker it is not just an instrument for describing the world, but rather the world itself; against the background of a philosophy that pivoted around the word and, with that, around writing, the "relevant"—in other words, ethical[4]—nature of translation reveals itself in the capacity to activate the "creative spirit of the people,"[5] and therefore to be able to modify common sense. It is again through translation that Gramsci conjugates Marxism in a cultural key, effecting a change of paradigm according to a secular and anti-deterministic trajectory.[6]

Analogously, Spivak's comments on Hegel's thinking of the method of philosophy may well relate to her broad notion of translation as an "activity of consciousness that moves of itself; this activity, the method of philosophical discourse, structures the philosophical text."[7] At the moment when the translator creatively contradicts these exigencies of this structure to appropriate a text, she is reminded by the early Derrida: that she, like all deconstructive readers, is pursuing "a discourse which borrows from a heritage the necessary resources for the deconstruction of that heritage itself."[8]

2010); Alessandro Carlucci, *Gramsci and Languages: Unification, Diversity, Hegemony* (Chicago: Haymarket, 2013).

4 "The philosophy of translation, the ethics of translation—if translation does in fact have these things—today aspires to be a philosophy of the word, a linguistics or ethics of the word" (Jacques Derrida, "What Is a 'Relevant' Translation?" [Lawrence Venuti trans.], Critical Enquiry 27[2]: 178).

5 Antonio Gramsci, Letter to Tanja Schucht of March 19, 1927, in *Letters from Prison*, VOL. 1 (Frank Rosengarten ed., Raymond Rosenthal trans.) (New York: Columbia University Press, 1994), pp. 83–84.

6 "Gramsci uses the term 'language' [*linguaggio*] in the sense of what, in a post-Kuhn era, may be defined as a paradigmatic discourse or, simply, a paradigm" (Derek Boothman, *Traducibilità e processi traduttivi. Un caso: Gramsci linguista* [Perugia: Guerra, 2004], p. 57).

7 Gayatri Chakravorty Spivak, "Translator's Preface" in Jacques Derrida, *Of Grammatology* (Spivak trans.) (Baltimore, MD: Johns Hopkins University Press, 2016), p. xxviii. Also, p. 6 in this volume.

8 Spivak, "Translator's Preface," p. xxxviii.

The ideal disinterested objectivity of the text according to Hegel's object of critique in the Phenomenology then become sublated into the negation of its negation, a critical engagement to a model of generalist humanism which must at the same time be actively contradicted by partisan interests.[9] Both define their respective heuristic trajectories starting off from the relation between languages and reality, in order then to expand their field of action and promote forms of social emancipation; Gramsci's project proposes the reconstruction, within the context of the hegemonic relation between State and civil society,[10] of the role of the intellectuals in the formation of a common feeling at national level, and the ability to translate "one philosophical system into the terms of another."[11]

Spivak has translated the work of one woman (a member of the caste-Hindu elite representing subalternity) and three men. The translation that established her reputation was that of the critique of "Eurocentrism" in the Algerian-French philosopher Jacques Derrida's *De la grammatologie*. Introducing Derrida's work required as much attention to an elite tradition of European philosophy as understanding woman-as-subaltern required attentiveness to the discourse of high Hinduism in "Can the Subaltern Speak?"

---

9 "One's anxiety is for one's responsibility to the text, not the other way round. [. . .] Have we not guessed that the early lesson of disinterested objectivity was in fact an unacknowledged partisanship for a sort of universalist humanism" (Gayatri Chakravorty Spivak, "At the *Planchette* of Deconstruction is/in America", in Anselm Haverkamp [ed.], *Deconstruction is/in America: A New Sense of the Political* [New York: New York University Press, 1995], p. 237).

10 See Peter Thomas, *The Gramscian Moment: Philosophy, Hegemony and Marxism* (Leiden: Brill, 2009), p. xix.

11 Antonio Gramsci, *Quaderni del carcere* (Turin: Einaudi, 1975), Q7§1, p. 851 [here, as afterwards, citations give the number of the notebook (Q), followed by the paragraph and page numbers]. See Gramsci, *Prison Notebooks, Volume III* (Joseph Buttigieg ed. and trans.) (New York: Columbia University Press, 2007), p. 153.

In her discussion of the work of Ranajit Guha, the editor of the South Asian historians' Subaltern Studies Collective, she makes clear the distinction between class and subalternity, pervasive in Gramsci, as follows:

> The starting point of a singular itinerary of the word "subaltern" can be Antonio Gramsci's Southern Question' rather than his more general discussions of the subaltern. Although Guha seems to be saying that the words "people" and "subaltern" are interchangeable [. . .] subaltern is a position without identity. [. . .] Class is not a cultural origin, it is a sense of economic collectivity, of social formation as the basis of action.[12]

As for woman as a special category of gendered subalternity, that relates to the denial of the public sphere—"[My] decision was based on a certain program at least implicit in all feminist activity: the deconstruction of the opposition between the private and the public."[13] Its best example is perhaps "Can the Subaltern Speak?"[14] In "In Response: Looking Backward, Looking Forward,"[15] Spivak gives her own sense of her relationship to Gramsci and Marx in thinking through the issue of women as a special subalternist category. Her current work with Ursula Apitzsch on the correspondence between Gramsci and the Schucht sisters (his wife and sister-in-law), while he was incarcerated, brings forth Gramsci's own thoughts on this issue.

---

12 Gayatri Chakravorty Spivak, "Scattered Speculations on the Subaltern and the Popular," *Postcolonial Studies* 8(4) (2005): 476.

13 Gayatri Chakravorty Spivak, *In Other Worlds: Essays in Cultural Politics* (New York: Methuen, 1987), p. 103.

14 Gayatri Chakravorty Spivak, "Can the Subaltern Speak?" in Cary Nelson and Lawrence Grossberg (eds), *Marxism and the Interpretation of Culture* (Urbana: University of Illinois Press, 1988), pp. 271–313.

15 Gayatri Chakravorty Spivak, "In Response: Looking Backward, Looking Forward," in Rosalind Morris (ed.), *Can the Subaltern Speak? Reflections on the History of an Idea* (New York: Columbia University Press, 2010), pp. 227–36.

Both Spivak and Gramsci make use of translation in order to bring out the contradictions internal to (the) political reason which is presented as the norm and often justified in metaphysical terms. Their writings are contingent. The critic Robert Young, generalizing from Spivak's study of a specific "backward" area of India and its transformation into "Indian history" in the early nineteenth century theorizes that, according to Spivak, "history is not simply the disinterested production of facts, but is rather a process of epistemic violence."[16] This epistemic violence goes through the Southern Question translated into the Subaltern Studies of Ranaijt Guha, following a relationship that travels from Italian history during the Risorgimento into the historiography of Indian nationalism. When in "The Southern Question," Spivak sees that "Gramsci considers the movement of historical-political economy in Italy within what can be seen as an allegory of reading taken from or prefiguring an international division of labor," she is of course not thinking of subalternity at all.[17] In this sense, the relation between the subaltern as a category for empirical exploration for Gramsci and the feminist inflection that Spivak gives to subalternity leaves both with the problem of representation: What are the limits and modalities of the representability of the Other? What are the genres and the narrations through which the Occident has created for itself an image of the other, consonant with its own needs and the capabilities of managing that selfsame image? The problem, heuristic and formal, is not alien to an

---

16 Robert J. C. Young, *White Mythologies* (London: Routledge 2010), p. 200. For "epistemic violence," see Spivak, "The Rani of Sirmur," in *A Critique of Postcolonial Reason: Toward a History of the Vanishing Present* (Cambridge, MA: Harvard University Press, 1999), pp. 198–246 and passim. "You don't leap into the subaltern, you sink into the subaltern [. . .] I like the word 'subaltern' for one reason. It is truly situational" (Spivak, "Negotiating the Structures of Violence" in *The Postcolonial Critic: Interviews, Strategies, Dialogues* [Sarah Harasym ed.] [New York: Routledge, 1990], p. 141).

17 Spivak, "Can the Subaltern Speak?," p. 283.

anthropological/folkloric inflection,[18] and is reproposed in the respective paradigmatic episodes centered on the charismatic figure of David Lazzaretti for Gramsci.[19]

Since the 1980s, Spivak's practice of imaginative activism in deep educating the Dalit—which remains to be related to translation in the broadest possible sense—has suggested, following Gramsci, that the subaltern is not generalizable and the effort to translate the voting subaltern into the rights and duties of citizenship would bring in a generality that can access political positions without identity.

Ferruccio Rossi Landi has put together fiction and historiography as raising the question of the function, modality, and instruments of translating, reconstructing a relationship of genetic and structural homology between translation and original, text and discourse, social behavior and ideology.[20] Can Spivak be taken as an example of this?

Gramsci certainly would have shared Spivak's opinion that "subalternity became imbricated with the idea of non-recognition of agency,"[21] since translation in the Notebooks cannot be considered separate from philological practice, and if to the subalterns one can acknowledge the status of political subjects, this is thanks to the pedagogical consequences that this research has regarding common sense.[22] Parallel to

---

18 See Kate Crehan, *Gramsci, Culture and Anthropology* (Berkeley: University of California Press, 2002), pp. 98–123.

19 "I believe becoming a cultural broker has been an unintended consequence of translating Mahasweta Devi, but surely not Jacques Derrida? And what 'culture' does Mahasweta represent?" (Spivak, "Questioned on Translation: Adrift" in this volume, p. 141).

20 See Ferruccio Rossi Landi, *Ideologia. Per l'interpretazione di un operare sociale e la ricostruzione di un concetto* (Rome: Meltemi, 2005).

21 Spivak, "Scattered Speculations," p. 447.

22 See Joseph Buttigieg, "Education, the Role of Intellectuals, and Democracy: A Gramscian Reflection" in Carmel Borg, Joseph Buttigieg, and Peter Mayo (eds), *Gramsci and Education* (New York: Rowman & Littlefield, 2002), pp. 121–32.

this, if "the translator's preparation might take more time [since she] must surrender to the text,"[23] in other words, if her formation has to allow her to enter into an "intimate" syntony with the text, this is because she will have to carry out an analogous task, through involvement and meticulousness, to that of the integral historian vis-à-vis the subalterns, or a mission not inferior, in its size, to the search through the archives that contain the demonstrations of colonial imperialism.[24]

23 Spivak, "The Politics of Translation" in this volume, pp. 39–40.
24 "Without succumbing to a nostalgia for lost origins, the critic must turn to the archives of imperialist governance" (Spivak, "Three Women's Texts and a Critique of Imperialism," *Critical Inquiry* 12[1] [1985]: 261).

Bibliography

ABEL, Lionel. "Jacques Derrida: His 'Difference' with Metaphysics." *Salmagundi* 25 (Winter 1974): 3–21.

ADAMI, Valerio. *Dessiner. La gomme et les crayons* (Jean-Paul Manganaro and Philippe Bonnefis trans). Paris: Galilée, 2002.

AKHTER, Farida. *Depopulating Bangladesh: Essays on the Politics of Fertility*. Dhaka: Narigrantha, 1992.

AMADIUME, Ifi. *Male Daughters, Female Husbands: Gender and Sex in an African Society*. London: Zed Books, 1987.

AMBEDKAR, B. R. "Castes in India," in *The Essential Writings of Ambedkar* (Valerian Rodrigues ed.). New Delhi: Oxford University Press, 2002, pp. 241–62.

AMIN, Samir. *Unequal Development: An Essay on the Social Formations of Peripheral Capitalism* (Brian Pearce trans.). New York: Monthly Review Press, 1976.

APPIAH, Kwame Anthony. "Digging for Utopia." *New York Review of Books* 68(20) (December 2021): 80.

APTER, Emily. "Afterword: Towards a Theory of Reparative Translation," in Francesco Giusti and Benjamin Lewis Robinson (eds), *The Work of World Literature*. Berlin: ICI Berlin Press, 2020, pp. 209–28.

———. "What Is Just Translation?" *Public Culture* 33(1) (January 2021): 89–111.

ARISTOTLE. *Poetics* (Stephen Halliwell trans.), Loeb Classical Library. Cambridge, MA: Harvard University Press, 1995.

BALIBAR, Étienne. *La proposition de l'égaliberté. Essais politiques, 1989–2009*. Paris: Presses Universitaires de France, 2010.

BANERJEE, Sumanta. *India's Simmering Revolution: The Naxalite Uprising*. London: Zed Books, 1984.

BARRETT, Michele, and Anne Phillips (eds). *Destabilizing Theory: Contemporary Feminist Debates*. Stanford, CA: Stanford University Press, 1992.

BARTHES, Roland. *Image-Music-Text* (Stephen Heath trans.). New York: Hill and Wang, 1997.

——. *S/Z* (Richard Miller trans.). New York: Hill and Wang, 1974.

BASU, Tapan, Pradip Datta, Sumit Sarkar, Tanika Sarkar, and Sambuddha Sen, *Khaki Shorts and Saffron Flags: A Critique of the Hindu Right*. New Delhi: Orient Longman, 1993.

BATESON, Gregory. *Steps to an Ecology of Mind*. Chicago: University of Chicago Press, 2000.

BECKER, Alton. *Beyond Translation: Essays Toward a Modern Philology*. Ann Arbor: University of Michigan Press, 1995.

BENJAMIN, Walter. *Illuminations* (Harry Zohn trans.). London: Fontana Press, 1973.

——. "The Task of the Translator" (Harry Zohn trans.), in *Selected Writings, Volume 1: 1913–1926* (Marcus Bullock and Michael W. Jennings eds). Cambridge, MA: Harvard University Press, 1996, pp. 253–63.

——. *The Work of Art in the Age of Its Technical Reproducibility* (Michael Jannings trans.). Cambridge, MA: Harvard University Press, 2008.

BENVENISTE, Emile. *Indo-European Language and Society* (Elizabeth Palmer trans.). London: Faber, 1973.

BERMAN, Sandra, and Michael Wood (eds). *Nation, Language and the Ethics of Translation*. Princeton, NJ: Princeton University Press, 2005.

BERTHOLF, Garry. "Listening to Du Bois's *Black Reconstruction*: After James." *South: A Scholarly Journal* 48(1) (Fall 2015): 78–91.

BHABHA, Homi K. "Democracy Derealized," in Okwui Enwezor (ed.), *Documenta 11, Platform 1: Democracy Unrealized*. Ostfildern-Ruit: Hatje Cantz, 2002, pp. 346–64.

——. *The Location of Culture*. New York: Routledge, 1994.

BOOTHMAN, Derek. *Traducibilità e processi traduttivi. Un caso: Gramsci linguista*. Perugia: Guerra, 2004.

BRAUDEL, Fernand. *Mediterranean and the Mediterranean World in the Age of Philip II*, 2 VOLS (Siân Reynolds trans.). New York: Harper & Row, 1972–73.

BROWN, Dee Alexander. *Bury My Hearth at Wounded Knee: An Indian History of the American West*. New York: Holt, Rinehart & Winston, 1971.

BUCK-MORSS, Susan. *Hegel, Haiti, and Universal History*. Pittsburgh, PA: University of Pittsburgh Press, 2009.

BURKE, Edmund. *The Writings and Speeches of Edmund Burke* (P. J. Marshall ed.). Oxford: Clarendon, 1981.

BUTLER, Judith. "The CounterText Interview." *CounterText* 3(2) (2017): 115–29.

———. "Gender in Translation: Beyond Monolingualism," in Jude Browne (ed.), *Why Gender?* Cambridge: Cambridge University Press, 2021, pp. 15–37.

BUTTIGIEG, Joseph. "Education, the Role of Intellectuals, and Democracy: A Gramscian Reflection" in Carmel Borg, Joseph Buttigieg, and Peter Mayo (eds), *Gramsci and Education*. New York: Rowman & Littlefield, 2002, pp. 121–32.

CARLUCCI, Alessandro. *Gramsci and Languages: Unification, Diversity, Hegemony.* Chicago: Haymarket, 2013.

CASANOVA, Pascale. *The World Republic of Letters* (Malcolm DeBevoise trans.). Cambridge, MA: Harvard University Press, 2007.

CASSIN, Barbara (ed.). *Vocabulaire européen des philosophies: Dictionnaire des intraduisibles.* Paris: Seuil, 2004. Available in English as: *Dictionary of Untranslatables: A Philosophical Lexicon* (Steven Rendall, Christian Hubert, Jeffrey Mehlman, Nathanael Stein, and Michael Syrotinski trans; Emily Apter, Jacques Lezra, and Michael Wood trans. trans. eds). Princeton, NJ: Princeton University Press, 2014.

CAWS, Mary. "*Tel Quel*: Text and Revolution." *Diacritics* 3(1) (Spring 1973): 2–8.

CÉSAIRE, Aimé. *A Season in the Congo* (Gayatri Chakravorty Spivak trans.). London: Seagull Books, 2005.

CHAKRABARTY, Dipesh. "A Small History of Subaltern Studies," in Henry Schwarz and Sangeeta Ray (eds), *A Companion to Postcolonial Studies* (Oxford: Blackwell, 2000), pp. 467–85.

CHATTERJEE, Partha. "Nationalism and the Woman Question," in Kunkum Sangari and Sudesh Vaid (eds), *Recasting Women: Essays in Colonial History* (New Brunswick: Rutgers University Press, 1990), pp. 233–53.

CHATTOPADHYAY, Gautam. *Communism and Bengal's Freedom Movement.* New Delhi: People's Publishing House, 1970.

CHIN, Tamara. "The Afro-Asian Silk Road: Chinese Experiments in Postcolonial Premodernity." *PMLA* 136(1) (January 2021): 17–38.

COETZEE, J. M. *Waiting for the Barbarians.* New York: Penguin, 1980.

CREHAN, Kate. *Gramsci, Culture and Anthropology.* Berkeley: University of California Press, 2002.

DAYAN, Joan. *Haiti, History, and the Gods*. Berkeley: University of California Press, 1995.

DE BOLLA, Peter. *The Discourse of the Sublime: Readings in History, Aesthetics, and the Subject*. Oxford: Blackwell, 1989.

DE MAN, Paul. "The Purloined Ribbon." Reprinted as "Excuses (Confessions)," in *Allegories of Reading*. New Haven, CT: Yale University Press, 1979, pp. 278–301.

DERRIDA, Jacques. *Acts of Religion* (Gil Anidjar ed.). New York: Routledge, 2002.

———. *The Animal That I Am* (David Wills trans.). New York: Fordham University Press, 2008.

———. *De la grammatologie*. Paris: Minuit, 1967. Available in English as: *Of Grammatology* (Gayatri Chakravorty Spivak trans.). Baltimore, MD: Johns Hopkins University Press, 2016[1976].

———. "The Force of Law: The 'Mystical Foundation of Authority'," in Drucilla Cornell, Michel Rosenfeld, and David Gray Carlson (eds), *Deconstruction and the Possibility of Justice*. New York: Routledge, 1992, pp. 3–67.

———. "Fors: Les mots de Abraham et Torok," foreword to Nicolas Abraham and Maria Torok, *Cryptonymie: Le verbier de l'Homme aux Loups*. Paris: Aubier Flammarion, 1976. Available in English as: "Fors: The Anglish Words of Nicolas Abraham and Maria" (Barbara Johnson trans.), foreword to Nicolas Abraham and Maria Torok, *The Wolfman's Magic Word: A Cryptonymy* (Nicholas Rand trans.). Minneapolis: University of Minnesota Press, 1986), pp. xi–xlviii.

———. *Given Time: I. Counterfeit Money* (Peggy Kamuf trans.). Chicago: University of Chicago Press, 1992.

———. *Glas*. Paris: Galilée, 1974. Available in English as: *Glas* (John P. Leavey and Richard Rand trans). Lincoln: University of Nebraska Press, 1990.

———. "L'archéologie du frivole," in Condillac, *Essai sur l'origine des connaissances humaines*. Paris: Galilée, 1973.

———. *La dissémination*. Paris: Seuil, 1972. Available in English as: *Dissemination* (Barbara Johnson trans.). Chicago: University of Chicago Press, 1978.

———. "La différance." *Bulletin de la société française de philosophie* 62(3) (1968): 73–101.

———. "La question du style," in *Nietzsche aujourd'hui?* VOL. 1. Paris: UGE, 1973, pp. 235–87.

———. "La question du style" and "Le facteur de la verité." *Poétique* 21 (1975): 96–147.

——. *La Voix et le phénomène: introduction au problème du signe dans la phénoménologie de Husserl* (Paris; Presses universitaires de France, 1967). Available in English as: *Speech and Phenomena and Other Essays on Husserl's Theory of Signs* (David B. Allison trans.). Evanston, IL: Northwestern University Press, 1973.

——. *L'écriture et la différence.* Paris: Seuil, 1967. Available in English as: *Writing and Difference* (Alan Bass trans.). Chicago: University of Chicago Press, 1978.

——. "Le parergon." *Digraphe* 2 (1974): 21–57.

——. "Le sens de la coupure pure (Le parergon II)." *Digraphe* 3 (1975): 5–31.

——. "Limited Inc" (Samuel Weber trans.). *Glyph* 2 (1977): 162–254.

——. *Marges de la philosophie.* Paris: Minuit, 1972. Available in English as: *Margins of Philosophy* (Alan Bass trans.). Chicago: University of Chicago Press, 1978.

——. *Of Spirit: Heidegger and the Question* (Geoffrey Bennington and Rachel Bowlby trans). Chicago: University of Chicago Press, 1989.

——. "Où Commence et comment finit un corps enseignant," in Dominique Grisoni (ed.), *Politiques de la philosophie.* Paris: Grasset, 1976, pp. 55–97.

——. *Positions.* Paris: Minuit, 1972. Available in English as: *Positions* (Alan Bass trans.). Chicago: University of Chicago Press, 1978.

——. *Sovereignties in Question: The Poetics of Paul Celan* (Thomas Dutoit and Outi Pasanen trans). New York: Fordham University Press, 2005.

——. *Voyous: deux essais sur la raison.* Paris: Galilée, 2003. Available in English as: *Rogues: Two Essays on Reason* (Pascale-Anne Brault and Michael Naas trans). Stanford, CA: Stanford University Press.

——. "What Is a 'Relevant' Translation?" (Lawrence Venuti trans.). *Critical Enquiry* 27(2): 174–200.

——. "White Mythology: Metaphor in the Text of Philosophy." *New Literary History* 6(1) (Autumn 1974): 5–74.

DEVI, Mahasweta. *Agnigarbha.* Kolkata: Karuna Prakashani, 1978.

——. "Breast-Giver," in *Breast Stories* (Gayatri Chakravorty Spivak trans.). London: Seagull Books, 2018[1997], pp. 34–69.

——. *Chotti Munda and His Arrow* (Gayatri Chakravorty Spivak trans.). Oxford: Blackwell, 2003 / London: Seagull Books, 2015[2002].

——. *Imaginary Maps* (Gayatri Chakravorty Spivak trans.). New York: Routledge, 1995.

——. "The Wet-Nurse," in Kali for Women (eds), *Truth Takes: Stories by Indian Women*. London: Women's Press, 1987, pp. 1–50.

Dhammapada. Ananda Maitreya (trans.). Berkeley, CA: Parallax, 1995.

"Dhvanyaloka" of Anandavardhana with the "Locana" of Abhinavagupta, The. Daniel H. H. Ingalls, Sr. (ed. and trans.), Jeffrey Moussaieff Masson and M. V. Patwardhan (trans). Cambridge, MA: Harvard University Press, 1990.

DJEBAR, Assia. *Loin de Médine*. Paris: Albin Michel, 1991.

——. *Women of Algiers in Their Apartment* (Marjolin de Jaeger trans.). Charlottesville: University of Virginia Press, 1992.

DU BOIS, W. E. B. *The Education of Black People: Ten Critiques, 1906–1960* (Herbert Aptheker ed.). Amherst: University of Massachusetts Press, 1973.

ELSTER, Jon. *Ulysses and the Sirens: Studies in Rationality and Irrationality*. Cambridge: Cambridge University Press, 1979.

ENROTH, Henrik, and Douglas Brommesson (eds). *Global Community? Transnational and Transdisciplinary Exchanges*. London: Rowan and Littlefield, 2015.

Fanon, Frantz. *Alienation and Freedom* (Jean Khalfa and Robert J. C. Young eds; Steven Corcoran trans.). New York: Bloomsbury, 2019.

FANON, Frantz. *Les Damnés de la terre Les de la terre*. Paris: François Maspero, 1961. Available in English as: *The Wretched of the Earth* (Richard Philcox trans.). New York: Grove Press, 2004.

——. *Peau noire, masques blancs*. Paris: Éditions du Seuil, 1952. Available in English as: *Black Skin, White Masks* (Charles Lam Markmann trans.). New York: Grove Press, 1967; *Black Skin, White Masks* (Richard Philcox trans.). New York: Grove Press, 2008.

FORBES, Jack D. *Black Africans and Native Americans: Color, Race, and Caste in the Evolution of Red-Black Peoples*. Oxford: Blackwell, 1988.

FOUCAULT, Michel. *The History of Sexuality*, VOL. 1 (Robert Hurley trans.). New York: Vintage, 1980.

——. "Nietzsche, Genealogy, History," in *Language, Counter-Memory, Practice: Selected Essays and Interviews* (Donald F. Bouchard ed.). Ithaca, NY: Cornell University Press, 1977), pp. 139–64.

FRANDA, Marcus F. *Radical Politics in West Bengal*. Cambridge, MA: MIT Press, 1971.

FREUD, Sigmund. "Die endliche und unendliche Analyse," in *Gesammelte Werke* (hereafter referred to as GW), BAND XVI, pp. 59–99. Available in English as: "Analysis Terminable and Interminable," in *The Standard Edition of the*

Complete Psychological Works of Sigmund Freud (James Strachey ed. and trans., with Anna Freud) (London: Hogarth, 1953–74), VOL. 23, pp. 209–53.

FROSINI, Fabio. *Gramsci e la filosofia. Saggio sui Quaderni del carcere.* Rome: Carocci, 2003.

GANGULY, Avishek. "Border Ethics: Translation and Planetarity in Spivak," *Intermédialités / Intermediality* 34 (Autumn 2019). Available at: https://doi.org/-10.7202/1070871ar (last accessed on January 13, 2022).

GHASSEM-FACHANDI, Parvis. *Pogrom in Gujarat: Hindu Nationalism and Anti-Muslim Violence in India.* Princeton, NJ: Princeton University Press, 2012.

GILE, Daniel, Gyde Hansen, and Nike K. Pokorn (eds). *Why Translation Studies Matters.* Amsterdam: Benjamin, 2010.

GOETHE, Johann Wolfgang von. *Conversations with Eckermann.* Washington, DC: Dunne, 1901.

GRAMSCI, Antonio. *A Gramsci Reader: Selected Writings, 1916–1935* (David Forgacs ed.). New York: New York University Press, 1988.

――. *Letters from Prison*, VOL. 1 (Frank Rosengarten ed., Raymond Rosenthal trans.). New York: Columbia University Press, 1994.

――. *Prison Notebooks,* VOL. 3 (Joseph Buttigieg ed. and trans.). New York: Columbia University Press, 2007.

――. *Subaltern Social Groups: A Critical Edition of Prison Notebook 25* (Joseph A. Buttigieg and Marcus Green eds and trans). New York: Columbia University Press, 2021.

HALEY, Shelley. "Be Not Afraid of the Dark: Critical Race Theory and Classical Studies," in Laura Nasrallah and Elisabeth Schüssler Fiorenza (eds), *Prejudice and Christian Beginnings: Investigating Race, Gender, and Ethnicity in Early Christian Studies.* Minneapolis, MN: Fortress Press, 2009, pp. 27–49.

HALPERIN, David. *Saint Foucault: Towards a Gay Hagiography.* New York: Oxford University Press, 1995.

HARRIS, Wilson. *The Guyana Quartet.* London: Faber, 1975.

HEGEL, Georg Wilhelm Friedrich. *Phänomenologie des Geistes.* Frankfurt am Main: Suhrkamp, 1970. Available in English as: *The Phenomenology of the Mind* (J. B. Baillie trans.). New York: Harper Torchbooks, 1967.

HEIDEGGER, Martin. *The Question of Being* (William Kluback and Jean T. Wilde trans). New York: New College and University Press, 1958.

HOMER. *The Odyssey* (A. T. Murray trans.). Cambridge, MA: Harvard University Press, 1995.

HORKHEIMER, Max, and Theodor W. Adorno. *Dialectic of Enlightenment* (John Cumming trans.). New York: Herder and Herder, 1972.

HOSSAIN, Rokeya Sakhawat. *"Sultana's Dream": A Feminist Utopia, and Selections from "The Secluded Ones"* (Roushan Jahan ed. and trans.). New York: Feminist Press, 1988.

HUSSERL, Edmund. *L'origine de la géométrie* (Jacques Derrida trans.). Paris: Presses universitaires de France, 1962.

HYPPOLITE, Jean. *Logique et existence*. Paris: Presses Universitaires de France, 1953. Available in English as: *Logic and Existence* (Leonard Lawlor and Amit Sen trans). Albany: SUNY Press, 1997.

———. "The Structure of Philosophic Language According to the 'Preface' to Hegel's *Phenomenology of the Mind*," in Richard Macksey and Eugenio Donato (eds), *The Languages of Criticism and the Sciences of Man: The Structuralist Controversy*. Baltimore, MD: Johns Hopkins University Press, 1970, pp. 157–68.

ILIAS, Akhtaruzzaman. *Chilekothar Sepai*. Dhaka: Dhaka University Press, 1995.

———. *Khoabnama*. Dhaka: Maola Brothers, 1996. Available in English as: *Khwab Nama* (Arunava Sinha trans.). New Delhi: Hamish Hamilton, 2021.

IVES, Peter. *Gramsci's Politics of Language: Engaging the Bakhtin Circle and the Frankfurt School*. Toronto: University of Toronto Press, 2004.

———, and Rocco Lacorte (eds). *Gramsci, Language and Translation*. Lanham, MD: Lexington Books, 2010.

JAFFRELOT, Christophe. *Hindu Nationalism: A Reader*. Princeton, NJ: Princeton University Press, 2007.

JAYAWARDENA, Kumari. *The White Woman's Other Burden: Western Women and South Asia During British Rule*. London: Routledge, 1995.

KAKAR, Sudhir. *The Inner World: A Psycho-analytic Study of Childhood and Society in India*, 2ND EDN. Delhi: Oxford University Press, 1981.

KANT, Immanuel. "Religion within the Boundaries of Mere Reason," in *Religion and Rational Theology* (Allen W. Wood and George di Giovanni eds and trans). Cambridge: Cambridge University Press, 1996, pp. 39–215.

———. *Religion within the Limits of Reason Alone* (Theodore M. Greene and Hoyt H. Hudson trans.). New York: Harper & Row, 1960.

KLEIN, Melanie. *Works*, VOLS 1–4. New York: Free Press, 1984.

KURGAN, Laura, and Xavier Costa (eds). *You Are Here: Architecture and Information Flows*. Barcelona: Museum of Contemporary Art, 1995.

LACAN, Jacques. "Du réseau des signifiants," in *Le Séminaire de Jacques Lacan Livre XI: Les Quatre Concepts Fondamentaux De La Psychanalyse* (Jacques-Alain Miller ed.). Paris: Éditions du Seuil, 1964, pp. 43–52. Available in English as: "The Network of Signifiers," in *The Seminar of Jacques Lacan, Book IV: Four Fundamental Concepts of Psychoanalysis* (Alan Sheridan trans.). New York: W. W. Norton, 1981, p. 42–52.

———. *Ecrits* (Bruce Fink trans.). New York: W. W. Norton and Company, 2006.

———. "The Line and Light," in *The Four Fundamental Concepts of Psychoanalysis* (Alan Sheridan trans.). New York: W. W. Norton, 1978.

———. "Seminar on 'The Purloined Letter'" (Jeffrey Mehlman trans.). *Yale French Studies* 48 (1972): 39–72.

LANDI, Ferruccio Rossi. *Ideologia. Per l'interpretazione di un operare sociale e la ricostruzione di un concetto.* Rome: Meltemi, 2005.

LÉVI-STRAUSS, Claude. *La Pensée sauvage.* Paris: Plon, 1962. Available in English as: *The Savage Mind.* Chicago: University of Illinois Press, 1966.

LÉVY, Bernard-Henri. *Bangla Desh: Nationalisme dans la revolution.* Paris: François Maspéro, 1973.

LIFSCHULTZ, Lawrence. *Bangladesh: The Unfinished Revolution.* London: Zed Books, 1979.

LORD, Albert B. *The Singer of Tales.* New York: Atheneum, 1965.

LYOTARD, Jean-François. *The Postmodern Condition: A Report on Knowledge.* Minneapolis: University of Minnesota Press, 1984.

MADSEN, Deborah. "The Making of (Native) Americans: Suturing and Citizenship in the Scene of Education." *Parallax* 17(3) (2011): 32–45.

MAJUMDAR, Binoy. *Gayatrike.* Kolkata: Protibhash, 2002.

———. *Ishwarir Swarachito Nibandha o Anyanya.* Kolkata: Pratibhash, 1995.

———. *Kabyoshamogro,* VOL. 1. Kolkata: Pratibhash, 1993.

MALLARMÉ, Stéphane. *Mallarmé* (Anthony Hartley ed. and trans.). Harmondsworth: Penguin, 1965.

———. *Quant au Livre, Oeuvres completes.* Paris: Pléiade edition, 1945.

MARX, Karl. *Capital: A Critique of Political Economy,* VOL. 1 (Ben Fowkes trans.). New York: Vintage, 1977.

———. *Capital: A Critique of Political Economy,* VOL. 3 (David Fernbach trans.). New York: Vintage, 1981.

———. *Surveys from Exile: Political Writings*, VOL. 2 (David Fernbach ed.). New York: Penguin / New Left Review, 1973.

MASON, Wyatt. Review of *Essays Two* by Lydia Davis. *New York Times*, December 3, 2021. Available at: https://nyti.ms/3tcephS (last accessed on January 11, 2022).

MATILAL, Bimal Krishna. *The Word and the World: India's Contribution to the Study of Language*. New Delhi and New York: Oxford University Press, 1990.

MATSUI, Yayori. *Women's Asia*. London: Zed Books, 1989.

MAZHAR, Farhad. *Ashomoyer Noteboi*. Dhaka: Protipokkho, 1994.

MAZUMDAR, Nirode, inspired by Ram Proshad. *Song of Kali: A Cycle of Images and Songs* (Gayatri Chakravorty Spivak trans.). Calcutta: Seagull Books, 2000.

McELENEY, Corey. "The Resistance to Overanalysis," *Differences* 52(2) (2021): 1–38.

MEHLMAN, Jeffrey. "Portnoy in Paris." *Diacritics* 2(4) (Winter 1972): 21–28.

MOONEY, James. *The Ghost-Dance Religion and the Sioux Outbreak of 1890*. Glorieta, NM: Rio Grande Press, 1973.

MORRISON, Toni. *Beloved*. New York: Plume Books, 1987.

MOUDELINO, Lydie. "Contextualizing Fanon, Again: On the Black Man and His 'Fellows' in 1950s France." Paper presented at "Seventy Years of *Black Skin, White Masks*," Modern Language Association Convention, Washington, DC, January 7, 2022.

NAPALJARRI, Peggy Rockman, and Lee Cataldi (trans). *Yimikirli: Warlpiri Dreamings and Histories*. San Francisco, CA: HarperCollins, 1994.

NIETZSCHE, Friedrich. *Untimely Meditations* (R. J. Hollingdale trans.). Cambridge: Cambridge University Press, 1983.

ORWELL, George. *Homage to Catalonia*. Orlando, FL: Harcourt Brace Jovanovich, 1952.

PLATO. *Euthyphro, Apology, Crito, Phaedo, Phaedrus* (Harold North Fowler trans.), Loeb Classical Library 36. Cambridge, MA: Harvard University Press, 1914.

POLYBIUS. *The Histories of Polybius* (W. R. Paton trans., F. W. Walbank and Christian Habicht revd.), Loeb Classical Library 128. Cambridge, MA: Harvard University Press, 2010.

PONTALIS, J.-B. *The Language of Psychoanalysis*. London: Hogarth Press, 1973.

PRASAD, Satendra. "Limits and Possibilities for Civil Society Led Re-democratization: The Fijian Constitutional Debates and Dilemma." *Prime* (2000): 3–28.

PROUST, Marcel. *A la recherche du temps perdu*. Paris: Pléiade edition, 1954.

RAMSEY, Kate. *The Spirits and the Law: Vodou and Power in Haiti*. Chicago: University of Chicago Press, 2021.

RAY CHOWDHURY, Malay. "Binoy Majumdar: Kabitar Bodhi Briksha." Available at www.binoy898180804.wordpress.com (last accessed on January 8, 2022)

SALIH, Tayeb. *Season of Migration to the North*. Boulder, CO: Lynne Rienner, 1997.

SANDERS, Mark. *Ambiguities of Witnessing: Law and Literature in the Time of a Truth Commission*. Stanford, CA: Stanford University Press, 2007.

SAUSSURE, Ferdinand de. *Course in General Linguistics* (Wade Baskin trans.). New York: Philosophical Library, 1959.

SEN, Dinesh Chandra. *History of Bengali Language and Literature*. Kolkata: University of Calcutta, 1911.

SEN, Samar, Debabrata Panda, and Ashish Lahiri (eds). *Naxalbari and After: A Frontier Anthology*, VOL. 2. Kolkata: Kathashilpa, 1978.

SEN, Taraknath. *A Literary Miscellany*. Kolkata: Avant-Garde, forthcoming.

SINGH, K. S. *Birsa Munda and His Movement* (1872–1901). Calcutta: Seagull Books, 2002.

SOYINKA, Wole. "Othello's Dominion, Immigrant Domain." *Savannah Review* 3 (May 2014): 1–20.

SPIVAK, Gayatri Chakravorty. "Acting Bits/Identity Talk." *Critical Inquiry* 18(4) (Summer 1992): 770–803.

———. *An Aesthetic Education in the Era of Globalization*. Cambridge, MA: Harvard University Press, 2013.

———. "At the *Planchette* of Deconstruction is/in America", in Anselm Haverkamp (ed.), *Deconstruction is/in America: A New Sense of the Political* (New York: New York University Press, 1995), pp. 237–49.

———. "Can the Subaltern Speak?" in Larry Grossberg and Cary Nelson (eds), *Marxism and the Interpretation of Culture*. Urbana: University of Illinois Press, 1988, pp. 271–313.

———. *A Critique of Postcolonial Reason: Toward the History of the Vanishing Present*. Cambridge, MA: Harvard University Press, 1999.

———. *Death of a Discipline*. New York: Columbia University Press, 2003.

———. "Deconstruction and Cultural Studies: Arguments for a Deconstructive Cultural Studies," in Nicholas Royle (ed.), *Deconstructions: A User's Guide*. New York: Palgrave, pp. 14–43.

———. "French Feminism in an International Frame," in *In Other Worlds: Essays in Cultural Politics*. New York: Routledge, 1998, pp. 184–211.

———. "From Lived Experience to a Step Beyond Hegel." Paper presented at "Seventy Years of *Black Skin, White Masks*," Modern Language Association Convention, Washington, DC, January 7, 2022.

———. "Global Marx?" in Theodore A. Burczak, Robert F. Garnett Jr., and Richard McIntyre (eds), *Marxism without Guarantees: Economics, Knowledge, and Class*. London: Routledge, 2017, pp. 265–87.

———. *Imperative to Re-imagine the Planet / Imperative zur Neuerfindung des Planeten*. Vienna: Passagen Verlag, 1999.

———. "In Response: Looking Backward, Looking Forward," in Rosalind Morris (ed.), *Can the Subaltern Speak? Reflections on the History of an Idea*. New York: Columbia University Press, 2010, pp. 227–36.

———. *Jukti o Kalpanashakti*. Kolkata: Anustup, 2018.

———. "Love, Cruelty, and Cultural Talks in the Hot Peace." *Parallax* 1 (November 1995): 1–31.

———. "Our Asias—2001: How to Be a Continentalist," in *Other Asias*. Oxford: Blackwell, 2007, pp. 209–38.

———. *Outside in the Teaching Machine*. New York: Routledge, 2009[1993].

———. "Planet-Think/Continent-Think." The Wellek Library Lecture delivered at the Critical Theory Institute, University of California–Irvine, May 25, 2000.

———. "Planetarity (Box 4, WELT)." *Paragraph* 38(2) (June 2015): 290–92.

———. *The Postcolonial Critic: Interviews, Strategies, Dialogues* (Sarah Harasym ed.). New York: Routledge, 1990.

———. "Psychoanalysis in Left Field and Fieldworking: Examples to Fit the Title," in Michael Munchow and Sonu Shamdasani (eds), *Speculations after Freud: Psychoanalysis, Philosophy and Culture*. London: Routledge, 1994, pp. 41–76.

———. "Race before Racism: The Disappearance of the American," in Paul A. Bové (ed.), *Edward Said and the Work of the Critic: Speaking Truth to Power*. Durham, NC: Duke University Press, 2000), pp. 51–65.

———. "Reading 'Pterodactyl,'" in Radha Chakravarty (ed.), *Mahasweta Devi: Writer, Activist, Visionary*. London: Routledge, forthcoming.

———. "Reading the Archives: The Rani of Sirmur," in Francis Barker (ed.), *Europe and Its Others*, VOL. 1. Colchester: University of Essex, 1985, pp. 128–51.